The Future of the Automobile

The International Automobile Program

Co-Directors: Daniel Roos and Alan Altshuler

National Team Leaders

France	Michel Frybourg
Italy	Patrizio Bianchi
Japan	Hideo Nakamura and Yukihide Okano
Sweden	Lars Sjöstedt
United Kingdom	Daniel Jones
United States	Alan Altshuler and Daniel Roos
West Germany	Meinolf Dierkes

Program Secretariat

Martin Anderson, Executive Officer (1981–1984)
Robert Greene, Executive Officer (1980–1981)
Mary McShane, Research Associate
James Womack, Research Associate
Rob Coppock, European Coordinator
Trish Fleming, Administrative Assistant

Acknowledgment

The international coordination of this program and the preparation of this volume were supported by the German Marshall Fund of the United States and the Lilly Endowment.

The Future of the Automobile

The Report of MIT's
International Automobile
Program

by

Alan Altshuler
Martin Anderson
Daniel Jones
Daniel Roos
James Womack

with contributions by

Hermann Appel
David Bayliss
Gunnar Hedlund
Masakazu Iguchi
Kazutoshi Koshiro
Harry Katz
Karl Ludvigsen
Mary McShane
Rémy Prud'homme
Wolfgang Streeck

The MIT Press
Cambridge, Massachusetts

First MIT Press paperback edition, 1986

© 1984 by the Massachusetts Institute of Technology

This book has been set in Palatino
by The MIT Press Computergraphics Department
and printed and bound by Halliday Lithograph
in the United States of America

Library of Congress Cataloging in Publication Data
Main entry under title:

The Future of the automobile.

Bibliography: p.
Includes index.
1. Automobile industry and trade. I. Altshuler, Alan A., 1936–. II. Massachusetts Institute of Technology. III. International Automobile Program.
HD9710.A2F87 1984   338.4′76292   84-12269
ISBN 0-262-01081-X (hard)
        0-262-51038-3 (paper)

Contents

Appendixes

Preface

The International Automobile Program

In 1979, in the midst of the second energy shock, we—like many others—began to wonder about the future of the automobile-based system of personal transportation. Were its resource demands sustainable, particularly in the light of its complete dependence on petroleum? Could the earth's environment tolerate ever-increasing amounts of auto travel? Would the world's citizens accept the safety and urban-amenity consequences of mass automobility over the long term? As energy prices soared, the first of these concerns in particular seemed to cast a shadow on the future of the automobile.

At the same time, the world economy was entering the worst economic downturn since the Great Depression, and the auto industry was among the hardest-hit sectors. It soon became apparent that, although the continuing spread of automobility might cause resource and environmental challenges, a major contraction in auto production was even more troubling to the world's advanced industrial economies. In addition, because the effects of the downturn in auto sales were felt in different degrees by the leading auto-producing nations, with some countries' auto industries faltering as others surged ahead, the world trading system was showing serious strains.

In this situation of crisis, we resolved to mount an examination of the automotive system that would be unusual in three respects. First, it would integrate the perspectives of those who focus on the automobile as a travel mode and those concerned with its production. Transportation, environmental, and resource analysts would be asked to collaborate with students of corporate organization and finance, labor relations, and international trade. Second, the study would be global in orientation. Third, its time frame would extend past the end of the century.

During 1980 we worked with leading research institutions in France, Italy, Japan, Sweden, the United Kingdom, the United States, and West Germany to develop a national research team in each country. (The members are listed in appendix A.) These seven nations, which we refer to as the Auto Program countries, account for three-fourths of the world's motor-vehicle production and two-thirds of new-vehicle sales. In addition, they are the home countries of all the transnational automobile manufacturers.

Our intent was to conduct a truly comprehensive examination, from many perspectives and with a view to the long-term future, of the social consequences of the automobile as a consumer product and on the auto industry as a central element of the world economy. To fully achieve our goal, we felt it was essential to understand the perspectives of the decision makers who shape the destiny of the automobile and the auto industry. We therefore solicited the thoughts of senior company executives, union leaders, and government officials concerned with the health of the auto industry in the seven Auto Program countries. We also sought out the views of leaders in industries closely involved with the auto sector, such as energy and finance, and those who deal with the side effects of auto use, including environmentalists, government regulators, and transportation planners. These individuals were asked to join the research teams in a series of forums held annually over a three-year period in the United States, Japan, and Europe. Those who accepted our invitation to participate are listed in appendix B.

The forums provided a mechanism for these individuals to talk frankly about important auto-related issues and to comment on Auto Program research findings. We should make clear that, although the forum participants have taken great pains to criticize drafts of this volume, for which efforts we are deeply grateful, there is no suggestion that they agree with or endorse our findings.

The Massachusetts Institute of Technology, jointly through the Center for Transportation Studies and the Center for International Studies, served as headquarters for the coordination of the overall program. (This does not mean, of course, that MIT as an entity endorses the findings of the program or of this report.) As program co-directors we worked intensively during the program's initial year to develop the concept, line up funding, and identify team leaders in the Auto Program countries. In subsequent years Daniel Roos administered the international program, planned the annual forums, and supervised the program's research activities in the areas of automobile technology and use. Alan Altshuler took responsibility for the overall integration of the program's research activities and supervised program research in the areas of industry analysis and public policy.

The ambitious nature and the international focus of the Auto Program required the cooperation and commitment of many institutions and individuals in seven countries. We wish in particular to acknowledge the dedicated efforts, over a four-year period, of the team leaders: Patrizio Bianchi, Italy; Meinolf Dierkes, West Germany; Michel Frybourg, France; Daniel Jones, United Kingdom; Hideo Nakamura and Yukihide Okano, Japan; and Lars Sjöstedt, Sweden. Others making important contributions to the administration of the program were Rob Coppock of the Science Center in Berlin, who coordinated many of the program's European activities, and Robert Whitford, who organized Auto Program research at Purdue University.

A research effort of this magnitude requires a large amount of financial support over a number of years. In addition to the support for the international coordination of the program provided by the German Marshall Fund of the United States and the Lilly Endowment, each national research team obtained funds from public and private organizations in its home country. We take this opportunity on behalf of our colleagues to gratefully acknowledge the many financial contributors who made the program possible.

The Present Volume

At the conclusion of four years of intensive research involving innumerable consultations and communications among academics, government officials, company executives, and union leaders, we believe that the International Automobile Program has accomplished the most comprehensive assessment ever conducted of a major world industry and its product. This volume is a report on the state of the automobile and the auto industry and their future prospects based on the findings of the program. It is not a consensus view of those participating in the program, nor is it a massive compilation of facts and figures. Rather, it is a collaborative interpretation and analysis by the principal authors which attempts to understand the problems inherent in ever-expanding automobility, the ways in which the auto industry may evolve in the future, and the future political economy of the automotive world.

As in any work of collaboration, a word about specific contributions is necessary. Alan Altshuler, James Womack, and Daniel Roos provided the overall direction and the editorial coordination to forge an integrated manuscript from a diversity of parts. James Womack prepared chapter 1 and, with Alan Altshuler, co-authored chapters 2 and 11. Rémy Prud'homme supplied the material in chapter 2 on the future of the auto industry in the less developed countries, and Daniel Jones contributed key concepts about the process of industry evolution. Chapter 3 was written by James Womack, drawing on materials prepared by Mary McShane in her role as coordinator of the program's automobile use studies. Chapter 4 was co-authored by James Womack and Daniel Jones, with contributions from Herman Appel, Masakazu Iguchi, and Lars Sjöstedt. Alan Altshuler wrote chapter 5, drawing on materials, including the program's demand model, prepared by David Bayliss. James Womack, Martin Anderson, and Daniel Jones were jointly responsible for chapters 6, 7, and 8. Chapter 9 was co-authored by Harry Katz and Wolfgang Streeck, with contributions from Kazutoshi Koshiro. Chapter 10 was prepared by Alan Altshuler. Appendix C is the work of Harry Katz, Wolfgang Streeck, David Marsden, and Stephen Wood. Gunnar Hedlund contributed Appendix D. Karl Ludvigsen edited the manuscript for stylistic consistency and continuity. However, these individual attributions must not obscure the fact that the volume has been a truly collaborative effort throughout.

Other Auto Program Research

Although this volume is the most comprehensive publication under the aegis of the International Automobile Program, it represents only a tiny fraction of the program's research findings. The working papers that provided most of the evidence for the interpretations presented in this volume are available from the MIT Center for Transportation Studies, Cambridge, Massachusetts 02139. In addition, several complementary volumes are in preparation by individual researchers participating in the program. These cover a wide range of topics, including trade policy, automotive technology, automobile use, labor relations, and the future of the automobile and the auto industry in the developing countries.

At the outset of the Auto Program we believed that the world faced a growing need for farseeing assessments of key industries and their social ramifications. We believed, further, that these assessments could be accomplished only through worldwide research and discussions, not just by academics in a single discipline but by academics in a wide range of disciplines comparing perspectives and consulting with government officials, industry executives, labor leaders, and user and public-interest groups. At the conclusion of our exploratory effort, we are firmly convinced of the utility of this approach. We have frequently found the process very difficult, as was inevitable with the high level of international tension surrounding a number of the issues, but we believe that even greater difficulties lie down a path of isolation and of failure to approach the world as a unified system. Thus, we hope that others will follow in our footsteps in assessing the auto industry and in examining other sectors of the world's industrial economy. Finally, on a personal note, we would like to thank our many colleagues who invested their time and energy in a unique experiment to increase international understanding. We hope the result justifies their initial faith.

Alan Altshuler and Daniel Roos

1   The Automobile and Its Industry under Siege

The world stands at the centenary of the automotive age. For nearly 90 years after the invention of a workable automobile in the mid 1880s, automotive development proceeded steadily. Use and ownership climbed ever higher, mass automobility spread to more and more nations, and new operating capabilities were continually perfected. Although new-vehicle sales and production dropped dramatically at times in response to broader economic and political conditions, they invariably rebounded and surged upward once more (figure 1.1). During the extraordinary worldwide economic boom in the three decades after the Second World War, the production of new vehicles and the total number of vehicles in use climbed year after year at a dizzying rate (figures 1.1 and 1.2). By 1980 the world's motor-vehicle fleet had grown to 320 million passenger cars and 82 million trucks and buses.*

In short, for nearly a century the automobile's future always seemed brighter than its past. Since the early 1970s, however, the predominant view has changed dramatically. Problems have piled one on top of the other, and many questions have been raised about the long-term prospects for the automobile and its industry.

The initial shift in expectations came with the dawning realization of what mass automobility on a world scale might mean for the earth's resource base and atmosphere. In the period between 1950 and 1980 the global motor-vehicle fleet grew by 472 percent. In 1980 the amount of personal travel by automobile worked out to 2,200 kilometers for every person on the planet, yet this was less than one-third the level

---

*Throughout this volume, "motor vehicles" will mean cars, trucks, and buses; "automobiles" will mean passenger cars only. It would be desirable in most cases to refer to automobiles alone, but such data are not available on a world basis for the early years of the automotive era.

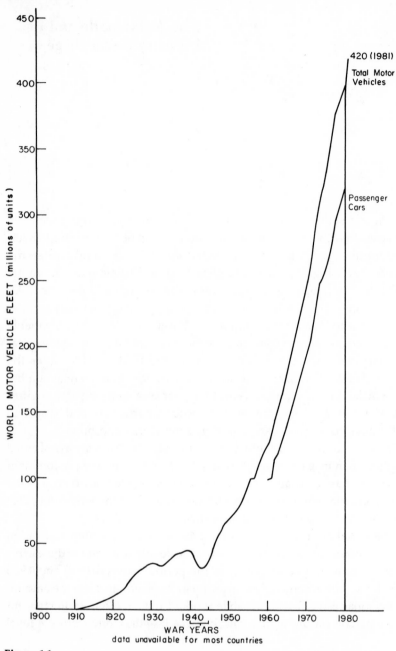

Figure 1.1
World motor-vehicle fleet, 1900–1981, and world automobile fleet, 1960–1980.
Source: *World Motor Vehicle Data*, 1982 edition, Detroit: Motor Vehicle Manufacturers
Association, 1982

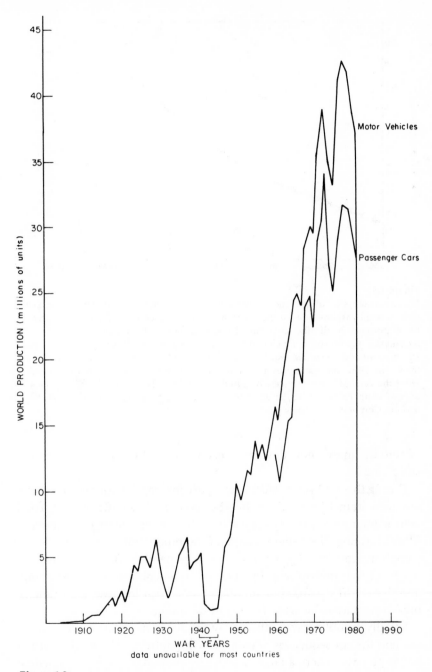

Figure 1.2
World motor-vehicle production, 1900–1981, and world automobile production,
1960–1981. Source: See figure 1.1

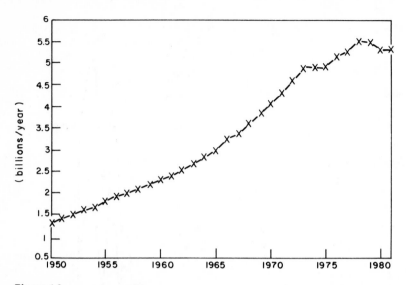

Figure 1.3
World consumption of gasoline by motor vehicles (in barrels), 1950–1981. Note: Data
include retail gasoline sales in the seven Auto Program countries and gasoline uses
for all purposes in all other countries. Thus, some non-motor-vehicle uses (such as
recreational equipment) are included in the data for the Auto Program countries, and
a number of additional uses (such as aviation) are included in the data for the rest of
the world. However, these uses are a tiny fraction of total consumption and do not
affect the general trend. Sources: *World Energy Statistics*, New York: United Nations,
various years; *BP Statistical Review of the World Energy Industry*, London: British Petroleum Corporation, various years.

of auto use in the most developed economies, where levels of use were
still rising.[1]

During these 30 years, world gasoline consumption for motor-vehicle
use grew from 1.29 to 5.32 billion barrels per annum (figure 1.3). Total
vehicular emissions nearly kept pace with growing energy consumption.
More alarming, the general shape of the production, use, energy-con-
sumption, and emissions curves was exponential. The absorptive capacity of the atmosphere, by contrast, was stable or even declining,
and the world's petroleum supplies, along with the reserves of many
other raw materials, were finite and declining.

Equally troubling were the safety implications of mass automobile
use and the consequences of ever-growing traffic for the world's urban
environments, where a larger and larger portion of the world's people
lived. Total fatalities due to auto accidents increased steadily, to more
than 250,000 per year worldwide in the late 1970s (figure 1.4).[2] Two

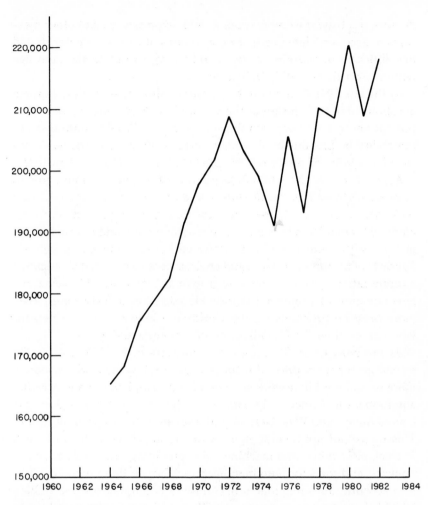

Figure 1.4
Motor-vehicle-related fatalities in 54 countries, 1964–1982. Note: These figures are the total for the 54 countries that consistently reported such fatalities during the period 1964–1982. These fatalities include pedestrians and cyclists struck by motor vehicles. The total of 255,212 fatalities in 1979 cited in note 2 is for the 96 countries reporting fatality data in that year. Sources: *World Road Statistics*, Geneva: International Road Federation, various years; *Demographic Yearbook*, New York: United Nations, various years.

decades of postwar experimentation with expressways and other measures to accommodate ever-growing streams of cars had demonstrated the difficulty of retrofitting the world's major cities to the auto age without sacrificing highly valued amenities of city life.

By the late 1970s, after two severe energy shocks, even more extreme questions about the future of the automobile were widely posed. Was the automotive system "running on empty"?[3] Would continued automobility be possible at all within perhaps 30 or 40 years, when the world's petroleum reserves were predicted to be largely exhausted?

At just this point the extraordinary period of postwar economic growth came to a close. Worldwide auto use and the demand for new cars suddenly leveled off in response to broader economic phenonema, many of them related to energy. The environmental and resource issues of the 1970s were temporarily deferred because the more ominous forecasts of resource shortages and environmental crises had all assumed a continuation of world economic growth at 1960s rates. However, the new situation of prolonged worldwide recession quickly raised even more pressing problems for the world auto industry and for persons who earned their livelihoods from auto manufacturing.

At the peak of world automotive production, in 1979, just as the second great energy-price adjustment began to slow the world economy, more than 3.6 million workers were directly employed manufacturing automobiles in France, Italy, Japan, Sweden, the United Kingdom, the United States, and West Germany (the seven Auto Program countries). This figure did not include many workers in related industries, such as steel, electronics, and machine tools, providing raw materials, components, and tools for auto manufacture. With all these workers taken into account, auto manufacturing in 1979 accounted for 5–6 million jobs in these nations and several million additional jobs elsewhere in the world.

By 1981 the number of directly employed auto workers in the seven Auto Program nations had declined by 400,000 and perhaps 600,000 other jobs were lost in raw-materials supply and component manufacturing. And this may have been only the beginning, since the effect of the new automated, flexible manufacturing systems in the auto industry was only beginning to be felt.

What is more, the impact on manufacturing employment was only a portion of the impact of the automotive system on employment and the total economy. In the United States, the country with the highest level of motorization, government data for 1979 indicated that 9.1

percent of the work force was employed in motor-vehicle-related occupations: 1.2 percent in manufacturing vehicles, 2.8 percent in selling
and servicing them, 1.0 percent in building and maintaining the highway
network, and 4.1 percent in hauling freight or passengers by means of
motor vehicles (many of them automobiles).[4] In other developed countries the percentages were somewhat smaller but still substantial.

Thus, it was apparent that shrinkage of the motor-vehicle system
could present even more urgent problems than rapid expansion. What
was more, a leveling off in motor-vehicle production combined with
changes in world energy prices suddenly raised the possibility of dramatic shifts in the location of employment within the worldwide vehicle-
manufacturing system, because national auto industries were very dif-
ferentially positioned to deal with the new world conditions of the
1980s.

During the period of rapid world growth from the end of World War
II to 1979, barriers to automotive trade between the developed countries
were progressively dismantled. This process was not terribly threatening
to any national auto industry because the types of vehicles demanded
in the American and Japanese markets and in the different European
countries varied markedly. International trade in automobiles was substantial and was increasing gradually, but most imports were in marginal
market segments that domestic producers could afford to ignore.

After 1979, all this changed. The types of automobiles demanded
across the developed world converged dramatically. This was particularly true in the United States, whose predominant "very large"*
automobile had been in a size class of its own. Suddenly every world
manufacturer was a potential threat to every other manufacturer in a
largely integrated world market. Worse, from the producers' standpoint,
it was a buyer's market, because the slump in demand due to the
slumping world economy created excess capacity for the world auto
industry in aggregate. Some national industries (notably in Japan and
parts of Europe) were able to produce cars of unchallenged quality or
at substantially lower cost, or both, and so a dramatic export surge
developed as the less competitive national industries reeled under a
flood of imports in addition to a deep slump in the overall market.

---

*Throughout this volume, we will categorize automobile by five size classes: small, light,
medium, large, and very large. The criteria defining each class are given in the note to
figure 6.1.

This new competition pitted against one another national auto industries organized on strikingly different principles, and it quickly generated trade imbalances of unprecedented magnitude for a manufactured good. The imbalance between Japan and the Western auto-producing nations was particularly marked. The net Japanese trade surplus in motor vehicles and parts with North America and Western Europe soared from \$2.9 billion in 1973 to \$17.6 billion in 1981.[5] Because the auto industry is the world's largest manufacturing activity and is widely perceived as a key industry for any developed economy, the prospect of additional dramatic shifts in the location of auto production, notably from the United States and some parts of Europe to Japan, quickly generated intense economic and political conflict within the developed world. Many observers analyzed this turn of events, if protracted, as the potential tip point whereby the United States, Europe, and Japan would revert from their postwar path of increasing economic integration back toward isolation and nationalism.

In the mid 1980s, in the midst of a modest recovery in the world economy, there is a strong desire on the part of governments, carmakers, and unions to assume that the recent trade and production crises are past. Most Western automakers are once again profitable, and sales have increased in most national markets in comparison with the lows of 1982. However, the fundamental imbalances between national production systems have not changed, and "temporary" trade barriers raised after 1979 are proving difficult to remove. Furthermore, even the most optimistic forecasts of economic growth in the remainder of this century are very low when compared with the postwar average. Thus, the next recession in auto sales may throw the automotive world back into intense turmoil, even if current trade barriers are relaxed for the next few years.

Finally, even with the assumption that current trade issues will be resolved and that sustained economic growth and expansion of the world auto industry will return, the earlier problems of resource constraints and environmental limits are commonly thought to lie in wait. Thus, the automotive future is surrounded with questions—questions about natural resources, about environmental acceptability, about the long-term demand for new cars, about the future location of auto production, about automotive employment, and about the very nature of economic and political relations among the major auto-producing nations.

This volume seeks to answer these questions in a time frame of the next 20 years. This is the period extending beyond the short-term economic and political fluctuations of the next few years, but near enough that government officials, industry executives, union leaders, and other informed opinion leaders in the key auto-producing nations must begin making plans now to deal with foreseeable problems.

Because new automobile designs require about 5 years to bring to market, will typically continue in production for 6–8 years, and will be driven by motorists for 12 or more years after leaving the factory, it is apparent that automobiles designed in 1984 will still be in use in large numbers in the year 2010. Thus, there is an extraordinarily long lag between the identification of problems in the automotive world and the point at which adjustments to the production system and the vehicle fleet are fully in place. This creates a need for great foresight on the part of those guiding the future of the automobile—a need this volume seeks to help meet. In addition, when our analysis identifies general trends that are adverse to the interests of the world community, particularly in the area of trade and international economic relations, new approaches with greater promise will be proposed.

We begin by examining the path of evolution in the automotive world from the bright beginnings of 100 years ago to the present crisis. The development of the world auto industry during this period shows a clear pattern involving recurrent crises that have led to creative shifts in course, which have been followed by renewed growth. Understanding this pattern provides a vital perspective on the current era. More important, it is the starting point for a consideration of productive paths to the future.

2   A Century of Transformations

The automobile as a basic concept has hardly evolved at all during its first century. A hundred years after the first practical vehicle, the automobile is still a four-wheeled, internally powered personal transport apparatus for road use, designed to carry a driver and a few passengers. Technical advances have provided utility, performance, operating economy, and personal comfort far beyond the dreams of the original automakers, but the concept of the automobile remains much as it was in the mid 1880s.

The auto industry, by contrast, has evolved through a series of dramatic transformations from a small group of artisans and tinkerers concentrated in France and Germany to a vast worldwide enterprise organized on totally different principles. The first of these transformations was the breakthrough by American producers around 1910 from custom building to a mass-volume industry. The second occurred in Europe in the 1950s when European producers combined mass production with an emphasis on product differentiation to challenge American-based production for the first time. The third commenced in Japan in the late 1960s, when Japanese auto producers made dramatic breakthroughs in production organization that soon yielded a lower-cost product of unexampled manufacturing accuracy.

Each transformation has had three elements: A creative breakthrough in some aspect of production systems or products has facilitated an explosion of demand in the domestic market and has quickly resulted in a sudden and powerful export threat to producers in the rest of the world. The transformations and their elements are summarized in table 2.1.

The consequence of each transformation has been that a new region of the world has seized the initiative in shaping the future of the world auto industry. Figure 2.1 shows the remarkable consequences of these transformations for regional shares of world motor-vehicle production.

Table 2.1
Industrial transformations in automotive history

Transformation	Date	Production or product innovation	Geographic area of rapid market growth	National or regional industry seizing initiative in shaping the world industry
I	1902 into 1920s	Standardized product, mass production system	U.S.	U.S.
II	1950s into 1960s	Product differentiation, emphasis on product technology	Europe	Europe
III	late 1960s through 1970s	"Just-in-time," total quality and corporate groups as a new system of production organization	Japan	Japan
IV (?)	late 1980s into 1990s	Concentrated production at low-factor-cost locations	Certain LDCs such as Korea, Mexico, and Brazil	?
or				
IV (?)	late 1980s into 1990s	Mass introduction of flexible manufacturing systems; new forms of "cooperative competition"	Many?	None, many, all?

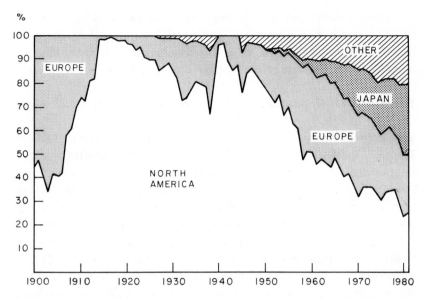

Figure 2.1
Shares of world motor-vehicle production by region. Note: The data are for motor vehicles, including cars, trucks, and buses. Data on cars alone are not available for the early years of the industry. Source: Calculated from *World Motor Vehicle Data Book*, 1983 edition, Detroit: MVMA, 1983

Each transformation within the auto industry has had a broader political dimension as well. Each transformation was at least partially a consequence of government policy in the nation or region of its origin, and each led directly to government policy responses in other countries affected by the resulting export surge. Understanding the process of transformation therefore involves keeping both the industrial and the governmental contribution continuously in view. The entire process, within industry and among governments, has in each instance taken many years to play itself out fully, with major consequences for the course of the world economy and for relationships among nations.

The third transformation is now well advanced, although its final outcome is far from clear. Whatever its resolution, it will doubtless have successors. Indeed, another transformation has been widely predicted for the next 20 years. This possibility, involving the rise of auto manufacturing in several less developed countries, has been viewed as a long-term threat to the vast auto industry of the developed world—including Japan. We have a different view about the future shape of the world industry, but it is quite correct to think that a key objective of this volume is to discern the outline of future transformations. In this chapter, we set the stage for this task by carefully examining the nature of the transformations that have occurred thus far.

The First Transformation: From Curiosity to Volume Production

The automobile was born in Germany and France in the mid 1880s. The early models were one-of-a-kind efforts—really experimental prototypes designed for the pleasure and amusement of the well-to-do. Production volumes gradually increased to batches of similar but seldom identical vehicles, and the automobile, even 15 years after its invention, was still no more an industrial product than are houses or bassoons.

Part of the problem was the lack of appropriate mass-production techniques. This in turn was due to the concentration on luxury designs for which there could only be a very small market and which therefore did not call for innovations in mass manufacturing. This design tendency was reinforced by the policy of a number of European governments of offering bonuses to those who purchased large, heavy-duty vehicles suitable for military use in the event of war.[1] Thus, although the European cars were often elegant in conception and finely crafted, their market was restricted to a tiny stratum of society.

By 1906, more than 20 years after the appearance of the first practical vehicle, French and German producers still accounted for 58 percent of worldwide production and were the acknowledged leaders in high-performance products.[2] However, the market was tiny; fewer than 50,000 vehicles were produced per year in all of Europe. Meanwhile, the stage was being set for a radical transformation that would transfer the momentum in the world auto industry to the United States.

In 1902, Ransom Olds initiated American series production with his "curved dash" Oldsmobile. This car was tiny in comparison with typical European products and was explicitly intended for a mass market. By 1906, Henry Leland had designed a Cadillac with completely interchangeable parts. This innovation won the Dewar engineering competition in England when three Cadillacs were completely taken apart by the judges, reassembled into three new vehicles, and driven 500 miles without mechanical failure. Although Leland's design was too elaborate for immediate mass-market success, it firmly established interchangeability as the design philosophy of the future.[3]

By 1908, Henry Ford and his associates were combining the design and manufacturing ideas of Olds, Leland, and many others into a new car, the Model T, which was to be backed up by a new manufacturing system. The Model T incorporated a number of advances in fabrication techniques and materials to simplify manufacture, hold down costs, and adapt the car to primitive rural driving conditions as well as the need for simple maintenance and repairs. The excellence of the design was soon augumented, in 1914, by the continuous production system that came to be called the assembly line. This united many years of experimentation in two separate aspects of production. New production machinery to facilitate the continuous flow of materials in the assembly process was married to a fully worked out "scientific management" approach to the division of manufacturing skills and the routinization of complex work.[4]

In short order, Ford used this new system of social organization and production machinery to lead the world auto industry into the age of mass production. From 1,700 vehicles in the company's first year (1903), production rose slowly to 10,000 in 1908, when the Model T was introduced, but then exploded to 300,000 in 1914, when the assembly line was fully installed. By 1923, when Model T sales peaked, Ford's U.S. production totaled 1.9 million. At that point, after the economic devastation of World War I had completely halted European production for 5 years and crippled the postwar economy, Ford was producing 44 percent of the world's output of automobiles from his American production base. In that year other American producers, notably the rapidly growing General Motors, accounted for additional 2.1 million units, bringing the American share of world auto production in 1923 to 91 percent.[5]

In the early 1920s, Alfred Sloan at General Motors perfected the decentralized organizational techniques needed to manage the giant enterprises the automakers had become.[6] American dominance of what had become one of the world's largest industries was then nearly complete. Throughout the 1920s the American share of world auto production remained at 84 percent or higher, and was generally in excess of 90 percent when American-controlled production in Canada was included.

Although the lion's share of the world auto market was also in the United States, the American producers were exporters as well. In 1929 they exported 10 percent of their production (546,000 units) and in the process captured 35 percent of the world automobile market outside the United States.

The European Response: Government Mediation

This remarkable American achievement did not mean that auto production in Europe and elsewhere was headed toward extinction, or that a number of smaller European producers did not continue to pioneer in the field of automotive technology. However, in view of the wealth and market power of the American automakers, some explanation is needed of why they did not eliminate their foreign rivals and concentrate practically all auto manufacture in the United States.

The answer lies partly with the primitive shipping systems of the early twentieth century. Transportation of fully assembled automobiles entailed high costs for crating and for repair of damage en route, compared with even low-volume final assembly near the point of sale. Thus, in the same way that General Motors and Ford established a large number of regional assembly plants in the United States by the mid 1920s, they also established regional assembly plants in many foreign countries. By 1929, Ford was assembling cars in 21 countries while General Motors had assembly plants in 16.[7]

The more basic reason, however, for the failure of U.S.-based production to capture practically the whole auto market was the reaction of governments in Europe to the American challenge. In the early days of the industry, European governments had permitted nearly free trade in cars. As late as 1913 the tariff on cars entering Germany was only 3 percent. In Italy it was 4 to 6 percent, and in France 9 to 14 percent. The U.K. applied its historic free-trade stance to cars, imposing no tariff on auto imports.[8] After World War I a broad consensus arose in Europe that there was a need to protect and promote domestic auto manufacture, including the production of major components such as engines. This called for domestic production facilities far beyond the relatively simple final-assembly plants the American producers were already building.

Even the United Kingdom adopted this philosophy, by retaining its wartime "luxury" tariff of 33.3 percent on imported cars. It also imposed a horsepower tax, calculated on the bore of the cylinders, which was highly disadvantageous to most American autos such as the Model T. Steep tariffs were also applied to tires and other components.[9]

Elsewhere in Europe during the 1920s, tariffs on finished units and parts were adjusted steeply upward, with the result that the major

Table 2.2
Tariffs on passenger cars, 1913–1983 (expressed in percent of customs value)

Year	U.S.	Japan	France	Germany	Italy	U.K.
1913	45.0	n.d.	9–14	3	4–6	0
1924	25–50[a]	n.d.	45–180	13	6–11	33.3
1929	10.0[b]	50	45	20	6–11	33.3
1932	10.0	n.d.	45–70	25	18–123	33.3
1937	10.0	70[c]	47–74	40	101–111	33.3
1950	10.0	40	35	35	35	33.3
1960	8.5	35–40	30	13–16	31.5–40.5	30.0
1968	5.5	30	0/17.6	0/17.6	0/17.6	17.6
1973	3.0	6.4	0/10.9	0/10.9	0/10.9	10.9
1978	3.0	0	0/10.9	0/10.9	0/10.9	0/10.9
1983	2.8	0	0/10.5	0/10.5	0/10.5	0/10.5

Notes: Ranges in this table indicate that tariffs varied by type of vehicle or reciprocally with foreign tariffs. For example, in the 1920s the U.S. tariff varied from 25 percent to 50 percent, being adjusted within that range to equal the auto tariff in the country of origin. The "slashes" in the entries for the European countries after 1968 (1978 in the case of the U.K.) indicate the elimination of tariffs within the EEC and a common external tariff.
a. 1922; b. 1930; c. 1940; n.d. = no relevant data available.
Sources: Motor Vehicle Manufacturers Association, *Digest of Import Duties Levied by Selected Countries*, Detroit: MVMA, 1974; Toyota Motor Sales Corporation, *The Motor Industry of Japan 1981*, Tokyo: Toyota, 1981; Daniel T. Jones, *Maturity and Crisis in the European Car Industry*, Brighton: University of Sussex Science Policy Research Unit, 1981; tariff schedules of GATT.

national markets were largely protected from imports (table 2.2). American producers were still able to sell to the non-European world despite tariffs, since there were no domestic manufacturers outside North American and Europe, but those producers wishing to sell in Europe had to establish full-scale manufacturing in each market in order to offer products at competitive prices. Ford and General Motors quickly moved to do this. In 1931, Ford opened a fully integrated manufacturing complex at Dagenham, England, modeled on its Rouge complex in Detroit. Similar plants on a smaller scale were opened at Cologne in 1931 and at Strasbourg in 1934. General Motors, which lagged behind Ford in developing overseas operations, adopted the alternative strategy of buying established automobile manufacturers in Britain (Vauxhall, in 1925) and in Germany (Adam Opel, in 1929) as the quickest way to gain access to European markets. Both GM and Ford would have moved even further if all European countries had been as open to direct foreign investment as Germany and the United Kingdom. GM's attempts to purchase a French manufacturer were resisted by the French government, and both GM and Ford were denied permission to establish manufacturing operations in Italy to compete with Fiat.[10]

The effect of the American investments was to diffuse American manufacturing know-how in Europe—particularly in Germany and the United Kingdom, the countries most open to direct investment. This also spurred efforts by indigenous European manufacturers to catch up with world "best practice," and to a considerable extent European manufacturing know-how came to equal that of U.S.-based producers during the 1930s. However, the markets in Europe were too small to afford manufacturers the full advantage of scale in auto production.

As the Depression set in, domestic markets stagnated and tariff barriers were raised even higher. As a result, before World War II, national auto markets in Europe were small, and no European manufacturer seems to have been able to produce an automobile, even in the most modern manufacturing complex, at a cost comparable to those of the Ford and GM operations in Detroit. Internal Ford Motor Company documents of the period clearly indicate that all of the company's European manufacturing operations, including the highly integrated, state-of-the-art Dagenham facility, had higher delivered costs in Europe (excluding tariffs, of course) than their counterparts in Detroit, even though the European facilities were 6,000 kilometers closer to the market and paid lower wages.[11] The problem was largely the simple lack of volume as a result of market isolation, but the solution—in the form of a common European market—was only discovered 20 years later after the lessons of the Depression, the accompanying trade wars, and World War II were put to creative use.

The Second Transformation: Volume Production plus Product Differentiation

In the early 1950s, as the European economic recovery commenced, the European auto industry consisted of a jumble of small producers. At the beginning of the decade they accounted for only 13.6 percent of world auto production, compared with North America's 85.1 percent (table 2.3 and figure 2.2). The Europeans fashioned domestically produced products for very different national market conditions, which were due to the wide variations in consumer incomes, vehicle taxes,

Table 2.3
Regional distribution of world auto production (thousands of units)

Year	North America	Western Europe	Japan	CPEs	ROW	Total
1929	4790.7	554.0	—	10.0	—	5354.7
1938	2143.4	878.6	—	51.9	—	3073.9
1950	6950.0	1110.4	1.6	99.1	6.7	8167.8
1955	8295.2	2486.2	20.3	154.3	58.6	11014.6
1960	7000.6	5119.7	165.1	272.5	427.3	12985.2
1965	10016.3	7519.4	696.2	410.3	639.3	19281.5
1970	7490.6	10378.6	3178.7	701.4	1006.2	22755.5
1971	9679.8	10932.0	3717.9	922.6	1120.5	26372.8
1972	9982.7	11152.8	4022.3	1146.4	1178.2	27482.4
1973	10895.0	11472.0	4470.6	1393.9	1377.5	29609.0
1974	8490.1	9943.7	3931.8	1634.4	1551.5	25551.5
1975	7762.0	9325.5	4568.1	1768.5	1532.6	24956.7
1976	9635.2	10775.2	5027.8	1868.0	1608.9	28915.1
1977	10376.1	11231.9	5431.0	1962.7	1575.9	30577.6
1978	10315.4	11320.8	5748.3	2065.3	1776.0	31225.8
1979	9421.4	11342.8	6175.8	2092.2	1980.6	31012.8
1980	7222.3	10371.8	7038.1	2117.8	1889.2	·28639.2
1981	7059.3	9816.3	6974.1	2007.6	1495.4	27352.7
1982	5860.3	10269.7	6886.9	1972.0	1616.5	26605.4

Notes:
This table includes auto production in those countries that fully manufacture cars. This is defined as 75 percent or more value added locally. A number of other countries such as Mexico, South Africa, and Nigeria assemble or partially manufacture substantial numbers of automobiles with lower amounts of value added locally. These countries have not been included here to avoid double counting since in many cases these cars are knocked-down kits, which are also counted in the production statistics of countries in this table. However, the reader should understand that available world data on auto production are notoriously imprecise. It is not possible to allocate auto production by region with absolute precision.
The producing nations within the regions are as follows:
North America: U.S. and Canada
Western Europe: Austria, Belgium, France, Germany, Italy, Netherlands, Spain, Sweden, and U.K.
Centrally Planned Economies: Czechoslovakia, East Germany, Poland, Rumania, and U.S.S.R.
Rest of World: Australia, Argentina, Brazil, India, South Korea, Turkey, and Yugoslavia.
— = fewer than 500 units
Sources:
MVMA, *World Motor Vehicle Data Book*, various years; SMMT, *The Motor Industry of Great Britain*, various years.

Table 2.3 (continued)

L'Argus de l'Automobile, *Statistiques Automobiles*
Automotive News, *Market Data Book Issue*
JAMA, *Motor Vehicle Statistics*
Comecon data 1980 and *Comecon foreign trade data 1980*, edited by the Vienna Institute
for Comparative Economic Studies, London: Macmillan, 1983 and 1982.

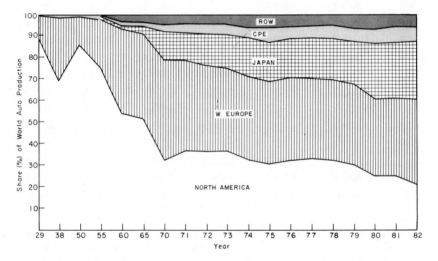

Figure 2.2
Share of world automobile production by region, 1929–1982. Source: See table 2.3

and geography among the European countries. In Italy, low incomes, high fuel taxes, and the concentration of population in ancient cities with narrow streets and limited parking combined to channel consumer demand toward very small cars. In Sweden, with its lower fuel taxes, higher incomes, less dense cities, and harsh winter driving conditions, consumers desired larger, sturdier cars, even at the expense of higher purchase cost and fuel consumption.

In addition, the numerous European manufacturers were pursuing many different technical solutions to the differing design requirements. Some producers favored large engines; others experimented with very small displacements and unusual cylinder layouts. Some producers used rear-engine/rear-drive arrangements, others offered front-mounted engines with rear-wheel drive, and still others concentrated on front-mounted engines with front-wheel drive. Unit bodies competed with chassis-on-frame designs, diesels vied with gas engines, and a myriad of suspension systems and body types were available. In contrast, the North American producers had standardized on a large, 6- or 8-cylinder, front-engine/rear-drive, gasoline-fueled, chassis-on-frame design, which they were intent on producing in the highest possible volumes.

To the American observer, the welter of European design approaches and the large number of small producers signaled only confusion in the marketplace and a failure by European producers to gain the advantages of high-volume production. So long as European markets were tightly sealed off by tariffs this was true. However, once the tariff walls in Europe began to come down in the late 1950s and early 1960s, the diversity of the European auto industry became its greatest strength. When each manufacturer could sell its specialized products in all the markets of Europe, adequate scale to capture full production economies was suddenly available. Table 2.4 indicates the extraordinary growth in intra-European auto trade since the 1950s. Real prices to consumers fell, demand surged upward, and the European industry advanced to the forefront of world motor-vehicle manufacturing.

An additional spur to the dynamism of the European auto industry was the continuing need to accommodate new participants in an expanded European community. Spain in particular provided a spur to competition as the Common Market's external tariff fell toward the end of the 1960s. Its low wages and openness to direct foreign investment proved particularly attractive to the American multinational corporations, which had no national allegiances within Europe but desired to increase their trans-European market share. Other European

Table 2.4
Auto trade within Western Europe

	Intra–W. European trade		Inter-producer trade in W. Europe	
	thousands of units	as percentage of production	thousands of units	as percentage of production
1929	39.0	7.0	13.9	2.5
1938	74.7	8.5	17.0	1.9
1950	200.6	18.1	67.1	6.0
1960	961.5	18.8	360.5	7.0
1970	2,676.0	25.8	1,277.0	12.3
1980	3,700.0	35.6	2,250.0	21.6

Notes:
"Inter-producer trade" is trade between the major auto producing countries in Europe: France, Germany, Italy, Spain, Sweden, and U.K. The growth of this type of trade is particularly significant because each of these countries is capable of meeting its needs internally and in the years before the EEC did so.
Sources:
See table 2.3

manufacturers expanded their Spanish production as well, and output soared from 40,000 units in 1960 to just over a million in 1980. Forty-five percent of production was exported to other European countries.[12]
  By the early 1970s the total European market was equal in size to the North American market (figure 2.3). However, the Europeans had already surpassed North America in production because the European producers, with their wide product range, were in a strong position to sell to the rest of the world. Tariffs fell dramatically throughout the world between 1950 and 1973, opening much of the world to relatively unfettered marketplace competition. The Europeans quickly took advantage of this, greatly aided by the fact that North American automobiles had grown so large that they were not suited to consumer incomes and energy prices in any other world market. American auto exports, which (except to Canada) had fallen to practically zero during the tariff wars of the 1930s, failed to grow significantly in the 1950s and 1960s, even as tariffs fell and American exports to most world markets were rapidly increasing in other sectors. Meanwhile, exports of European automobiles to points outside of Europe and the European share of world exports grew rapidly (table 2.5 and figure 2.4). This was most dramatically illustrated in U.S.-Europe auto trade, where the pre-war American tariff was largely eliminated by the 1950s and European

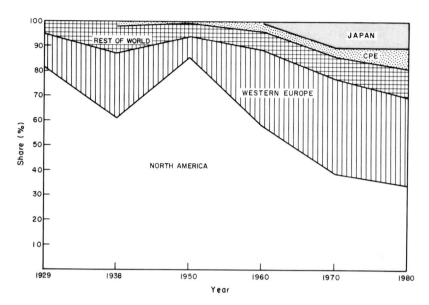

Figure 2.3
Share of world automobile market by region, 1929–1980. Source: See table 2.3

Table 2.5
Extraregional auto exports

	Exported from		
	N. America	W. Europe	Japan
Units (thousands)			
1929	400.0 (est.)	55.9	—
1938	149.2	96.3	—
1950	116.7	375.7	—
1960	107.3	1212.6	7.0
1970	76.0	1889.1	725.6
1980	170.6	1276.4	3947.2

— = fewer than 500 units
Sources: See table 2.3

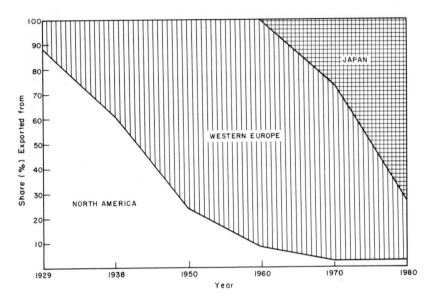

Figure 2.4
Share of extraregional auto exports, 1929–1980. Source: See table 2.3

tariffs were on their way down. Although American exports of finished units to Europe never approached even 1 percent of the European market in the postwar era, after 1956 the European share of the American market began to grow rapidly (table 2.6).

The Europeans' initial success in the American market came among buyers of the smallest cars, to whom they offered products from the low and intermediate segments of their European lines (typified by the Volkswagen Beetle). The Europeans in fact "invented" this market segment in the United States, as these customers had been ignored by the American producers. However, an 8.1 percent European share during the 1958 recession was enough to provoke a response by the Americans, whose "compact" models soon drove the European share back to about 5 percent.

As the American market segments served by the European producers grew as a percentage of the total American auto market in the late 1960s, the European threat to American-based production grew once again, reaching a new peak of 10.5 percent of the market in 1970.

Table 2.6
Import share of the American, European, and Japanese auto markets

Imports to	U.S.			Europe	Japan
Exported from	Europe	Japan	World	Japan	World
1950	0.3	—	0.3	n.d.	n.d.
1955	0.8	—	0.8	n.d.	n.d.
1956	1.6	—	1.6	n.d.	n.d.
1957	3.4	—	3.4	n.d.	n.d.
1958	8.1	—	8.1	n.d.	n.d.
1959	10.2	—	10.2	n.d.	n.d.
1960	7.6	—	7.6	n.d.	n.d.
1961	6.5	—	6.5	n.d.	n.d.
1962	4.8	0.1	4.9	n.d.	n.d.
1963	5.0	0.1	5.1	n.d.	n.d.
1964	5.8	0.2	6.0	n.d.	n.d.
1965	5.8	0.3	6.1	n.d.	n.d.
1966	6.8	0.5	7.3	n.d.	n.d.
1967	8.2	0.9	9.1	n.d.	n.d.
1968	8.9	1.6	10.5	0.6	n.d.
1969	8.7	2.5	11.2	n.d.	n.d.
1970	10.5	4.2	14.7	1.1	n.d.
1971	9.0	5.9	14.9	1.6	n.d.
1972	7.6	5.7	13.3	2.7	n.d.
1973	9.0	6.2	15.2	3.6	n.d.
1974	9.0	6.7	15.7	4.0	n.d.
1975	8.9	9.3	18.2	5.2	1.7
1976	5.6	9.2	14.8	5.6	1.7
1977	6.3	12.0	18.2	6.2	1.7
1978	5.9	11.9	17.8	6.3	1.9
1979	5.6	17.0	22.6	7.2	2.1
1980	5.4	22.8	28.2	9.8	1.6
1981	5.8	23.0	28.8	9.1	1.1
1982	5.4	23.2	28.6	8.6	1.2

Notes:
— = less than 0.05 percent; n.d. = no relevant data available
Europe = all countries in Western Europe
Sources:
For U.S.: MVMA, *Automobile Facts and Figures*, various years; Automotive News, *Market Data Book*, various years. For Europe: SPRU Databank on the Western European Auto Industry. For Japan: Japan Automobile Manufacturers Association, *The Motor Industry of Japan*, various years.

Unionized American auto workers, and American labor more generally, began to voice concerns about this trend and about the continuing investments of American multinational corporations in foreign production facilities.

Had the growth of European automakers' share of the U.S. market continued, a new round of government mediation of trade flows—this time from the American end—might have ensued. However, instead the American producers responded with another round of new small cars. Aided by rising European wages and the dollar devaluation of 1971, they gradually pushed down the European share to the 5–6 percent range. The demands for government mediation gradually abated, lessened also by the continuing boom in the world economy, the boom in the world auto market in particular, and the decision by Volkwagen in 1974 to assemble its low-priced models for the North American market in the United States.

Despite their setback in small cars, the European producers had other cards to play because of the diversity of their products and their technology. They refocused their U.S. marketing on cars originally designed as "larger" models for the European market. Although these were still smaller than dominant U.S. designs, the European producers' emphasis on luxury, sporty performance, and operating economy (through the introduction of diesel passenger cars to the U.S. market) gradually permitted them to redefine the U.S. luxury market and capture practically all sales in the price class above $20,000. In 1980, in fact, although Europe's unit volume to the United States and Canada was only 30 percent of Japan's, the dollar value of Europe's motor-vehicle exports to North America was 54 percent of the Japan's.[13]

By the early 1970s, the second transformation had largely worked its way through the transatlantic auto industry. Government protection and aid in the 1930s, thorough assimilation and refinement of American manufacturing techniques by the European industry, and the concerted effort to remove trade barriers in the 1950s and 1960s had permitted the European producers to take advantage of their natural strengths in products. The result was rebalanced competition. The European and American markets were open both internally and to each other by the early 1970s, and the volume of automotive trade within Europe and across the Atlantic was substantial. Table 2.7 summarizes these trends in world automotive trade.

In addition, large amounts of direct investment in manufacturing facilities occurred in both directions—from the United States to Europe

Table 2.7
Production and trade in automobiles by major area, 1929–1980 (millions of units)

Imports to	Exports from					
	N. America	W. Europe	Japan	CPEs	ROW	Total
1929						
N. America	0.1	—	—	—	—	0.1
W. Europe	0.2	—	—	—	—	0.2
Japan	—	—	—	—	—	—
CPEs	—	—	—	—	—	—
ROW	0.2	0.1	—	—	—	0.3
Total exports	0.5	0.1	—	—	—	0.6
Production	4.8	0.6	—	—	—	5.4
1938						
N. America	—	—	—	—	—	—
W. Europe	—	0.1	—	—	—	0.1
Japan	—	—	—	—	—	—
CPEs	—	—	—	—	—	—
ROW	0.2	0.1	—	—	—	0.3
Total exports	0.2	0.2	—	—	—	0.4
Production	2.1	0.9	—	0.1	—	3.1
1950						
N. America	—	0.1	—	—	—	0.1
W. Europe	—	0.2	—	—	—	0.2
Japan	—	—	—	—	—	—
CPEs	—	—	—	—	—	—
ROW	0.1	0.3	—	—	—	0.4
Total exports	0.1	0.6	—	—	—	0.7
Production	7.0	1.1	—	0.1	—	8.2
1960						
N. America	—	0.6	—	—	—	0.6
W. Europe	—	1.0	—	—	—	1.0
Japan	—	—	—	—	—	—
CPEs	—	—	—	—	—	—
ROW	0.1	0.6	—	—	—	0.7
Total exports	0.1	2.2	—	—	—	2.3
Production	7.0	5.1	0.2	0.3	0.4	13.0

Table 2.7 (continued)

Imports to	Exports from					
	N. America	W. Europe	Japan	CPEs	ROW	Total
1970						
N. America	0.9	1.0	0.4	—	—	2.3
W. Europe	—	2.7	0.1	0.1	—	2.9
Japan	—	—	—	—	—	—
CPEs	—	—	—	0.1	—	0.1
ROW	0.1	0.8	0.2	—	—	1.1
Total exports	1.0	4.5	0.7	0.2	—	6.4
Production	7.5	10.4	3.2	0.7	1.0	22.8
1980						
N. America	1.1	0.6	2.0	—	—	3.7
W. Europe	—	3.7	1.0	0.1	—	4.8
Japan	—	—	—	—	—	—
CPEs	—	—	—	0.5	—	0.5
ROW	0.1	0.7	0.9	—	0.2	1.9
Total exports	1.2	5.0	3.9	0.6	0.2	10.9
Production	7.2	10.4	7.0	2.1	1.9	28.6

Notes: To determine exports from a region, read down the column. For example, in 1980 Japan exported 2.0 million automobiles to North America, 1.0 million to Western Europe, and 0.9 million to the Rest of the World, for a total of 3.9 million. To determine imports, read across the rows. For example, in 1980 North American countries imported 1.1 million units from other North American countries, 0.6 million from Western Europe, and 2.0 million from Japan, for a total of 3.7 million. Intra-regional trade flows (e.g., Canada to U.S., France to West Germany, Brazil to Uruguay, Poland to Hungary) are indicated by boxes. To determine production in a region, read down the column to the row labeled "Production." For example, production of autos in Western Europe totaled 10.4 million units in 1980. The regions are as follow: N. America = U.S. and Canada; W. Europe = OECD member countries in Europe; CPEs = U.S.S.R., Eastern Europe, and People's Republic of China. Values are rounded to nearest 100,000. — = fewer than 50,000 units. Sources: See table 2.3.

in the 1960s and from Europe to the United States in the 1970s. This caused disquiet in Europe in the late 1960s about a new "American challenge" in which American multinational corporations would seize a controlling interest in European industry. However, the actual effect was soon realized to be a further transfer of American managerial expertise to Europe, this time for the purpose of developing integrated, trans-European manufacturing systems. The key evidence was that the two firms that actually achieved this (Ford and GM) prospered in Europe and pushed their European competitors to think in similar trans-European terms. The firm that failed (Chrysler) was never able to integrate a number of nationally oriented subsidiaries into a trans-European entity.

In the 1970s Volkswagen moved its production of lower priced models for the North American market to the United States, Renault took a controlling interest in American Motors, and a number of European auto producers (including Volvo, Daimler-Benz, and Renault) bought smaller American truck manufacturers. In addition, a number of component and aftermarket suppliers (including Michelin and Robert Bosch) established American manufacturing operations. Thus, despite occasional strains, the competitive balance between the United States and Europe was relatively stable by the 1970s. Integration of the two regional industries continued to grow, and auto trade ceased to be a transatlantic political issue.

The Third Transformation: Another Breakthrough in Volume Production

As the trade barriers were coming down within Europe and across the Atlantic in the 1950s and 1960s, they were also coming down all over the world. The Kennedy Round of trade negotiations in 1962 pushed the process ahead rapidly, with the result that the European external tariff on automobiles was reduced to 10.9 percent by 1973 while the American tariff was reduced to a nominal 3.0 percent. In a competitively balanced world auto industry, this meant mainly that consumers had access to most of the world's automotive products without paying large excise taxes. It also meant that international auto trade in general increased at a rapid rate. However, when a new approach to production organization was pioneered in Japan, the relatively low tariff barriers provided the opportunity for another dramatic transformation in the world auto industry.

The first transformation in the auto industry (from custom to volume production) was experienced in Japan at the beginning of its auto age— an era ushered in by the Americans. Ford and General Motors established Japanese plants in 1924 and 1927, respectively, to assemble kits of parts produced in Detroit. For a number of years, Japan offered a striking example of the American dominance of the world auto industry. In 1929, Ford and GM assembled 29,338 vehicles in Japan, and 5,018 additional vehicles were imported in fully finished form (mostly from the United States), while only 437 vehicles were manufactured in Japan to Japanese designs.[14]

During the 1930s, however, the Japanese government's concern about foreign domination grew. The army in particular was anxious that indigenous Japanese industry be capable of full-scale auto manufacturing. The Law Regarding Automobile Manufacturing Enterprise of 1936 made this intent clear, and by 1939 both Ford and General Motors had closed their operations. However, the focus on war production and then the war itself foreclosed any immediate possibility of Japanese-owned producers building up an internationally competitive auto industry.

In the immediate postwar period, the Japanese government vacillated about the desirability and particularly about the feasibility of developing an independent auto industry. However, by the end of the American occupation in 1952 it had determined to include the auto sector in the list of industries to be favored with low-cost bank credit, preferential tax treatment, and careful protection of the domestic market.[15] In addition, it reaffirmed the prewar practice of requiring that Japanese auto plants be Japanese-owned. Without this last requirement, GM, Ford, and perhaps some of the European firms would presumably have once more dominated the domestic industry. Indeed, Ford acquired a new plant site in Yokohama in the hopes of being allowed to resume its prewar activities.[16]

Progress in building an indigenous domestic industry was slow as the Japanese producers used scarce foreign currency to obtain designs and tooling from a number of Western producers. In the early 1950s, as the Japanese producers experimented with organizational techniques, there were severe labor difficulties at Nissan. Progress in developing the product toward the minimal standard of quality and comfort for consumer acceptance in the United States and Europe was arduous.

However, by around 1960 the Japanese auto industry had begun to export. In addition, an organizational model had been found in industrial and conglomerate groups. A new labor-relations model had been developed in the form of company-based unions with lifetime employment, augmented later by "quality circles" and other approaches to worker participation. Finally, a new manufacturing philosophy, based on the concepts of "just-in-time" and "total quality," had taken hold. Together, these developments represented a major breakthrough in production organization that soon made it possible for the Japanese to build a car of a given specification with fewer hours of human effort than had previously been thought possible and to attain a previously unknown level of manufacturing accuracy in mass-market products. This was the key to the third transformation.

Over the next 20 years, as these manufacturing techniques were refined, the progress of the Japanese auto industry was continuous. Japan's share of Western markets jumped in several years (notably 1970, 1975, and 1979), and this drew the attention of the automotive world to Japan. However, these share increases were due to sudden shifts in the type of car demanded and slumps in Western markets resulting from recessions and energy price hikes rather than to sudden leaps in competitiveness by the Japanese producers, whose progress was continuous.

During this period the Japanese government gradually shifted its role from promotion and protection (which had been essential for the development of an independent Japanese industry) to guidance (which was of more questionable value). In the 1950s and 1960s the Ministry of International Trade and Industry (MITI) stressed the conventional view of the auto industry as a high-volume business above all else. To foster high volume it continually tried to consolidate the industry into two or three firms, each specializing in a single size segment of the market. MITI officials argued that in this way Japanese producers could quickly obtain the necessary volume to reduce their costs, expand volume in the domestic market, and break into world competition as low-cost producers on the basis of high volume and low wages.

In practice, Japan's success did not follow this path precisely. The initial Japanese efforts around 1960 to export a very basic product sold on the basis of very low price were not successful. These cars were not up to a minimum international standard and could not be sold merely on the basis of price. Instead, Japan's export success came through fine-tuning manufacturing systems to combine high-volume output with high quality and low labor content. This was the incremental task of many years.

The role of the Japanese government in building this manufacturing system, beyond assistance in building volume by completely protecting the domestic market from foreign products, was negligible. MITI did not invent the industrial or conglomerate groups, the new labor-relations model, the "just-in-time" manufacturing system, or the concept of "total quality." Indeed, MITI resisted the desire of a number of the conglomerate groups to maintain a role in auto manufacture. If left to its preferences, it might well have dampened the extraordinarily dynamic competition between the large number of firms in the Japanese domestic market. Thus, the Japanese breakthrough would not have been possible without government nurture; however, government aid alone was far from sufficient, and excessive government guidance might well have led to a poorer performance in export markets.

By 1973 the Japanese auto industry was well on its way to world leadership in manufacturing technique, but it was concentrating on the production of small cars and was not a cause of wide concern among producers in other regions. In the United States, the growing Japanese market share in the early 1970s was coming mostly at the expense of European small-car imports.

Then the first energy shock shifted the pattern of demand, particularly in the United States, in precisely the direction for which the Japanese producers were prepared. Japan's auto exports and market share zoomed upward, and the automotive world quickly took notice. After the 1979 energy-price adjustment pushed demand patterns even further in the favor of Japanese manufacturers, Western producers began to speak of the "Japanese challenge." By the late 1970s, the Japanese automakers were adding a net 400,000 units of production capacity per year and the fear began to grow in the United States and Europe that Japanese-based production would expand to supplant much of the production in the historic auto-producing regions.

The European-American Response: A New Round of Government Mediation

The early 1970s marked the culmination of remarkable progress toward open trade in automobiles among the Auto Program countries. By 1973 the American auto tariff had fallen to 3 percent, the Japanese tariff to 6.4 percent, and the Common Market external tariff to 10.9 percent. In addition, with the exception of Italy (which retained a unit limitation on Japanese automobiles), there were no import quotas barring auto trade.[17] This openness was the result of a wide perception that competition within the developed world was reasonably balanced and that open trade would lead to no dramatic relocation of auto production.

After 1973, however, the perception of rapidly growing Japanese capability in auto manufacture, coupled with economic slumps and stagnation (particularly in the U.S. auto market), reversed this trend and ushered in a new period of government mediation. One Western auto-producing nation after another retreated from open trade in the specific case of Japanese imports. This retreat commenced in 1975 when the British government encouraged the negotiation of a private agreement between Britain's auto-industry association and its Japanese counterpart that effectively limited Japanese passenger-car imports to 11 percent of the British market. France was next in 1977, with a 3 percent cap on Japanese market share. The other Auto Program countries followed in 1980–81 in the midst of the world economic slump. The U.S. government negotiated a "voluntary" restraint agreement whereby the Japanese government accepted responsibility for limiting passenger car exports to 1.76 million units (including station wagons and vans) in the year beginning April 1, 1981. This was a drop of 7.7 percent from the previous 12-month period. The agreement held imports to the same level in the two succeeding years. After further negotiations in the fall of 1983, the ceiling was increased to 1.94 million for the year beginning April 1, 1984.

After the agreement between the United States and Japan, Germany (long the bastion of free trade in the EEC) secured an informal promise that the Japanese auto producers would limit the rate of increase in their share in the German market. Belgium soon followed with an agreement to reduce Japanese imports to Belgium by 7 percent in 1981 compared with 1980. The Netherlands limited Japanese imports in 1981 to the 1980 level. In early 1983 Sweden warned that it would carefully monitor Japanese sales in Sweden to ensure that Japanese vehicles would not be diverted from other Western markets. In mid 1983, European auto protectionism took on a multilateral aspect for the first time as the European Economic Community reached agreement with the Japanese government that Japanese auto exports to the EEC market as a whole would be "moderate in relation to past export and market performance and future market developments." This was widely taken as a warning that if the Japanese share increased substantially beyond the 9 percent EEC-wide level achieved in 1982 the European countries were likely to take further actions to limit imports.

The measures taken to date in response to Japanese exports focus on a single country, have limited durations in some cases, and generally seek to cap Japanese unit sales or market shares rather than dramatically reduce them. Nevertheless, they raise questions about how far government mediation of the auto market will go in response to the third transformation and what the long-term effects may be for the world auto industry and the world economy. European mediation in the 1920s and 1930s did eventually yield an auto industry competitive with that of the United States, but only after a depression and a world war. Thus, many observers, including the authors, have worried that the current retreat from a unified world market can easily spiral out of control.

In sum, a pervading sense of crisis has emerged in the 1980s about the future direction of the world auto industry and the resolution of the competitive imbalance resulting from the third transformation. Will government actions ostensibly aimed at adjustment have the effect of rebalancing the world industry on a higher competitive plane, or will they instead lead to stagnation and permanent market isolation with spillovers in other aspects of international relations?

A Fourth Transformation?

North America, Western Europe, and Japan account for 87 percent of the world's automobile production but for only 16 percent of the world's population.[18] Is it possible that additional transformations in the auto industry will occur as automobility spreads to new regions?

It is clear that the world outside the three major auto-producing regions accounts for a growing share of the total world auto market. It is also apparent that the governments of many of these countries are determined that production for their markets will occur locally and that local production has been increasing (tables 2.3 and 2.8). Thus, there is no question that these regions will play a larger role over time in the world industry.

Of greater interest, however, is the possibility that some combination of government assistance and industrial dynamism is even now laying the groundwork that will permit additional nations or regions to break through into export markets, as Japan did most recently, to initiate a fourth transformation in the world auto industry.

Two countries outside the major auto-producing regions have had substantial auto industries for 30 years, fostered by a long history of government efforts to promote local manufacture. However, neither

Australia nor South Africa has developed an export industry, and it is difficult to see any competitive superiority developing in these locales, which share the disadvantages of relatively high wage rates, small domestic markets, long shipping distances to major markets, and low labor productivity compared with Japan.

This leaves the low-wage developing countries and the Soviet bloc as the prime prospects for the emergence of a new force in the world auto industry—the former on the basis of low wages, the latter because governments can set export prices at arbitrarily low levels. For those whose thinking is influenced by theories of the product cycle, the emergence of export industries in at least a few of these countries seems highly likely, perhaps before the third transformation is fully resolved.[19] Indeed, the Japanese challenge is often portrayed as the spur to the relocation of auto production to low-wage locales for export back to the developed countries, because this offers a ready means for American and some European producers to deal with competitive shortcomings highlighted by the Japanese.

To date, however, the efforts of a number of Soviet-bloc and developing countries to play an expanded role in the world auto industry have met with limited success. In the Soviet bloc the 1970s might be labeled the decade of the false transformation. Mass manufacture of motor vehicles had been carried on in the Soviet Union since the 1930s, when Ford first provided the necessary technical assistance. However, the domestic automobile markets of the U.S.S.R. and its Eastern European satellites remained very small through the first two decades of the postwar era. In addition, the indigenous production systems and product designs were not competitive with Western offerings, and the local producers gave no evidence of innovative dynamism that might boost them onto the world stage.

In the late 1960s the U.S.S.R. and a number of the Eastern European nations embarked on a new course calling for large-scale imports of Western manufacturing know-how, tooling, and vehicle designs. These imports were to pay for themselves by means of automotive exports to the West, often in the form of buy-back arrangements wherein tools and designs would be exchanged for finished autos and components. For example, Lada in the Soviet Union bought tooling from Fiat to produce on license the 124 model, which the Italian manufacturer was phasing out. Soon Lada was exporting to Western Europe. Several other producers in Poland and Rumania soon followed the Russian example, obtaining designs and tooling from Fiat, Renault, and Citroen in return

Table 2.8
Auto production and assembly outside the three primary producing regions (thousands of units)

	1950	1960	1970	1975	1980	1981	1982	Approx. local content (1980)
Centrally Planned Economies								
China	n.d.	n.d.	n.d.	n.d.	22.0	n.d.	n.d.	100%
Czechoslovakia	24.5	56.2	142.9	175.4	183.7	180.6	170.0	100
East Germany	10.0	64.1	126.6	159.1	176.8	176.5	176.0	100
Poland	0	12.2	64.1	164.3	351.0	247.5	250.0	100
Rumania	0	1.2	23.6	68.0	79.3	79.0	91.0	100
USSR	64.6	138.8	344.2	1201.7	1327.0	1324.0	1285.0	100
Rest of World								
Australia	0	305.1	330.0	351.0	318.0	358.4	411.5	80
Argentina	0	30.3	163.4	185.7	215.6	139.4	106.9	95
Brazil	0	62.3	343.7	772.1	977.7	621.1	718.3	98
Chile	0	0	20.7	4.9	25.2	20.6	7.9	40
Colombia	0	0	7.7	23.1	32.3	24.7	26.5	50
India	6.7	19.1	37.4	23.1	30.5	42.1	42.7	100
Indonesia	0	2.0	2.0	30.8	41.0	n.d.	n.d.	40
Iran	0	2.5	31.8	90.0	80.0	n.d.	n.d.	50
Malaysia	0	0	7.5	28.3	81.0	87.8	85.3	50
Mexico	0	24.8	136.7	237.1	303.1	355.5	300.6	60
Nigeria	0	0	7.1	6.5	151.0	n.d.	n.d.	30

Philippines	0	2.9	7.6	—	26.6	25.0	n.d.	70
South Africa	0	87.4	195.0	—	277.0	301.5	n.d.	50
South Korea	0	0	14.5	17.5	57.2	68.8	94.5	90
Taiwan	0	0.4	n.d.	—	132.1	137.6	133.7	60
Thailand	0	0	6.6	15.6	25.0	n.d.	n.d.	35
Turkey	0	0	5.0	—	32.0	26.0	31.2	80
Venezuela	0	6.5	48.0	92.0	94.0	82.8	93.9	40
Yugoslavia	0	10.5	112.2	183.2	255.2	239.6	211.4	76

Notes:
This table includes all countries in the world that manufactured, partially manufactured, or assembled more than 20,000 passenger cars in 1980. Because those countries with less than a 75 percent local-content requirement are not included in table 2.3, the "rest of the world total" in that table is substantially smaller than in this table. The difference lies in assembly and partial manufacture in a number of countries yielding vehicles which are often also counted as production in a developed country where most of the parts were manufactured. n.d. = no relevant data available

Sources:
MVMA, *World Motor Vehicle Data Book* (various years); SMMT, *Motor Industry of Great Britain* (various years); United Nations *Statistical Yearbook* (various years); Rémy Prud'homme, "The Location of the World Automotive Industry," paper prepared for the Future of the Automobile Program, International Policy Forum, 1983. Local content estimates are also based on research by Rémy Prud'homme utilizing the replies of French government commercial attachés throughout the world to an official questionnaire.

for cash or shipments of components and finished vehicles back to the Western firms for sale in the West.

Because Western producers would not sell their current designs and tooling for export production, it was inevitable that the Eastern Europeans and the Russians would always lag one product generation behind in Western markets. However, the theory was that a substantial market existed in the Western industrialized economies for extremely low-priced autos even if not very stylish or up to the latest Western standards—in essence, a market for "brand-new used cars." For a while this approach seemed to promise a major impact on the world auto industry, and through most of the 1970s Eastern-bloc exports to the West grew steadily, although from a tiny base. However, the Eastern producers showed little capacity to independently develop new designs and manufacturing systems, and in the late 1970s some of the buy-back arrangements misfired when the Eastern European products offered as repayment for tools and designs were judged to be of inadequate quality for sale in the West. This and the deterioration of détente made Western producers wary of further buy-back arrangements just at the point when stagnation in the world economy and a decline in Eastern-bloc export earnings made purchases of Western technology with hard currency difficult or impossible. Thus, Eastern-bloc exports to the West have stabilized at a modest level, accounting for 1–2 percent of the new-car market in Western Europe during 1979–1982.

The developing world includes a vast array of countries with widely differing cultures, political systems, and levels of industrial infrastructure. A number of these countries have developed substantial auto industries in recent years, and some are now exporting, mostly to other developing countries, at low volumes. A review of every country with potential to participate in the world auto industry at some point in the future would require a book of its own, but two examples can be cited to show the problems facing countries with developing domestic auto markets and export ambitions.[20]

In Brazil, automobiles had been assembled with a low level of local content since the 1920s by Ford and General Motors. In 1957 the Kubitschek government launched a new plan for the auto industry that spurred auto sales and required that a very high proportion of the manufacturing process occur within Brazil. "Brazilianization" of the auto industry was to proceed under the supervision of the multinational auto producers, who were to be offered access to a totally protected growth market with favorable tax treatments in return for greatly increasing their investments in Brazilian auto-manufacturing facilities. Seven multinational producers found the prospect of access to a large growth market attractive and accepted the government's terms. By 1962 the average automobile sold in Brazil had 93 percent local content on the basis of manufacturing value added. However, this came at a high price for local consumers. In 1967 Brazilian cars cost 60 percent more than similar products produced in the United States and Europe, despite much lower wages.

The problem was the large number of producers sharing a very small market, a classic case of a scale-economy cost penalty. The government, however, had considerable ability to spur demand, which it did by creating a nationwide financing system for auto purchases at attractive interest, by holding vehicle purchase and use taxes very low, and by fostering a skewed income distribution which created a middle class with ample incomes for buying cars. Finally, the importing of vehicles manufactured elsewhere was prohibited.

By the early 1970s, auto production was zooming upward in Brazil, to the point where oil imports for motor vehicles were becoming a major burden on the Brazilian trade balance. The government had already sensed that Brazil might be able to join the ranks of world auto exporters because the cost of Brazilian cars was dropping dramatically as volume increased. The Special Fiscal Benefits Program for Exports, initiated in 1972, took the bold step of using the appeal of access to the growing Brazilian market to compel the multinational corporations to begin exporting from Brazil. In this way, it was hoped, Brazil could continue to expand domestic auto use while covering oil-import bills with earnings from auto exports. The program involved individual agreements with multinational companies offered large tax breaks on domestic sales and the right to add new product lines or total capacity for the Brazilian domestic market in return for promises to export given volumes of finished units and components over the following decade. The result was a rapid increase in Brazilian auto exports to the world, from only 2,000 at the start of the program in 1972 to 135,000 in 1981 (table 2.9).

In this achievement Brazil stands alone among the less developed countries, but its future as a major auto exporter is far from assured for a number of reasons. A fundamental one is that the Brazilian industry has made no breakthrough in production systems or products beyond low wages. However, because the amount of labor needed in Brazil to manufacture a product of given specification and quality seems to be

Table 2.9
Brazilian auto production and exports

	Production (thousands)	Exports (thousands)	Exports as a percentage of production	Value of exports (millions of current dollars)		
				Vehicles	Parts	Total
1960	62.2	—	—	n.d.	n.d.	n.d.
1965	138.7	—	—	n.d.	n.d.	n.d.
1970	343.7	—	—	n.d.	n.d.	n.d.
1971	437.7	2	0.5	5	20	25
1972	508.8	14	2.8	33	36	69
1973	600.1	25	4.2	40	37	76
1974	708.6	66	9.3	116	71	186
1975	772.1	73	9.4	193	124	317
1976	827.2	80	9.7	219	295	514
1977	771.6	70	9.1	242	508	750
1978	919.9	96	10.4	408	143	551
1979	961.5	105	10.9	493	208	701
1980	977.7	n.d.	n.d.	774	265	1039
1981	621.1	135	21.7	830	n.d.	n.d.
1982	718.3	n.d.	n.d.	n.d.	n.d.	n.d.

— = <500 units or 0.1 percent; n.d. = no relevant data available.

Sources:
Production data from Motor Vehicle Manufacturers Association, *World Motor Vehicle Data*, 1982, p. 285; export data from Rémy Prud'homme, "Motor Vehicle Production and Use in Developing Countries: A Case Study of Brazil," p. 11.

higher than in the developed countries, and particularly higher than in Japan, the Brazilian industry seems in fact to have no competitive superiority, particularly in finished units. Also, since Brazil's domestic market demands a considerably simpler automobile than the markets of the developed world, most of its exports have been to other developing countries.[21]

The failure to develop any true competitive edge means that the ability of the Brazilian government to compel increasing levels of exports by the multinational automakers, particularly of finished units, depends on the continuing attraction of access to the Brazilian domestic market. In the past few years this market has collapsed, leaving many of the multinational producers with large losses in Brazil and doubts about the future strength of the market. In addition, a large part of the problem with the Brazilian auto market is the very high dependence of Brazil on imported oil, which accounts for more than 80 percent of total consumption. This makes the future market for petroleum-fueled automobiles doubtful in Brazil in any case, even if auto exports zoom and the country's foreign-debt problems can be resolved.

The energy situation requires thought about alternative fuels—in this case alcohol, the use of which the Brazilian auto industry has been pursuing at a rapid rate under market and government pressure. However, alcohol-fueled engines currently have no market in the rest of the world. Thus, the Brazilian industry faces a clouded future in which its vehicle design is diverging from the rest of the world at just the point where the Brazilian government wants to push auto exports even faster to deal with the foreign-debt crisis.

Korea is a second example of an industrializing nation eager to break into the international auto market as an exporter. Korea's industry began to develop later than Brazil's and it followed the alternative path of building up domestically owned producers with limited ties to the multinational automakers.

In 1962 Korea prohibited imports of completely built up cars. At the same time, the government decreed that only firms with majority domestic ownership would be licensed to produce cars in Korea. From this point, local-content requirements were raised gradually as the domestic producers showed the capacity to meet them. Auto production increased slowly to 9,100 units in 1974, when the government announced an ambitious plan for a major leap in auto production. Motor-vehicle production, including cars, trucks, and buses, was to jump from about 30,000 units in 1974 to 500,000 in 1980 and 1 million in 1985.

Table 2.10
Korean auto production and exports

	Production (thousands)	Exports (thousands)	Exports as a percentage of production
1965	0.1	n.d.	n.d.
1970	14.5	n.d.	n.d.
1971	12.4	n.d.	n.d.
1972	9.5	n.d.	n.d.
1973	12.8	n.d.	n.d.
1974	9.1	n.d.	n.d.
1975	17.5	n.d.	n.d.
1976	25.6	n.d.	n.d.
1977	42.3	n.d.	n.d.
1978	85.7	16.4	19.1
1979	113.6	18.7	16.5
1980	57.2	14.7	25.7
1981	68.8	17.2	25.0
1982	94.5	14.1	14.9

n.d. = no relevant data available

Source: MVMA, *World Motor Vehicle Data*, 1983, pp. 97, 100.

A large portion of this output was to be exported, boosting the Korean producers into the front ranks of world auto exporters in only a decade. The boldest part of the plan was the intention of Hyundai, one of the two firms producing autos, to rapidly design and market an indigenous product to be sold in world export markets in direct competition with the established multinational producers.

The actual performance of the Korean auto industry was considerably less spectacular than planned. Production peaked at 114,000 in 1979 before the severe contraction in the Korean economy in 1980 cut auto output nearly in half. A modest recovery has followed, but it is clear that the process of building Korea into an automotive export giant will take much longer than planned (table 2.10).

Part of the problem was that the Korean government's policy of supporting domestic auto producers with credit, favorable taxes, and export assistance was not coordinated with its domestic treatment of auto purchases. In fact, the government's consumption/demand policy was essentially anti-auto. Purchase taxes were assessed at 45 percent of the retail price ex-tax, annual registration taxes were more than 10 percent of purchase price, and gasoline was taxed at one of the highest rates in the world (218 percent of the price ex-tax in 1977, 168 percent in 1982). Finally, the income distribution in Korea is much more egalitarian than that in Brazil, so the middle class does not have the income to purchase new cars.

The consequence was that the Korean domestic market at its demand peak in 1979 called for only 89,000 units, spread among six domestically produced models. Scale economies were therefore unavailable, and production costs were very high despite very low labor costs per hour worked. The Korean Ministry of Commerce estimated in 1979 that Hyundai's production cost for the Pony, its indigenous design made up of a number of components produced on license from various world manufacturers, was $3,972. This compared with an estimated cost for Toyota's most basic Corolla of $2,300. Thus the Pony faced a $1,700 manufacturing-cost disadvantage in export markets. In addition, because the Pony was not as sophisticated a design as the Corolla or other Japanese offerings in this size range and because it had to overcome consumer unfamiliarity with the model and the producer, the car had to be sold by underpricing Japanese producers.

About 19,000 Ponies were exported in 1979, at a large loss to Hyundai. The company will have great difficulty sustaining an export offensive in the long run, even with generous government export assistance, unless the domestic market grows enough that Hyundai achieves scale economies fully and takes advantage of its lower labor costs. Since scale economies probably require combined production of about 500,000 units per year by Hyundai and its domestic rival Daewoo, it is apparent that the Korean market must grow very rapidly for this to occur in the near future.

Thus, the experience to date with auto manufacture in less developed countries and in Eastern-bloc countries is mixed. Their domestic markets and production were growing rapidly before the worldwide economic slump of the early 1980s, and their share of the total world industry will doubtless increase in the next 20 years. However, they have not made the leap into the world arena as major exporters of finished units or components, nor have they shown any special dynamism in their domestic industries that might combine with lower wages to shift the initiative in the world auto industry outside the established producing areas (particularly Japan). The limits of government assistance in seizing the initiative, particularly in the absence of some sort of creative dynamism within domestic industries, are also apparent from the cases cited. However, the potential of one or more of the less developed countries to become a major player in the world industry (particularly as a supplier of components) cannot be dismissed lightly, and any success they do find will be at the expense of the established producers in the developed countries.

Transformations in Summary

From this review of the first century of automotive history, it appears that transformations of the sort currently unbalancing the world industry are the norm rather than the exception in the history of the automobile. Each transformation has commenced within a set of supportive conditions laid down by a nascent industry's home government, and each has been fueled by an extraordinary dynamism within the emergent industry. Two of the three (the emergence of the United States and the rise of Japan) have led to mediation of the competitive dynamic on the international level by governments in countries whose existing producers have been threatened by the upstarts on the world scene.

The nature of future transformations is far from obvious. The day of new entrants on the world scene producing and exporting whole vehicles, with the transforming consequences of the Americans, the Europeans, and the Japanese, may even be past. But this does not mean that the process of transformation and adjustment is at an end. To the contrary, the central questions for intelligent thought about the future continue to be about the nature of transformations to come and about the resolution of the third transformation, which is still in progress.

More Pressing Issues?

These topics require further investigation. However, is it possible that concentration on these issues is a case of focusing on the specific details of a future whose broad outline is not even remotely feasible? Can it be that the future of the whole auto industry, wherever located, is in serious jeopardy because of changes in the auto industry's broader environment? Indeed, as the question was posed in chapter 1, can the world's natural resources and environment support automobility at whatever level in the long term? Will the world's citizens tolerate the undesirable side effects of ever-expanding automobility? In short, are there constraints on the future of the automobile that take precedence over the issues posed above of which auto industries in which locations will prevail in world competition? These questions must be answered clearly before the future shape of the world auto industry can be discussed further.

Can Automobility Endure?

Do conditions loom in the foreseeable future that can be dealt with only by reducing the mass use of automobiles for personal travel? Many analysts have judged that they do, grouping potential threats to the future of automobility under two headings. The most pressing, in many assessments of the situation, are physical shortages of energy and limits on the capacity of the atmosphere to absorb auto emissions. If these problems can be surmounted, it can still be argued that the unpleasant side effects of automobility, such as traffic congestion and noise in urban areas, will become so great that societies will decide that the gain in personal mobility is not worth the cost to the community. Restrictions on auto use or decisions not to build the roads needed for growing traffic might follow. Further in the future, other challenges to automobility may come from improved urban transit systems, cheaper or faster air and rail links for intercity travel, or electronic communications systems that may reduce the desire for personal travel. Collectively these might halt or reverse the growth in auto use. But are these truly threats to widespread auto use in the long term, or are they only problems for certain vehicle technologies and operating practices?

Energy and Air-Quality Constraints on Automobility

In 1979 the second jump in energy prices raised the prospect that the petroleum-fueled auto transport system was living on borrowed time. One influential analysis assessed the situation as follows: "Whether world fleet growth can continue will be determined by three factors: the level of oil production, the share of fuel allotted to automobiles, and efficiency improvements in the world automobile fleet. As oil production levels off, the share available for cars is likely to decline in the face of expanding claims from high priority uses. If the increase in world fleet efficiency is rapid enough to offset the decline in automotive fuel, the fleet can continue to grow. If not, growth in the world fleet is likely to come to a halt."[1]

The authors of *Running on Empty* elaborated on these points by arguing that oil production was unlikely ever to exceed the 1979 level, not only because proven reserves were declining but also because the oil-producing nations of the Middle East could meet their fiscal needs without pumping at full output. In addition, a "depletion psychology" was predicted that would convince oil-exporting nations that oil left in the ground would be worth more in the future than any possible investment of the currency received for pumping it today. It was also argued that other oil users would have a stronger claim on oil supplies than motorists when shortages and price escalations forced governments to make allocational decisions about uses of oil.

Thus, the whole burden of the automotive future seemed to rest on improvements in vehicle fuel efficiency. The authors of *Running on Empty* and a number of other analyses performed at that time did not claim to have analyzed the potential for efficiency improvements in detail. Nevertheless, they concluded that automobility would probably never spread to countries not yet in the auto age and that continued automobility in the developed countries would become progressively more precarious over the next 20 or 30 years.

Five years later it is apparent that these arguments were overstated. The trend in oil production has been downward since 1979 because of conservation and the slump in the world economy following the oil price increases. However, the world's proven reserves have been roughly constant since 1973 (figure 3.1). In 1982 there were 34 years' worth of proven reserves at current pumping rates under the assumption of no new discoveries—a figure exactly the same as for the period 1969–1971, before the world was aware of any energy crisis. Furthermore, it is apparent that the amount of proven reserves will continue to be remarkably sensitive to energy prices. Ninety percent of world petroleum exploration, expressed either in wells or in footage drilled, has occurred in the United States, which contains only 23 percent of the world's surface area thought likely to cover oil reservoirs.[2] Equally intense drilling activity over the rest of the earth is almost certainly capable of maintaining proven reserves at current levels for many years to come, even if aggregate petroleum consumption increases above the peak of 23 billion barrels reached in 1979.

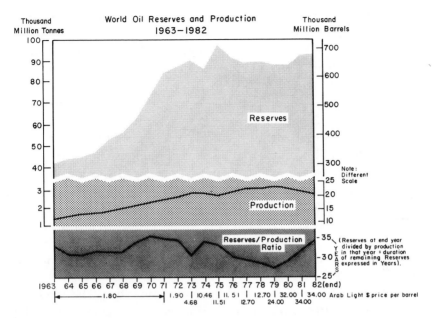

Figure 3.1
World oil reserves and production, 1963–1982. Source: *Statistical Review of the World Energy Industry*, London: British Petroleum, 1982, p. 2.

Oil in the ground is, of course, useless to the motorist, and the willingness of oil-exporting nations to pump their reserves is subject to many factors, political as well as economic. However, 5 years' experience with high oil prices has shown that national appetites for consumption are likely to thwart the development of a "depletion psychology." Saudia Arabia, Kuwait, and the United Arab Emirates, with roughly half the world's proven reserves, have such high ratios of reserves to population that they may well choose to restrict output at points in the future. However, even these countries have found ways to spend as much as or more than they have earned since the price jump of 1979, and the remainder of the OPEC producers (all with low reserves in relation to population) have never had the luxury of a depletion psychology.

A second discovery of the past 5 years has been that other users of oil are much more sensitive to price increases than motorists. In space heating, electricity generation, industrial process energy, and agriculture, conservation and switching to other fossil fuels have been dramatic. In the United States the petroleum share of the total energy consumed in the transport sector has remained constant at around 95 percent. However, the oil share of electricity generation has fallen from 18 percent in 1973 to 8 percent in 1982. Residential and commercial users have also switched, decreasing the oil share of energy use in these sectors from 18 percent in 1973 to 10 percent in 1982. All together, fuel switching in nontransport sectors has decreased petroleum consumption in 1982 by 27.2 percent from what it would have been if petroleum's share of energy needs in these sectors had remained at the 1973 level. This means that 23 percent of oil use in the transport sector in 1982 was in effect obtained from fuel switching in other domestic sectors and without need for additional oil production.[3] In Japan, consumption of residual fuel oil for power plants and boilers fell 37 percent between 1979 and 1982, mostly because of fuel switching. This reduced oil consumption for those purposes by 800,000 barrels per day, an amount slightly greater than total daily gasoline consumption in Japan in 1982.[4]

A major adjustment in the world's refining capacity will be necessary to accomodate these shifts in uses, since most refineries outside the United States have been designed to convert crude oil to large amounts of residual fuel oil and small amounts of gasoline. Adjusting world refining capacity to the standard U.S. configuration would yield roughly twice as much gasoline from present crude-oil consumption. In addition, advances in refining technology are expected to soon increase the proportion of gasoline that can be obtained from a barrel of crude oil from the current 50 percent to 65 percent.[5] Also, it will be possible over time to switch the source of process energy in the world's refineries from residual oil to natural gas, freeing an additional 4 percent of current oil consumption for motor-vehicle use.[6]

Because of supply trends in alternate fuels, including coal and natural gas, it appears that switching in other sectors will continue and that the world's remaining oil will be used increasingly by the transport sector. This suggests that the amount of driving that can be done with the remaining oil is much greater than was thought only 5 years ago. This is even more likely in light of the findings of the past 5 years about the capacity of the auto industry to improve the fuel economy of the auto fleet. Much has been achieved in a short period with simple improvements to conventional auto designs that greatly reduce fuel consumption without sacrificing key attributes of the vehicle, such as carrying capacity. In the United States (the extreme example), the average fuel economy of new cars sold has increased from 14.2 miles per gallon in 1973 to 26.0 in 1983.[7]

There are numerous additional near-term technological opportunities to adapt the automobile to changing energy availability. One promising approach is to refine methanol from the natural gas now being extracted but flared in many parts of the world as a by-product of oil production. Methanol can be burned in automobiles with only minor engine and fuel system modifications and may make pollution control easier as well. Gradually, as the world's natural gas supplies are depleted, the raw material used for methanol production could be changed to coal, a resource in abundant supply for the forseeable future. In the longer term ethanol may be a promising fuel as well since it also can be burned with only minor engine modifications and can be produced from wood and other plant matter which are renewable. These possibilities and others suggest that automotive technology is unexpectedly robust and provides a powerful defense against energy starvation even if the real price of oil climbs steadily during the next 20 years.

If the search for new energy sources and improvements in the energy efficiency of automobiles of given carrying capacity, performance, and amenities prove inadequate to meet the energy challenge, the automotive system has a last defense: to decrease the average capacity and performance of the autos in the world fleet. This would be a real sacrifice for motorists but one less severe than most alternatives to auto use, and it could yield large increases in travel per gallon of fuel. The smallest cars on the market today—vehicles the size of the Honda Civic, the Ford Fiesta, and the VW Polo—can achieve 50 miles per gallon on the U.S. Environmental Protection Agency's composite cycle. Substituting small cars for the world's current fleet, which averages around 25 mpg on the same test, would reduce energy consumption by 50 percent with no technological advances whatever and no need for a reduction in driving.

Thus, the "energy problem" is not the problem it has been commonly thought to be. Fuel prices may well rise in real terms over the next 20–30 years and will almost certainly rise over the very long term. However, the auto industry has had ample warning and stands well prepared to deal with this situation as it develops, primarily through the orderly introduction of new technologies in the vehicle that will reduce fuel consumption while preserving the auto's familiar utility and amenities.

This approach does have one major flaw: It cannot deal with political disruptions in major oil-exporting nations that cut supplies without warning and drive prices up drastically. If this should occur again, as it did twice in the past decade, the shortages must be accommodated by reductions in auto travel in the short run while the energy intensity of the fleet is reduced.

Because the average car in the developed countries is driven for more than a decade, the true automotive energy problem is the long lead time needed to re-outfit the fleet in response to sudden price increases. This is particularly so because the short-term response of most motorists to energy-price increases is to maintain their level of spending on personal transport by deferring auto purchases. In the United States, the percentage of personal-consumption expenditures devoted to automobile purchase and use moved only within a range of 11.2–13.5 percent during the period 1960–1980. The energy-price increases of 1974 and 1979 hardly affected total personal spending on automotive transportation, because the increase in gas prices was offset by reduced spending for new cars.[8] For the auto industry, this means that sudden shifts in energy prices reduce sales dramatically just when investments must be made in new tooling for more fuel-efficient models. However, the industry is gradually remedying part of this problem with advances in flexible manufacturing systems that permit rapid shifts in the product mix from less to more fuel-efficient vehicles without the need for major capital expenditures. Thus, although dramatic drops in vehicle sales and painfully slow responses to ratchets in energy prices may recur, the system of automobility itself and the continuing growth in automobile use will not be threatened by energy shortages in the near future.

The "energy crisis" will have an effect on the automotive world during the next 20 years, however. The growth in new-car demand will be less than was anticipated before 1979, because of the general sluggishness of the world economy as it makes the transition to other fuels while autos continue to burn oil.

A second potential constraint on automobility is the ability of the atmosphere to absorb and disperse the by-products of auto use. In the 1970s, concern focused on the major pollutants emitted by gasoline engines: hydrocarbons (HC), carbon monoxide (CO), nitrogen oxides (NO_x), and lead. The common fear was these would have such severe health consequences and be so intractable to technical solutions that the public would face a clear choice between personal mobility and good health.

Technical problems in developing satisfactory emission-control systems on tight timetables led to much heated discussion, particularly in the United States, about restricting motor vehicle use in major urban areas. However, by the late 1970s three-way catalyst systems able to reduce emissions to very low levels had been perfected, and aggregate emissions of HC, CO, NO_x, and lead began to decline in the most developed countries. In the United States the current emission-control regulations will cause aggregate motor-vehicle emissions to decline at least through the early 1990s as vehicles with advanced controls enter the fleet. At that point total emissions nationwide are predicted to be approximately 60 percent (HC), 50 percent (CO), and 20 percent (NO_x) below the levels of 1970.[9] In addition, the use of lead in motor fuels will have been largely eliminated. Past this point the trend in aggregate emissions, if current regulations are not tightened, depends on the rate of growth in vehicle use and the types of inspection and maintenance performed on emission-control systems. Although these reductions are still less than desired by many of the participants in public controversies about air quality, the trends are strongly in the direction of improvement. In consequence, the political debates of the 1970s about restraining motor vehicle use as an essential step toward clean air have ceased.

Despite these successes, however, new emission problems have been emerging. Strong consumer interest in diesels in the immediate wake of the 1979 energy-price adjustment has led to questions about the health effects of the particulates in diesel exhaust. In addition, concern has been growing in the 1980s about acid rain and about increasing carbon dioxide in the earth's atmosphere. Do these loom as constraints on auto use in the years ahead?

The dimensions of the diesel-particulate problem are not fully understood. In particular, the health effects of these sooty by-products of combustion in diesel engines are difficult to determine. A 1981 study by the National Research Council in the United States found no clear evidence that diesel particulates in the air harm human health beyond the established effects of the other hydrocarbon emissions they resemble.[10] However, this study also reported that sophisticated epidemiological studies of humans exposed to particulates are lacking and that many substances in particulates have been found to be toxic, mutagenic, or carcinogenic in animal tests.[11] Research on these questions is continuing, and there is no consensus about the probable outcome.

In the auto industry, the immediate realization in 1979 was that particulates may be a major problem and that a technical fix could require 5–10 years to perfect. This estimate was based on the industry's experience in developing catalyst systems from a paper concept to hardware that was reliable in daily use in production vehicles. Thus, it was important to push ahead with work on ways to reduce particulates before a new jump in energy prices greatly increased the demand for diesels and thus total particulate emissions. If epidemiological findings called for a cleanup at that point, when the industry had become heavily dependent on diesel sales, it might be necessary to move faster on reductions than technology permitted. Restraints on diesel-car production would be the only alternative.

In the United States, technical fixes have also been necessary to meet government standards introduced in 1982 and scheduled for major tightening in 1987.[12] Changes in engine and fuel-injection system designs were sufficient to meet the 1982 standards, but the 1987 reductions will require some type of cleanup apparatus in the exhaust system, at least for large cars. This is particularly so because standards for diesel NO_x emissions are being strengthened at the same time. In general, the amount of NO_x and the amount of particulates in diesel exhaust are inversely related, so an effort to reduce both at the same time requires new technologies.[13]

Because little systematic thought had been given to passenger-car diesel particulates before 1979, there were many unexplored avenues toward a technlogical fix but a long distance to be traveled along any path. A number of competing technologies have been developed to the working-prototype stage; each of these uses some sort of trap in the exhaust stream to catch the particles, followed by an oxidation reaction to fully combust them in the trap. There is no question that such traps can remove a large portion of the particles. Current prototypes can clean up to 90 percent of the particles from the exhaust stream, a level more than adequate to meet the 1987 U.S. standard. Their shortcomings lie in reliability, durability, and manufacturing cost.

The ceramic monolith trap is one example. This device uses a porous ceramic material to filter the exhaust. As the trap begins to fill, however, backpressure on the engine rises, causing an increase in fuel consumption and eventually stalling. Thus, the particles must be removed from the trap periodically. One way to do this is to add an organometallic material to the fuel. When this material reaches the trap it reduces the combustion temperature of the particulates below the normal temperature of the exhaust stream, with the result that the particles burn completely, cleaning the pores of the trap. There are problems with this system, however. Temperatures in the trap are likely to vary widely as the particles burn, and the trap may shatter under thermal stress. In addition, the organo-metallic compounds that catalyze the oxidation may be highly toxic. They will probably have to be installed in the engine compartment in a container sealed for the life of the vehicle. Finally, the trap raises engine backpressure even when clean, increasing fuel consumption by 1–4 percent. A first cost to the consumer of up to $400 added to increased fuel consumption produces an extra cost of up to $550 over the life of the vehicle. Thus, this trap in its current state of development may solve the diesel-particulate problem largely by making diesel cars so expensive to buy and operate that they will lose their market appeal to all but the buyers of the most expensive cars. Other prototype trap technologies currently exhibit different but equivalent drawbacks.

The more significant point, and the reason we have cited this example in detail, is that automotive technology usually advances incrementally. Because present state-of-the-art hardware is in only its first generation of development, much further progress will probably be possible. In 1979, filtration systems were beyond the state of the art. By 1981, engineers had developed prototypes of workable traps that were effective filters but were complex and unreliable. By 1983, the traps were much simpler and more durable but still expensive. Recent advances suggest that it may be possible to oxidize the particles in the trap with engine exhaust heat alone, without need for the organo-metallic catalyst. This would be another major simplifying step. Continuing experimentation with manufacturing techniques will probably reduce production costs substantially as designs become standardized.

Thus, it now seems likely that the particulate problem can be managed over a period of years without constraints on the use of passenger-car diesels, even if particulates are found to be dangerous to public health and more rigorous cleanup efforts are necessary. The key requirement, however, is that development efforts on the ceramic system and a number of competing concepts continue at a steady rate so that environmental events do not overtake the feasible pace of technological advance.

Acid rain is also a potential concern for the automobile-dominated transport system. As with many other environmental problems, its significance has become apparent rather suddenly despite increasing acid in rainfall for many years. This is because its effects on forests and lakes are not apparent before a threshold is reached but then quickly become highly visible. Thus, the problem has recently emerged in several countries as a major environmental crisis.

The acid in the rain comes from sulfur and nitrogen oxides placed in the air by the burning of fossil fuels. The amount of acid and the proportion of the total traceable to auto use probably varies considerably by region of the world. In the United States as a whole, in 1981 the passenger-car contribution to the total acid in rainfall was quite minor, only about 5.3 percent.[14] In some regions (such as southern California) where sulfur dioxide emissions from power plants are lower and auto use is higher, the auto contribution may be greater but is probably still a small fraction of the total. This is probably also true for northern Europe and other regions of the world where concerns about acid rain are strongest.

The true significance of acid rain is not yet understood. However, it is clear that reductions in the automobile's contribution, if they should prove necessary, are within the grasp of auto technologists. The three-way closed-loop catalyst systems introduced in the United States and Japan in the past few years to reduce NO_x emissions in gasoline engines below the current government standard (1.0 grams per mile) are capable of considerably lower emission levels.[15] In fact, a small number of models were certified by the U.S. Environmental Protection Agency for model year 1983 at NO_x levels below 0.2 grams per mile, and a considerable number emitted less than 0.4 grams per mile.[16] Similarly, electronic engine controls and exhaust-gas recirculation in combination with particulate trap–oxidizers will probably be capable within a decade of reducing NO_x emissions by passenger-car diesels to levels considerably below the 1.0 gram per mile required by the U.S. government for model year 1985.[17]

The key question for the long term is therefore not whether NO_x emissions can be reduced but whether there will be any need to do so and whether reduction efforts will interfere with the auto technologists' need to extract the maximum amount of energy from the available fuel. The answer to the latter part of this question is not known and will probably not be known for many years as technologists continue to innovate with spark-ignition and diesel engines. However, it is clear that none of the major efficiency-boosting innovations currently under consideration, such as "lean-burn" spark-ignition engines and adiabatic diesel engines, are ruled out by insurmountable problems with NO_x emissions.[18]

An atmospheric problem potentially much more ominous than particulates or acid rain and due in part to auto emissions is the rising level of carbon dioxide (CO_2). This is the result of fossil-fuel combustion along with a reduction in the earth's forests and other green areas which convert atmospheric carbon to solid form. The rise of carbon dioxide levels during the past 25 years is well documented, and continuing increases are a foregone conclusion for the years immediately ahead. Scientific opinion is widely divided on the likely consequences of more CO_2 in the air, but some of the possibilities are quite frightening.[19]

The worst scenario that has scientific support projects that, if CO_2 levels continue to rise at the rate of the past 25 years for the next century, the average air temperature at the earth's surface will rise by about 5 degrees centigrade. Because the increase will be much greater at the poles (about 12 degrees) than at the equator, glaciers in the northern hemisphere and the West Antarctic ice shelf will melt. Dramatic climate changes will follow and the world's oceans will rise by 6–7 meters. In the absence of heroic feats of civil engineering, many agricultural areas might be drought-striken, the world's coastal cities would be inundated, and the land area available for human habitation would be sharply reduced. However, this is only one possibility. Other scientists believe that the increases in CO_2 (which are agreed to be occurring) will cause only modestly higher temperatures and that continued use of fossil fuels may therefore have only modest and acceptable effects on the environment.

Atmospheric scientists holding optimistic views and those holding pessimistic views acknowledge the need for better atmospheric models, first to determine precisely the relationship between the CO_2 level and air temperature and then to establish the precise consequences of any given rise in temperature, particularly for the distribution of rainfall. Thus, an intense period of research is just beginning, and it will be some years before the extent of the problem is fully known. Nevertheless, it is prudent to ask what contribution automobile use makes to the CO_2 "problem" and what might be done if CO_2 emissions must be limited. In considering this question two differences between CO_2 and other emissions problems should be noted. First, CO_2 is the product of complete combustion in which hydrocarbon fuels are converted to CO_2 and H_2O. Therefore, no cleanup measures of the sort devised in the 1970s for other emissions are possible. Indeed, catalytic converters in auto exhaust systems reduce HC and CO emissions by "converting" these products of incomplete combustion to CO_2 and H_2O. The only approach to CO_2 reductions, therefore, is to reduce fuel consumption, since CO_2 production is directly proportional. The second difference between CO_2 and other auto emissions is that the effect of CO_2 is cumulative. HC, NO_x, and CO gradually break down in the atmosphere. Control techniques only need reduce the amount emitted per unit time to a level the air can disperse. However, fossil-fuel combustion in cars transports carbon found in the earth into the atmosphere, where it remains permanently in the absence of reconversion by plants. Thus, reducing fossil-fuel use per unit time delays any CO_2-related problems but cannot prevent them. If mankind proposes to eventually burn all of the world's oil in motor vehicles and for other purposes, all this carbon will wind up in the atmosphere, with whatever consequences for the climate.

Thus, the long-run need, if rising CO_2 is shown to produce unacceptable environmental consequences, will be to run automobiles on nonfossil energy sources or on alcohols produced by organic processes. There are many technical possibilities for doing this, but for the time period under study in this volume the more likely requirement (even if alarming scientific findings are forthcoming) will be to retard the growth in automotive fossil-fuel consumption to delay the warming trend while new energy sources are developed. Fortunately this approach is quite compatible with consumers' and manufacturers' desires to reduce energy consumption per vehicle-kilometer in order to offset rising oil prices. Continuing improvements in passenger-car fuel efficiency could permit continuing increases in total travel even if automotive fossil-fuel consumption had to be constrained near current levels for environmental reasons. This approach, stressing conservation over the intermediate term, seems particularly reasonable because the automobile's contribution to the total CO_2 problem is relatively minor. Fossil-fuel combustion each year releases about 5 billion tons of carbon into the air. Deforestation in tropical areas adds another 1.8–4.7 billion tons. Of the fossil fuel contribution, 47.2 percent comes from oil; automobiles consume about 25 percent of the oil. Thus, if one takes the conservative estimate of the contribution of deforestation (1.8 billion tons), it appears that auto use accounts for 8–9 percent of the total carbon contribution to the atmosphere.[20] Because it may be easier with current technologies to switch other energy users to nonfossil (e.g., nuclear or solar) sources or to halt the cutting of the world's forests and to institute reforestation, the situation of the auto sector may be similar to that concerning oil use. If other fossil-fuel users find ways to reduce CO_2 emissions, the period for which fossil-fuel use by automobiles is environmentally acceptable may extend far into the future even if CO_2 proves to be a serious long-term problem.

So, although the automobile by no means receives a perfect bill of health, it appears that no energy shortages or environmental threats will halt automobility in the time frame under study if automotive technology continues to address problems in a timely manner. This does not mean, however, that societies in the future will choose to tolerate pervasive auto use, particularly in crowded urban areas, or to carry out disruptive road-construction programs to accommodate an ever-swelling stream of cars. Might constraints on motor-vehicle use be a consequence?

Infrastructure Constraints on Automobility

In the 1970s a number of actions by governments in many countries suggested that societies might respond to the problems of growing automobility by constraining vehicle use. In almost all of the developed countries, freeway building (particularly through urban areas) was sharply curtailed. In hundreds of cities, areas were set aside as auto-free zones. In these same cities and in many others, parking regulations were tightened so that a shortage of vehicle storage began to constrain the number of vehicles that could be operated.

A decade after these trends first became visible, however, it is apparent that their net effect on the spread of automobility is minor. In the most developed countries the existing roadway networks have proved capable of accommodating growing motor-vehicle traffic without unacceptable congestion. This has been the case partly because government policies and underlying economic factors have also halted the growth of the largest cities in the developed countries during this period. The new urban growth, concentrated in satellites of major urban complexes and in smaller regional cities, can generally be accommodated by the arterial and feeder roads needed to offer access to individual buildings without the need for expensive and disruptive freeways. When freeways are needed, they are needed on the urban fringe, where they are more environmentally acceptable.

The effect of auto-free zones has been similar. To develop them on a small scale has no discernible effect on automobile use, but the exclusion of cars from large areas creates the twin problems of internal circulation and diversion of vehicles into surrounding areas. The experience of the past 15 years has been that large-scale diversions of traffic from urban centers are acceptable only if ring roads are already in place or can be built. This is not generally the case. Even if all urban cores restricted auto access, the effect on the overall auto system, where half of all driving is intercity and much of the remainder is from suburb to suburb, would be modest.

Shortages of parking are perhaps the most powerful force in suppressing motor-vehicle use. In very crowded cities such as Tokyo it is apparent that parking shortages rather than street congestion will be the long-term constraint on auto ownership and use. It is also apparent that the effect of storage costs and availability on the upper limit of auto use is substantial. In very crowded countries such as Japan and the Netherlands and in city-states such as Singapore and Hong Kong, the ultimate level of auto ownership per capita, even if consumer income ceases to be a constraint, will be much lower for this reason than in the United States, Canada, and Scandinavia. However, in all areas except the city-states mentioned it is also apparent that saturation due to space limitations will not be reached within the next 20 years.

The automobile has made peace with a number of its most vociferous critics in the 1970s. Reductions in emissions, improvements in safety equipment, agreements in many countries to share the proceeds of auto taxation with transit systems and other travel alternatives, and the growing perception of the economic importance of a healthy auto industry have largely diffused the political forces that once threatened to constrain the automobile.

Rivals for the Automobile's Function

Even if auto use in the future is unconstrained by shortages and social dicta, consumers may not choose to spend their fixed number of dollars on motoring. They may choose to travel, but not by car; or they may choose to communicate by newly developed electronic means rather than travel; or their tastes and preferences may change, causing them to travel less for pleasure or to put less money into the amenities installed in the vehicles they drive.

In urban areas the prime alternative to auto use is some form of mass transit, and it is apparent that governments in most of the developed countries have stepped up investments and operating subsidies for their urban transit systems during the past decade. In intercity travel, the prime alternatives are high-speed trains and aircraft for high-income travelers and low-speed trains and buses for those wishing to spend less but willing to take longer. In much of the world, air, rail, and bus systems have been extensively reorganized and improved in recent years. In the United States, these changes have been particularly far-reaching, with dramatic improvements in the intercity rail system and major reorganizations of the airline and bus systems after deregulation. These changes do not significantly reduce travel time in most cases but do offer the prospect of reduced travel costs relative to the automobile.

Thus far, however, there is no evidence of a shift in mode share away from automobiles in any of the developed countries, and for the longer period under consideration in this study we have found no convincing arguments that probable improvements in service and reductions in costs for competing modes will have any noticeable effect on the purchase and use of automobiles. The same can be said for electronic alternatives to travel, at least for the next twenty years. All evidence indicates that better voice communications increase business travel because they make feasible commercial tie-ups that formerly seemed too complicated. They also permit friendships to continue and grow, despite physical separation, to the point that personal contact is desired. Over the long term it may prove possible to develop television and other electronic linkups that will be "better than being there", but to date progress has been modest and it is hard to imagine that difficult personal or business affairs will soon be conducted without face-to-face contact.[21] What does seem likely in the next 20 years is that the role of first-class mail and the physical shipment of documents ranging from manuscripts to checks will be supplanted by electronic alternatives. However, the effects of these developments on the demand for and the use of automobiles are unlikely to be detectable.

Two additional questions about the long-term demand for automobiles concern the possibility of changing preferences for activities where the automobile is needed and is changing attitudes toward outfitting the vehicle. Suppose, for example, that the incipient trend toward working at home, aided by electronic links to the office, should intensify greatly. Similarly, home entertainment systems might improve to the point that viewing an event at home really is better than being there. Thus far, however, all predictions that television will supplant live entertainment, that home video systems will eliminate movie theaters, and that the office of the future will be located in the home have proved unfounded. In the period under review here it is difficult to imagine any technological advances that could make such a qualitative difference that widespread reductions in auto travel would occur, especially in view of the increasing propensity for weekend and vacation travel by car as leisure time and income grow.

But what if consumers lose interest in the nontransportation aspect of the automobile? The typical car sold in the developed countries now includes a large number of convenience, comfort, and entertainment features, which account for as much as half the vehicle's value but are hardly essential. What is more, much of the expectation in the auto industry about the future dollar volume of the business (in comparison with the unit volumes, on which the press and transport planners focus) rests on assumptions that auto designers will continue to develop new items for cars which consumers will purchase in lieu of other consumer goods. What if all of this changes over the next 20 years? This obviously entails much speculation and is not susceptible to a marshaling of evidence. The excitement value of automobiles depends in part on consumers' tastes and in part on new product offerings in other sectors. However, it also depends on what new features the auto producers are able to offer. No long-term flagging of consumer interest has been detected. While motorists are keeping their cars longer (partly in response to recent economic conditions and partly because vehicle durability has improved greatly in the past 10 years) they are also buying vehicles with higher levels of interior appointments and options. For the future, auto manufacturers envision a wide range of new technologies and functions for installation in motor vehicles.

Future Trends in the Harmful Side Effects of Automobility

The evidence cited indicates that automobility faces no serious threats over the next 20 years from energy shortages, environmental crises, social unacceptability, or rival modes of travel, provided that auto technologists continue to improve the product and to address changing operating conditions. This means that motor-vehicle use will continue to grow. Unfortunately, a number of undesirable side effects are sure to result, including large numbers of fatalities and injuries, undesirable environmental conditions (even if not at levels immediately imperiling public health), and inequities for citizens in highly motorized societies who are unable to use cars. What are the trends in these areas? What remedies are available by improving vehicle and roadway designs, changing driver behavior, or providing transportation alternatives? How do societies go about addressing these issues, and what may we expect in the way of future social demands?

Social responses to the problems of automobility during the past 20 years suggest that many factors interact to produce predominant national attitudes about the seriousness of problems and the appropriate solutions. The trend in objective conditions—number of fatalities, amount of pollutants in the air, proportion of citizenry with access to motor vehicles—is clearly central. For example, in Japan during the period 1964–1970 the risk of being killed per vehicle-kilometer of travel fell by 66 percent. However, the average amount of motor-vehicle travel by each Japanese grew so rapidly that the risk per year of being killed in a motor-vehicle accident increased by 20 percent.[22] With other causes of mortality on the decline, auto fatalities were perceived as an increasingly important threat to public health, and a massive national campaign for highway safety was launched in 1970.

However, knowledge of objective conditions and their consequences often can be obtained only by the commitment of major social resources to careful investigation. For example, for many years little thought was given to air pollution, which was viewed largely as an esthetic problem. Then new scientific findings, of an ambiguous but provocative nature, suggested not only that there was a threat to public health from auto fumes but that this threat, at the point of its discovery in the mid 1960s, was growing rapidly. A flurry of government actions followed in the United States, Japan, and Europe.

Similarly, knowledge of the seriousness of problems often depends on technological advances. New technologies may suddenly make new problems seem serious that previously went unnoticed and old problems seem "solvable" that were previously thought of simply as unpleasant conditions to be endured. For example, problem detection in air quality was aided by the development of inexpensive and accurate sensors to measure parts per million of pollutants in the air, as well as by more sophisticated epidemiological research techniques and new laboratory tests that showed that pollutants could be harmful even at low concentrations.

Other technological advances may suddenly offer new solutions to old problems. Auto safety provides many examples. When no one knew how to prevent skidding in panic stops, this was simply a condition to be avoided by careful driving. As microelectronic anti-skid systems become technically mature and relatively inexpensive, public pressure to make anti-skid brakes standard equipment will probably grow.

General economic conditions also effect the way problems are perceived. Just as poorer countries seem less inclined to worry about reducing air pollution and accidents than rich countries, the citizens of rich countries in boom times seem much more anxious for society to progress along environmental, safety, and equity dimensions than during times of economic stagnation.

Broader social conditions also have a major bearing on societal attitudes. Beginning in the mid 1960s, the United States, Western Europe, and Japan experienced a remarkable period of demand by citizens for environmental improvement. This could be traced to many causes, including the arrival at adulthood of the first postwar generation and the growing integration of the developed world which caused concerns in one region to quickly spread to other regions.

The fit between the solutions perceived as available and society's willingness to employ them is also a vital element in how problems are addressed. For example, the United States has often made dramatic advances with engineering solutions to problems connected with auto use. However, when these are unavailable or prohibitively expensive the United States often seems paralyzed by its decentralized government and by its citizens' distrust of direct regulation of personal behavior. Other countries where government regulation of behavior is accepted (seat-belt-use laws are perhaps the best example) may meanwhile make rapid progress.

The relations between governments and the degree of international coordination and integration bear on the approaches to problems and the pace at which remedies are implemented. For example, the openness of the U.S. auto market to foreign producers and their considerable sales volumes in the U.S. market have had a strong tendency to make American standards world standards. This is partly because some design features in vehicles (such as crashable structures) are so basic that it is easier for the producer to include the feature in all models produced than to design a special "American" version and partly because the development of cars meeting stringent American standards for export to the United States has made it easier for other governments to require these features for vehicles sold in their markets. As long as the Americans were pressing ahead with new vehicle regulations, this tended to foster their introduction in other developed countries as well. International coordination of vehicle standards might have the opposite effect, with poorer countries resisting new standards that would increase the cost of cars. Governments wishing to go faster in this situation would probably choose to regulate the behavior of their citizens.

In practice all these factors are linked. Scientists began to discover the effects of air quality on health when governments began to finance the search. Auto technologists began to discover new technical breakthroughs in safety and air quality when pushed to look for them during the same period of social restlessness in the 1960s. The United States was the world's richest society for much of the postwar period and thus the best able to implement technical fixes, an approach that fitted underlying American attitudes which accepted regulation of producers but resisted regulation of drivers. These interconnections mean that predictions about trends in environmental and safety regulation during the next 20 years are very difficult. However, several underlying factors that promise to be important can be foreseen. In particular, the ebullient growth of the first three postwar decades is unlikely to return. This growth often made almost any social improvement seem affordable— a state of mind we may remember fondly but with increasing distance. Thus, the recent emphasis on demonstrating that social improvements "pay for themselves" is likely to continue for many years. On the other hand, the capacity of technology both to discover problems and to devise solutions continues to grow. This alone will guarantee continuing action on the environmental and safety front. Perhaps the greatest question for the future concerns the degree of integration in the economies of the developed world. If the extraordinary movement toward open markets (which reached its zenith in the early 1970s) regains strength and trade in automobiles increases, the pressure for auto producers to achieve the highest world standard in the key export market (the United States) and to standardize regulations across the developed world will increase. If, on the other hand, markets are increasingly isolated, movement toward world standards on the American model and/or toward harmonization may atrophy.

On the basis of these general considerations, what can be said more specifically about future trends and social demands in the key areas of motor-vehicle safety, environmental protection, and equitable treatment of those unable to use the auto-dominated transportation systems of the developed countries?

Automobility and Safety

In every nation, progress in road safety seems to be a race between injury and fatality rates per vehicle-kilometer of travel, which invariably decline as automobility spreads, and the growth in total risk due to increasing travel per capita. As the experience of the average driver has increased and roadway systems have been improved, fatality rates seem to have fallen rapidly in every country where data have been collected. The United States experienced a decline in the fatality rate per 100 million vehicle-kilometers of travel from 11.3 during 1923–1927 (the earliest period for which data are available) to 3.3 in 1968 (the year a major government safety campaign focusing on vehicle hardware was commenced). Japan had a decline in the fatality rate from 18.0 in 1964 (the earliest date for which reliable data are available) to 11.2 in 1969 (just before the commencement of a major national safety campaign focusing on driver and pedestrian safety consciousness).[23] Experience in all other countries seems to parallel these examples.

Improvements in the safety performance of the auto-roadway system per kilometer traveled are generally more than offset by the growth in kilometers of travel, so that fatalities and injuries per capita rise dramatically for many years as automobility increases within a nation. In the United States, motor-vehicle fatalities per capita rose steadily through the postwar era until the early 1970s despite a 50-year history of widespread motorization. Experience in other developed countries was similar.

However, since about 1970 the developed countries seem increasingly to have been winning the safety race. Although figure 1.4 indicates a steady increase in worldwide motor-vehicle fatalities, this trend masks a striking decline in fatalities in the advanced industrial economies (table 3.1.). Fatalities declined 19 percent between 1970 and 1981 even as the number of motor vehicles in use in these countries increased by 59 percent.[24] It follows that the fatality rate per vehicle-kilometer of travel fell even faster than vehicle use increased, as is shown in table 3.2. The net result was that motor-vehicle-related fatalities per capita fell by 26 percent during this period (table 3.3).

What can account for these dramatic improvements in highway safety, which more than offset the increased travel per capita and which reduce

Table 3.1
Motor-vehicle-related fatalities in developed countries, 1970, 1976, and 1981

Country	1970	1976	1981	% change 1970–1981
Australia	3,798	3,583	3,322	−12.5
Austria	2,507	2,131	1,898	−24.3
Belgium	2,949	2,488	2,216	−24.9
Canada	5,080	5,262	5,410	+ 6.5
Denmark	1,208	857	662	−45.2
Finland	1,055	804	555	−47.4
France	16,387	14,799	13,287	−18.9
Germany	19,193	14,820	11,674	−39.2
Greece	1,043	1,192	1,516	+45.3
Ireland	540	525	572	+ 5.9
Italy	10,923	9,552	8,637	−20.9
Japan	21,795	12,654	11,335	−48.0
Luxembourg	132	100	100	−24.2
Netherlands	3,181	2,431	1,807	−43.2
Norway	560	471	338	−39.6
Portugal	1,842	3,372	2,950	+60.2
Spain	5,456	6,187	6,409	+17.5
Sweden	1,307	1,168	784	−40.0
Switzerland	1,694	1,188	1,165	−31.2
United Kingdom	7,771	6,570	6,069	−21.9
United States	52,627	45,523	49,268	− 6.4
Total	161,048	135,677	129,974	−19.3

Note:
These data include all fatalities occurring within 30 days of involvement in a motor-vehicle accident. Because some fatalities occur more than 30 days after an accident these figures are a slight undercount.
Source:
European Conference of Ministers of Transport, "Statistical Report on Road Accident Trends," Paris: ECMT (data for 1970 and 1976 from 1980 edition, 1981 data from 1982 edition).

Table 3.2
Motor-vehicle-related fatalities per 100 million vehicle-kilometers of travel, 1968, 1976, and 1980

Country	1968	1976	1980	% change 1968–1980
Australia	5.5	3.6	3.0	−45.5
Belgium	12.3	7.7	5.3	−56.9
Canada	4.7	3.0	2.7	−42.6
Denmark	n.d.	3.3	2.5	n.d.
Finland	n.d.	4.8	2.2	n.d.
France	10.4	6.2	4.5	−56.7
Germany	7.7	5.5	4.2	−45.5
Italy	9.9	4.5	4.1	−58.6
Japan	13.0	4.2	3.0	−76.9
Netherlands	8.2	4.4	3.3	−59.8
Norway	n.d.	3.2	1.9	n.d.
Spain	n.d.	8.0	7.5	n.d.
United Kingdom	3.8	2.7	2.3	−39.5
United States	3.3	2.0	2.2	−33.3

Note:
Because of the different national methods of estimating total vehicle-kilometers of travel and a lack of national estimates of average occupancy per vehicle-kilometer of travel it is difficult to use these data to compare nations. The data are useful in indicating the steady decline in fatalities per vehicle-kilometer in every nation.
n.d. = no relevant data available
Source:
Motor Vehicle Manufacturers Association, *Motor Vehicle Facts and Figures*, various years.

Table 3.3
Motor-vehicle-related fatalities per one million population, developed countries, 1970, 1976, and 1981

Country	1970	1976	1981	% change 1970–1981
Australia	304	257	224	−26.3
Austria	339	284	253	−25.4
Belgium	305	253	225	−26.2
Canada	238	228	223	− 6.3
Denmark	245	169	129	−47.3
Finland	229	170	116	−49.3
France	323	280	246	−23.8
Germany	316	241	189	−40.2
Greece	119	130	156	+31.1
Ireland	183	163	166	− 9.3
Italy	204	170	151	−26.0
Japan	209	112	96	−54.1
Luxembourg	388	278	278	−28.4
Netherlands	244	177	127	−48.0
Norway	144	117	82	−43.1
Portugal	213	349	297	+39.4
Spain	162	172	170	+ 4.9
Sweden	163	142	94	−42.3
Switzerland	274	187	180	−34.3
United Kingdom	140	118	109	−22.1
United States	257	209	214	−16.7
Total	238	191	176	−26.1

Source:
Calculated fron fatality data from table 3.1 and population estimates in United Nations *Demographic Yearbook*, New York: U.N., 1977, 1981.

the threat automobility poses to public health? A number of factors seem to be involved. One is the growing average age of motorists in the developed countries since the baby-boom generation reached driving age in the late 1960s. Another is the continuing improvements in road-way systems, along with the efforts to separate pedestrians and bicyclists from motor vehicles. These, along with continuing improvements in medical care, would presumably have contributed to the long-term trend toward lower fatalities per vehicle-kilometer. However, a con-siderable portion of the credit for the steep drop in fatalities per vehicle-kilometer after 1970 must also go to government safety programs de-signed to improve automobiles (in "primary safety" or crash avoidance and in crashworthiness) and to regulate the behavior of drivers and pedestrians.

After 1973 practically all governments reduced speed limits on high-ways in order to conserve energy. However, the more dramatic effect was to reduce fatalities. Of the 21 countries listed in tables 3.1–3.3, 18 have adopted some type of seat-belt-use law since 1969.[25] Automakers in practically all countries have been influenced in their vehicle designs by the series of crash standards imposed by the U.S. government on automobiles sold in the United States.

Can these favorable trends continue during the next 20 years? It seems certain that they can. One important factor is that the rate of growth in vehicular travel in the developed countries is likely to be slower than during the past 20 years. Another is that new vehicle technologies such as anti-skid brakes, rupture-resistant gas tanks, and more crashworthy structures in small cars will continue to be perfected.

One of the most common predictions of the 1970s about the trend in highway safety has failed to come true: The shift to smaller cars in the United States, Canada, and some countries in northern Europe since 1973 has been marked by substantial declines rather than dramatic increases in fatalities per vehicle-kilometer. And it is apparent that vehicle technologists have only begun to explore ways to cushion pas-sengers involved in crashes in small vehicles. Thus, the transition to still lighter vehicles in the years ahead does not have to carry a public-health risk if auto technologists are continually prodded to address the challenge of cushioning passengers from crash forces even as vehicle weight is reduced.

Despite these positive factors, a glance at motor-vehicle fatalities by category of road user (table 3.4) indicates two continuing problems for enhanced road safety in the long term. One is the large proportion of

Table 3.4
Distribution of motor-vehicle-related fatalities by categories of road user, 1982

Country	Pedestrians	Bicycle riders	Moped and motorcycle riders	Automobile occupants	Bus and truck occupants[a]	All motor-vehicle occupants	Total
Austria	18.9	6.7	16.6	53.6	4.2	57.8	100.0
Belgium	18.6	12.0	13.9	52.1	3.4	55.5	100.0
Denmark	24.8	14.6	15.1	41.4	4.1	45.5	100.0
Finland	27.4	14.4	8.3	45.0	4.9	49.9	100.0
France	16.1	4.5	15.8	58.6	5.0	63.6	100.0
Germany	22.3	9.3	17.1	48.3	3.0	51.3	100.0
Japan	30.4	9.9	22.4	24.8	12.5	37.3	100.0
Netherlands	14.9	21.6	14.6	46.5	2.4	48.9	100.0
Norway	22.4	8.7	10.0	51.4	7.5	58.9	100.0
Sweden	18.7	10.8	11.6	53.3	5.6	58.9	100.0
Switzerland	23.4	6.3	25.4	38.9	6.0	44.9	100.0
United Kingdom	31.5	4.9	18.0	41.5	4.1	45.6	100.0
United States	16.6	1.9	10.1	52.8	18.6	71.4	100.0

a. This category also includes a few fatalities of miscellaneous classification, such as horse riders and occupants of rail vehicles struck by road vehicles.

Source: European Conference of Ministers of Transport, *Statistical Report on Road Accident Trends*, Paris: ECMT, 1983.

fatalities occurring outside motor vehicles. In Japan, to take the most extreme case, 63 percent of highway fatalities are pedestrians, bicyclists, and motorcyclists. Better vehicle designs can have only a marginal effect on such fatalities, and the ability to separate pedestrians from bicyclists and bicyclists from automobiles and trucks is often limited by lack of space. Thus, continuing efforts to improve the safety consciousness of drivers and pedestrians will be essential. A country at the other extreme in terms of the predominant type of fatality is the United States, where 71 percent of those killed are occupants of cars and trucks. Though greater crashworthiness is important, safety experts are already finding evidence that more protective vehicles are of little use in the absence of some type of passenger restraint.[26] Fewer than 10 percent of Americans use their seat belts at present, and all government campaigns to date to voluntarily increase belt use have had little effect.

A debate has been underway since 1968 about the mandatory installation in new cars of air bags (or other "passive restraint" devices) that function automatically in a crash to cushion the occupants' impact with the steering wheel and dashboard. However, there is no sign that these will be required, despite their technical maturity and clear evidence from limited fleet tests that the reduction in fatalities would be dramatic. Similarly, recent public acceptance of stepped-up enforcement of laws against drunk driving has raised the prospect that seat-belt-use laws might be acceptable at some point in the future. However, in the United States these must be enacted on a state-by-state basis, and no state has yet seriously considered such a law. A number of European countries may therefore be in the best position to continue recent progress in highway safety, because the concept of mandatory seat-belt use is well established and a majority of motor-vehicle fatalities are vehicle occupants. Motorists who wear their belts will be the chief beneficiaries of continuing advances in vehicle crash protection.

Automobility and Environmental Quality

Earlier we asked whether air-quality problems might threaten the continuation of the automobile-dominated system of personal transportation in the next 20 years. We concluded that they will not, but this finding still leaves a broad range of air-quality issues in regard to which citizens must decide how high a quality of air to demand. For example, diesel particulates are not only a potential threat to health; they also smell bad and reduce visibility. Similarly, levels of nitrogen oxides that have no demonstrable long-term effect on well-being in healthy individuals may still cause irritation in breathing and impair the activities of those with lung diseases. What will society demand in the way of air quality as a matter of amenity in the years to come?

The first point to note is that air quality is improving in the United States and Japan, partly because of the emission standards adopted in the 1970s for HC, CO, and NO_x and the reduced use of leaded gas. This trend will continue well into the 1990s on the strength of current regulations as the vehicle fleet is renewed with post-1981 vehicles meeting the highest emission standards. The downward trend may continue even further if emission inspection is implemented on a wide scale. Therefore, it is unlikely that additional standards will be proposed for these pollutants in the United States and Japan in the next 20 years. Even if more stringent standards are adopted (notably for NO_x, to deal with acid rain) it seems likely that the present three-way closed-loop catalyst systems in combination with electronic engine controls can meet more stringent requirements without further alterations to existing engines. Similarly, the proposed U.S. diesel-particulate standard for 1987 is quite rigorous and is likely to be the highest level required for many years to come unless particulates are found to be particularly dangerous and the diesel market share increases dramatically.

Thus, the key air-quality issue in the developed countries in the next 20 years may well be whether European emission standards for HC, CO, and NO_x and the use of lead will come to approximate those of Japan and the United States, and whether other countries will follow the United States lead in limiting particulate emissions from passenger-car diesels.

A straightforward comparison of the American, Japanese, EEC, and other European standards on permissible emissions per kilometer traveled is not possible because of wide variations in the test cycles used. However, it is generally agreed that the United States and Japan have very similar standards for HC, CO, and NO_x and that these are at the highest level of stringency. To meet them, nearly all producers use catalyst systems which are poisoned by lead in gasoline. The current EEC standards, by contrast, are quite moderate in terms of the cleanup technology manufacturers need to install in the vehicle, being roughly equivalent to the American and Japanese standards of the mid 1970s. Sweden and Switzerland occupy an intermediate position just short of the level requiring catalyst systems.

Recently there has been much discussion in the EEC about removing lead from gasoline and reducing emission levels for HC, CO, and NO_x. Because lead is widely viewed as a serious long-term health problem, it seems likely that steps will be taken soon to begin the transition to lead-free fuel. (This process will take a number of years because cars now on the road cannot be modified to run on lead-free gasoline; full elimination of lead will occur only as vehicles needing leaded fuels are scrapped.) It also seems likely that standards for the other pollutants will be significantly tightened for new cars before the end of the decade. Current discussions center on what new standards to adopt and the best technical means of achieving them. One approach is to enact the current American-Japanese standards, which would require equipping European cars with catalysts. Another approach involves a search for new technologies that might reduce the emissions of new cars somewhat less than catalysts could but that would avoid their fuel-consumption penalty, their high manufacturing cost, and the tendency for their performance to deteriorate sharply as vehicles age. One possibility is "lean burn" technology, which increases the air-to-fuel ratio and improves the mixing of the two before combustion to reduce the production of pollutants in the engine and thus the need for cleaning the exhaust. Other techniques are under study as well, and a breakthrough in emission-control technology is an attractive research goal for the European auto industry. Development of better control techniques would enhance the industry's image as a technological leader and provide a competitive lever against the dominant American catalyst technology, particularly in developing countries, where pollution problems are growing but catalyst systems seem prohibitively expensive.

With regard to diesel particulates, the Europeans may also require important reductions during the period of this study. This is particularly so because the diesel share of the passenger-car market is much higher in Europe than in the United States and because several of the European producers are leaders in particulate-control technology, which they have been developing with vigor to defend their highly profitable North American diesel sales.

Air quality is, of course, only a portion of the environmental picture. It seems likely that other environmental demands will be placed on the automobile in future years—particularly in Europe, where the combination of old, compact cities and high volumes of auto traffic creates the worst amenity problems. The leading areas of advance are likely to be noise regulations for diesel cars and further exclusions of automobiles from dense city centers. Technologies are being developed to deal with the former, largely by enclosing and insulating the engine compartment. These techniques are simple in principle but may be costly, particularly if fitted to models already in production. With regard to auto exclusion, it is clear that the auto is not suited for use in many crowded areas and equally clear that further restraints of the sort pioneered in Göteborg, Munich, Copenhagen, and Amsterdam will have no measurable impact on the overall auto transportation system or the auto industry. Thus, it seems certain that experiments in finding the proper role for automobiles in crowded city centers will continue.

Automobility and Equality

A paradox of growing automobility is that persons without cars become less mobile as a large portion of society begins to travel predominantly by car, partly because transit options are cut back as riders switch to driving and partly because urban areas and essential travel destinations tend to spread out as auto use becomes more universal. In the United States, which has long been the leader in auto use and which now has a very low growth rate in auto ownership, 15.3 percent of households, as of 1977, had no motor vehicle (car, light truck, motorcycle, or moped).[27] Some of these households lacked the financial means to operate a motor vehicle, but many householders are physically unable to drive. Thus, it seems clear that society will never reach a point where everyone will want or be able to use his own independent means of transport. What can be done about growing immobility in the midst of auto-dominated societies?

Solutions fall in three distinct classes. One is to keep urban areas compact so that transit alternatives are attractive to use and relatively cheap to provide. A second is to adjust incomes and vehicle operating characteristics so that low-income and handicapped citizens may have auto access. The third, and the most promising in the near term, is for government to underwrite the expense of basic mobility, even at a high cost. Basic mobility is likely to be costly in fully auto-dependent societies, because conventional fixed-route transit systems will not be able to serve essential destinations. The alternative will be some sort of demand-responsive transit system, perhaps based on taxis. There has been much experimentation with such systems in the past decade in the United States, Japan, and Europe. A key finding is that, even with sophisticated methods of grouping trips to maintain high occupancies, such services are labor-intensive and costly. Nevertheless, they are a key social requirement to maintain equity in an auto-dominant society. For the longer term, motor vehicles that can be more easily used by elderly or handicapped citizens are a promising alternative.

The Need for Continuing Adaptation

This review suggests that the long-term prospects for automobility are bright because of a capacity for continuing adaptation to a changing operating environment. Particular promise seems to lie in the area of vehicle technology. In fact, technological advances are the most promising means of dealing with energy costs, continuing air-quality and safety problems, and long-term dilemmas of immobility for those unable to use the current generation of automobiles. But what determines the rate of improvement in auto technology, and will it be adequate to deal with foreseeable problems over the next 20 years?

4   Technological Opportunities for Adaptation

The automotive world has never lacked for "bright ideas." Concepts for electric cars, turbine cars, steam cars, and even flying cars have been around for many years, and working prototypes of these and a myriad of other concepts have been built. In the area of individual components—ceramic engines, carbon-fiber composite bodies, all-plastic tires—still more bright ideas exist in prototype form. Yet only a fraction of the many concepts proposed ever find their way into mass production.

How do ideas become realities in the world of the automobile? Is the world auto industry's bundle of bright engineering ideas able to cope with the future challenges of a changing operating and competitive environment discussed in chapter 3? In view of the process by which promising technical concepts become realities, what areas seem to promise the greatest advances in automotive technology in the years to come?

The Technology Process: How Innovation Occurs

New engineering ideas are developed and incorporated in automobiles in two ways. In the overall planning of a new vehicle, prototype systems and technologies are fitted into and harmonized with the total vehicle package, which itself may be either traditional or radically different. This is the work of the designers and engineers in the final-assembler firms, who continuously scan the "shelf" of available technologies—within the firm, across the supplier industry, and in other sectors—for new ways to perform old functions and ways to give automobiles new capabilities.

The placement of new component technologies on the shelf results from the research-and-development process of conceiving new concepts and bringing them up to proven prototype status. This is often the work of technologists in supplier companies who develop new components and then convince vehicle designers to use them. In the case of long-term development of radical technologies, this task may also require government support.[1] However, the process also works in the other direction when vehicle designers discover new needs and search for suppliers willing to develop suitable prototypes.

The Process of Designing Vehicles

The design process begins with the product designers and engineers in the final assembler firm, whose task is to master the complex and increasingly modular nature of the modern automobile. The basic structure (the body, in everyday language) serves as an armature for a growing number of essential systems. These include the power train to get it going, brakes to stop it, suspensions to mediate between the passengers and the road, and lighting and windshield wiping to make the auto usable around the clock. Other vital systems permit the driver to manage the vehicle (the steering wheel and linkage, the gas and brake pedals), the vehicle to communicate with the driver (the instruments), and the systems within the vehicle to communicate with each other (the transmission controls that adjust the shift pattern depending on the engine's operating mode). In addition, modern vehicles contain a host of comfort and convenience features and such necessities as emission controls and occupant crash protection.

The vehicle designer's challenge is to tune these systems to work together harmoniously, each taking account of the others' needs. Because interactions among the many systems are increasingly complex, harmony would be difficult to achieve in each new model even if the technology of the systems never changed. However, a key objective for the designer must be to change the very nature of the individual systems in order to improve the overall vehicle. Because the development of new technologies for the automobile's various systems proceeds at different speeds and in different directions, creating overlaps and conflicts, the maintenance of harmony at a time of technical change is a true art relying on much accumulated know-how and experimentation.

How does the vehicle designer go about his art? First, he must respect a long time scale. Just to incorporate a new component system—after it is fully developed in prototype form—into a new model takes 4 years on average. Part of this time is needed to design, build, and install production tools. This occurs after half or more of the time has been expended trying the new system out on test beds and then in prototype and pre-production vehicles to see what happens to the performance of the whole when something new is added. Since the results are likely to be a mixture of bad and good, several time-consuming iterations are usually needed to bring the complete vehicle up to a standard the consumer will accept.

All this can take place only after a system technology has reached the stage of a fully developed prototype. Getting it from a concept on paper to a prototype that really works can be an even more time-consuming process. In the cases of many new technologies it has taken a decade or more. The risks are so great throughout this process that in many cases the journey is never completed or is indefinitely delayed by technical obstacles or shifts in market conditions.

After a new technology enters production in a new model, feedback from users often leads to additional tuning of the system. It may even require expensive and embarrassing recalls if performance is grossly deficient. More significant, the cost of developing a new system and incorporating it in a new vehicle is such that the design must promise to sustain its appeal in the market for a considerable period of time.

These constraints mean that the designer cannot casually introduce a new technology. It cannot be done overnight, whatever consumer fads or government fiats may dictate, and any new concept must have sufficient staying power to return its investment cost. Thus, the auto designer must be visionary but sober in his attitude toward new technologies.

To meet these criteria, vehicle designers tend to add new systems one at a time or to apply new technologies to one area at a time. For example, microprocessor controls were added to engines beginning in the mid 1970s, to transmissions in the early 1980s and suspensions in the mid 1980s. This is the preferred course of the assembler because it builds step by step on experience, minimizing the chance of wasted development funds and the risk of a disastrous error.

Usually, the vehicle designer's approach to innovation is even more conservative than the foregoing example suggests. It draws upon experiments with four segments of consumers around the periphery of the mass market before a new concept is offered across the product line: The utilitarian consumers, looking for a vehicle that can perform new functions such as off-road operation, provided the initial market test of such concepts as four-wheel drive for passenger cars. The performance-minded consumers, desiring a vehicle at the cutting edge of performance in acceleration, handling, and braking, eagerly performed the initial on-the-road testing of disc brakes, fuel injection, low-profile tires, turbocharging, four-valve cylinder heads, and a host of other innovations. The economy-minded motorists, seeking to reduce operating costs to the minimum, made the pioneering purchases of automotive diesels. The luxury consumers, wanting new comfort and convenience features and willing to pay practically any price for them, made up the tiny initial market for such items as automatic transmissions, air conditioning, and trip computers. This approach allows the vehicle designer to introduce options in these peripheral segments with the expectation that the consumer will value the new attribute so highly that he will be willing to accept quirks in its operation or interference with other systems in the car. Early diesels were hard to start in cold weather; disc brakes were subject to warping and rapid pad wear; four-wheel-drive designs gave a rough ride and markedly increased fuel consumption; early auto air conditioners could only be produced and offered at what would later seem an absurd price. In such cases, because the consumer was willing to put up with one step backward in some area to take two steps forward in another, vital on-the-road experience could be gained and the designer could be aided by articulate feedback from highly interested users. Gradually, the innovation was refined for introduction in vehicles closer to the heart of the mass market, and at some point many innovations become "standard equipment" for the whole industry.

It is not surprising that the vehicle designer's nightmare is the prospect of putting an entirely new technology into the whole product line on short notice. With the experience in the United States during the 1974 and 1975 model years with emission controls, the nightmare became real as government-imposed timetables of only one or two years and a lack of suitable technologies fully developed as prototypes forced manufacturers to conduct on-the-road product proving. Although the auto industry was widely condemned by the public for its technical ineptitude, the more proximate cause of the problem was the gross violation of the industry's tried-and-true incremental approach to the introduction of innovations.

A final problem faced by the vehicle designer in what might be called the conventional innovation process is the need to nurse along the consumer who is accustomed to a familiar product that is already sat-

isfactory in most respects. A 1980s example is the emphasis on aerodynamics. The aerodynamically tuned auto body can look "different,"
indeed decidedly strange, to many consumers. The designer's challenge
is to bring the producer's traditional purchasers along while also attracting progressive-minded buyers through the gradual introduction
of aerodynamic features so that eventually the product feels "right"
again.

There are alternatives to incrementalism in innovation that offer
producers the prospect of greater rewards but with substantially greater
risks. One is to look at the shelf of available technologies and put
together a dramatically new package. Each piece in the new vehicle
may be familiar or only a slight advance, but the overall effect, when
a bundle of familiar systems are harmoniously recombined, may be
something quite new and may provide an enormous competitive advantage. Henry Ford's Model T is the archetypal example of what can
happen when this strategy works. Ford combined a number of features
that had recently been introduced by other producers, such as a four-
cylinder gasoline engine mounted longitudinally in the front, a drive-
shaft running in a torque tube to the rear wheels, and a steering wheel
on the left to correspond with standard road use in the United States.
To these Ford added several innovations of his own, among them
vanadium alloy steel in chassis parts to reduce weight, a three-point
engine-mounting system to isolate the engine from the twisting forces
absorbed by the frame and to allow the frame to be lightened further,
and a new engine block and head design that was cheaper to machine.
None of these advances was striking by itself, but when the whole
package was put together, the Model T was much cheaper to make,
more durable, and more versatile than any of its rivals. When this
design of 1908 was combined with advances in manufacturing systems
introduced by 1914, Ford had singlehandedly fashioned the first great
transformation in the world industry, very nearly *becoming* the entire
world auto industry in the process.[2]

In Ford's case the rewards were enormous because the advances in
the product were made with careful attention to production economics
and manufacturability as well as vehicle performance. The result of a
dramatic repackaging can also be a new product that is widely praised
by technologists as a brilliant advance but is unsuccessful in an economic
sense. In the BMC Mini design of 1959, designer Alec Issigonis en-
visioned a new minicar smaller than any of the existing models in the
British market. To achieve this he rethought the entire vehicle package,

placing the engine transversely in the front and coupling it to the front wheels by means of a new transaxle design. He spread the wheels as far toward the front and the rear as possible to make room for four passengers and give an acceptable ride in a very short vehicle, and he incorporated a new rubber suspension system to give adequate ride quality and handling while saving space and weight. The resulting Mini was a new type of car with extraordinary interior room and drive-ability in a tiny package. The problem with the Mini was that it would appeal to only a small market segment unless it could be priced well below existing models. The car's design and BMC's production system did not permit this to be done at a profit. The company produced the Mini for many years at a loss, hoping mainly to defend its market share at the low end and to attract first-time buyers to its marque.

The eventual beneficiaries of the philosophy represented by the Mini were the companies introducing second-generation designs, beginning with the Fiat 127 in 1971. These vehicles took the basic concept worked out in the Mini, simplified it, and developed a more rational manu-facturing system. By the time Volkswagen and Ford introduced the third generation of this concept in the 1974 Polo and the 1976 Fiesta, the product had been so improved that it could be sold for slightly less than the next larger size class and so was able to capture a large share of the European auto market. This was of small consolation to the original innovator: BMC (now merged into BL) did not enjoy comparable success with its own evolutionary developments of the Mini concept.

Another alternative to technological incrementalism, with even higher risk and potential payoff, is to select a new technology of a truly radical nature and build a new vehicle around it. This tantalizing avenue for would-be entrants to the auto industry has been followed most recently in the area of electric vehicles, notably by the Sinclair project in Great Britain. However, the history of the industry is littered with noble failures of such efforts. One bold innovator was André Citroën, who introduced a revolutionary car in 1934 built around the then-radical principle of front-wheel drive. Though the car went on to become successful, even legendary, the difficulties of launching it and curing its early mechanical problems bankrupted the company. Another ex-ample is the heavy commitment of Toyo Kogyo to the Wankel rotary engine. The use of the rotary engine made its Mazda cars world-famous as leaders in technology, and continues today to set the RX-7 sports car apart from all its competitors. But the Wankel rotary, and with it Toyo Kogyo, only narrowly escaped extinction in the mid 1970s, when high fuel consumption suddenly made Mazda's RX-3 and RX-4 models uncompetitive in the world market. A great innovator in other fields, the American William Lear, saw steam power as the creative force behind his planned entry into auto production in the early 1970s. The steam or Rankine-cycle engine seemed highly attractive at that time by virtue of its low emissions of pollutants. Its fuel efficiency was too low, however, to meet market needs after 1973, and the project had to be abandoned.

These examples help highlight the troubles with this approach. One is the need for the new technology to be considerably superior to the existing proven alternatives without displaying major offsetting faults. The other is the requirement that the vehicle package incorporating the innovation be comparable in other respects to existing products. Otherwise the most the vehicle designer can hope for is a tiny "enthusiast" market. Enthusiasts are valuable in introducing innovations in individual vehicle systems in otherwise conventional designs, but "enthusiasm" at the whole-vehicle level is much less useful since it usually cannot generate the necessary scale economies.

The potential for more sharp shifts in the automobile's operating environment and for the development of dramatic new technologies outside the auto industry (as occurred in the 1970s with the microprocessor) make success through radical innovation during the next 20 years a possibility. However, the problems facing the radical innovator, in particular the need to get a very complex product "right" on the first try, loom very large. Thus, the primary pattern of innovation in the industry during the period under study will continue to be the incremental introduction of new technologies and systems in what will appear to be rather traditional vehicles. Over time, as in the case of a growing child, this approach can almost imperceptibly produce something dramatically different.

The Research-and-Development Process for New Vehicle Systems

If the incremental incorporation of new system technologies into vehicle packages will continue to be the main source of technological advance in the auto industry, this prompts an obvious and important question: Where do these new systems and technologies come from, and how do they evolve into prototypes suitable for incorporation by the auto designer?

In some cases the vehicle designer in the assembler firm lays out the performance specification for a needed function and either sets to work on it in house or selects an outside vendor to perform the task. A notable example of recent years is the catalyst exhaust system General Motors called into being to meet emission rules. After doing the basic research on catalyst technologies, GM selected vendor firms to take a hand in the development of prototype and production hardware. This approach may be followed more often in the future, because the world's final assemblers have greatly increased their R&D outlays and patenting in recent years.

However, the auto industry is still predominantly a borrower of new technologies developed elsewhere. These technologies are often developed from paper concepts or converted from applications in other types of products by the industry's major systems suppliers, such as Robert Bosch (Germany), Nippondenso (Japan), Lucas (U.K.), and Bendix, Eaton, and TRW (U.S.). This process involves the adaptation of materials and technologies to the special needs of auto use, and it is sometimes performed by supplier firms on the speculation that they can convince auto designers to incorporate the new technologies in their products. Two examples will illustrate the problems that can be encountered along this path. The microprocessor was developed far from the auto industry, initially for specialized defense applications. It seems fair to say that it would have been developed at about the same time whether or not there had been an auto industry, and that its incorporation in auto products was not a foregone conclusion. However, the new technology raised such attractive possibilities for new automotive functions and for easier ways to perform old functions that experimentation with it by auto designers was certain. Adapting the microprocessor to real-world autos was not easy, though. A technology originally designed to work in a vibration-free, air-conditioned environment had to go under the hood of a car in conditions of thermal shock, extreme vibration, relentless grime, and electromagnetic interference as intense as enemy jamming in military use. In addition, the systems needed to be fail-passive so that the auto would continue to operate, though at a reduced level, in the event of system failure. Although the industry has made great strides in dealing with all these problems, fine tuning and system harmonization continue, particularly as more and more microprocessors controlling more and more functions are added to the vehicle. Another example of the technology-adaptation process is the turbocharger, a device that uses the energy of the exhaust stream to turn a turbine which pumps air into the cylinders at high pressure, increasing the power available from a small engine. The technology has been under development almost as long as there have been internal-combustion engines and has been incorporated in aircraft engines for some 60 years. However, in aircraft use the turbocharger operates at nearly constant output throughout a flight, can be easily cooled in flight by airflow through the engine nacelle, is carefully run up to operating temperature before takeoff, and can be shut down to cool after landing when its contribution to power is no longer needed. In automotive use none of this applies. The output of the turbocharger is needed instantly at irregular intervals for acceleration. The unit is often run hard while cold and shut down while hot. In some installations made in cars before the effects of these conditions were fully appreciated, the result was severe bearing wear caused by hard running before lubrication was adequate and by "coking" of lubricant due to heat spikes after the engine was shut down while hot. Auto technologists are nearly a decade into second-generation applications of the turbocharger. However, they have still not mastered all the problems of these applications, problems that demand solution as turbochargers are incorporated in a much wider range of vehicles in quest of adequate performance with the smaller-displacement engines now needed to improve fuel economy. Mass-market customers will be less impressed with the "turbo" label on the side of the car than with durability and driveability, so one may expect the technologists to redouble their efforts in this area.

A different sort of problem that may plague the supplier attempting to convert a technological concept into a system that will function in a car is the frequent need to pioneer new manufacturing methods to complement the new product. A current example is the use of plastic parts in place of steel stampings for body exteriors. Plastics can save weight—a valuable attribute—but for some years their adoption was blocked by the lack of suitable manufacturing techniques. Recently, however, plastic suppliers have sharply improved such methods as reaction injection molding to the stage where plastic panels for the hood of the Citroen BX, the front fenders of the Honda CRX, and the skin of the Pontiac Fiero can be produced at competitive cost.

The ability to produce a new system at a competitive cost with adequate quality is the key to moving it from the specialty market to the mass market once its performance in the vehicle has been perfected. For example, current turbochargers use rotary parts made of steel alloys, which are difficult and expensive to cast and machine. Recent development work by ceramic firms has focused on the substitution of ceramics because the raw materials are cheap and the manufacturing process may prove to be simpler. A breakthrough in production costs could lead to the use of turbochargers in a very wide range of automotive products.

It should be clear by now that the restocking of the "shelf" of prototype components and technologies is marked by much trial and error and many dead ends. The process also tends to leave many bits and pieces and half-finished designs on the shelf awaiting breakthroughs in other areas or shifts in market conditions. The continuously variable transmission (CVT) is a good example. Such devices are able to vary the gear ratio between the motor and the driving wheels practically instantaneously over a continuous range. This contrasts with the three, four, or five ratios available in current manual and automatic transmissions and the need to uncouple the motor from the drive wheels while shifting. If properly programmed to keep the engine working at its most efficient speed, whatever the speed of the vehicle, a CVT is capable of yielding substantial efficiency gains. CVTs were first developed and even produced in the early years of the industry (Cartercar, B.M., Certus), and a simple CVT was introduced in the late 1950s in the Dutch Daf, a small car designed to appeal to first-time drivers with qualms about shifting. However, to achieve the CVT's potential for higher efficiency, a more sophisticated management system has been needed to coordinate the engine, the fuel supply, and the transmission, and more durable materials have been needed for the transmission friction surfaces. Also required was a jump in energy prices so that the CVT's fuel economy would offset its higher manufacturing cost. The perfection of the microprocessor and more durable surface materials have combined with higher energy prices, to move CVT development ahead rapidly. Commercial mass production will be achieved in the mid 1980s.

Fortunately, the long history of experimentation in the auto industry, along with the perfection of the microprocessor, meant that the auto industry had a large shelf of technologies available when its operating environment changed radically in the 1970s. It was precisely for this reason that popular assumptions that the automobile could not adapt to new conditions were grossly pessimistic. In fact the adoption of technologies that had long languished on the shelf (diesels, fuel injection, turbochargers, high-strength steels, aerodynamic bodies, front-wheel drive, etc.) has been sufficient to ensure a bright future for the automobile.

Why Innovation Occurs

The energy shocks and air quality mandates of the 1970s illustrate one of the key reasons why new technologies are taken off the shelf and put into cars. However, these are by no means the only reasons, nor does a changing environment explain why technologies are put on the shelf in the first place. Technical advances do not occur without cause; rather they are a result of three conditions.

The first condition, as just discussed, is a dramatic change in the automobile's operating environment that demands new design approaches if the familiar product, with which the consumer is reasonably content, is to continue to be available. New technologies introduced in this circumstance might be termed "coping innovations" and will ideally be invisible. The designer's objective is to alter the car under the skin and inside the engine compartment so as to retain its utility in a changed environment without the user's noticing that a major change has been necessary.

In the 1970s, when the auto technologists succeeded with emission-control innovations the users noticed no change; when they failed the users noticed a deterioration in performance. Designers received little recognition for the former and much blame for the latter. Outside observers also perceived the industry as unimaginative and unable to innovate—this at the precise time when the industry's historic rate of innovation was taking a dramatic upturn.

In the 1970s the key changes in the operating environment were mandates for safety, lower emissions, and improved fuel economy in any given package of vehicle attributes. From its shelf of available technologies, the industry was able to respond rapidly; in fact it seems to have leapfrogged these problems. Many additional fuel-enhancing technologies, for example, are ready or nearly ready for production, but the current trend in fuel prices does not demand their immediate introduction. Similarly, safety and emission mandates appear unlikely to advance beyond current Japanese and American levels (although European emission standards may catch up), particularly so long as many national industries are facing severe competitive pressures. Despite this, the shocks of the 1970s are still being felt in auto technology, because the world's manufacturers experienced a severe scare about the technological adequacy of their product in a rapidly changing environment. They will not feel comfortable, therefore, until the shelf of technological opportunities is fully renewed to provide a vital cushion in the event of another dramatic environmental shift. The industry has also felt a need, on the basis of its experience since 1973, to go much further in the direction of bringing technologies from concept to prototype than it has historically. This is shown by its increased spending on intermediate-range research in the gap between basic science and direct engineering applications. This may in turn generate new technologies that may be adopted without specific environmental motivation.

A second impetus to innovation is intense competition in the auto marketplace. Competitive innovation is likely when there are many firms with a technical orientation competing in a relatively mature market. It becomes more likely still when automakers are anxious to add value to their products to compete with each other and with other sectors for the fixed number of consumer dollars, and when a number of suitable technologies are becoming available as a result of developments outside the industry. All these conditions are highly probable in the years ahead. Thus, competition will be an important driver of the auto industry's technical evolution, which will continue to be quite rapid by the standards of the postwar era.

One of these competitive conditions, the large number of firms in a relatively mature market, is itself partially due to an environmental change: higher energy prices, which have brought the product mix in the developed countries' auto markets into closer alignment. In this situation, companies can hope to compete in a number of ways, of which product differentiation and a superior manufacturing system are the most obvious. And both have technological dimensions. By introducing technological innovations in its products, a manufacturer can hope to offer an automobile that does things its competitors cannot. Even better, these innovations may be protected from immediate imitation by patents or know-how. In its production systems, an automaker may hope to introduce new manufacturing systems that reduce costs while improving quality and increasing flexibility, and these innovations may be protected by patents and offer the potential for the manufacturer to sell its process technology to competitors.

Paradoxically, success in developing new production systems may make it possible to reduce the cost and price of a product of a given description while creating a desire on the part of the producer to add value to the car. After all, the auto producer is not motivated to sell a low-cost car as such, but rather to sell an expensive car, in which the expense is derived not from manufacturing cost but from the addition of features and options. New technologies that offer new capabilities—entertainment, high performance, communication, even navigation—are the obvious way to do this. If these new technologies are not incorporated in autos, the producer fears a competitive threat from two directions: Other producers may offer them first, or the consumer may consume them elsewhere, leaving fewer dollars for auto consumption.

Innovation is not possible, however, without the potential for finding new technical "wrinkles." As noted above, even with its increased spending on research and development the auto industry remains as much a user of technologies developed elsewhere as an originator of new concepts. Thus, the general rate of creation of new technologies in society is a critical limiting factor on the rate of automotive innovation.

This leads to the third condition for innovation, which is the exogenous development of new technologies with applications in the auto industry. When a truly epochal innovation such as the microprocessor comes along, its adoption across the industrial landscape seems irresistible, even in the absence of environmental changes or intense competition. The intellectual challenge of something new seems to create fads in industry, just as among consumers, so that applications are found for such new technologies even where the greatest ingenuity is required to discern a true need. In the current era, microprocessors are proving to have enormous appeal to vehicle designers and production-process engineers. New materials derived from research into basic molecular structure may have a similarly broad attraction. In any event, it appears that new technologies now in sight will keep auto innovators busy for the foreseeable future.

Probable Areas of Future Innovation

This review of the "how" and "why" of automotive innovation is likely to have provoked curiosity about the "what." What are the most probable areas of technical advance in the years ahead? Several of the academic technologists participating in the Program have conducted assessments of future prospects in automotive technology. The following analysis is based on their findings.[3]

The clearest indication of future trends can be obtained by comparing the pressures for innovation with the technical potential for advance in each area. As noted earlier, technical advance will be slow even in the presence of extreme necessity if no new ideas are on the shelf, but may be very rapid in less pressing areas simply because new concepts can be easily introduced.

Environmental pressure to further enhance safety and reduce emissions is not likely to be so great in the future as in the 1970s, but the full application of microelectronics and new materials will make continuing progress a practical possibility. In the case of safety, the full introduction of microelectronics into vehicles will make it possible over the next 20 years, largely to eliminate skidding during braking, acceleration, and turning. Microprocessor-controlled anti-skid braking systems were developed initially for aircraft. These are now in their second generation of automotive use, having been introduced on top-of-the-line performance-oriented models. Anti-slip acceleration systems are entering the prototype testing phase and are anticipated to be available in a few years on "up-market" models, particularly those with rear-wheel drive. The logical completion of this process, perhaps beyond the period of this study, would be anti-skid steering systems that would sense and react to sideslip to preserve driver control in emergency maneuvers.

In managing crash energy, new plastic and composite materials may make it possible to increase survivable crash speeds substantially without increasing vehicle weight. New materials for windscreens, now in their first generation of consumer use, may largely eliminate lacerations from broken glass. Advances in microelectronics and manufacturing techniques may make possible low-cost passive restraints for front-seat and rear-seat passengers.

The real question about the rate of progress in auto safety lies not so much in the technical feasibility of the new systems as in public attitudes toward the problems they address. If consumer demand is the driving force, the adoption of these measures may be very slow (because they appeal primarily to performance-minded and safety-conscious market segments), and they will not be cheap even in high-volume production. In the absence of product regulation, only a small fraction of vehicles might encompass the full range of technical possibilities by the year 2000. Alternatively, governments may mandate them as "standard equipment" if it is perceived that other approaches to safety, based on altering driver behavior and improving road networks, are not workable. Government action becomes more likely if the health of the auto industry and the economies of the developed countries seem to permit innovations that will necessarily increase the price of new cars, and if the innovations are perceived as reliable in everyday use.

The last is a particularly important issue for technologists, because most new systems (such as passive restraints and traction control) function by instantly assessing situations. Microprocessors, with their associated impact and acceleration sensors, make this possible. They also bring an unsettling potential for "false positives" (system action when not wanted) and "false negatives" (no response when needed). Experience in the past decade indicates that such problems, and the public's perception of them, must be fully overcome before consumers will accept regulatory mandates. Thus, the perception that these systems are fully reliable will tend to increase pressure for their adoption.

The emission situation is similar. The standards set in the 1970s may be adjusted slightly (e.g., the phasing out of leaded gas in Europe accompanied by more stringent emissions standards), but it is entirely possible that the next 20 years may pass without a raising of standards to levels which demand new technologies. Indeed, the main technological challenge in this area may lie in maintaining existing levels of emission control while making progress in other areas such as performance, noise, and fuel economy.

An important issue may concern passenger-car diesels. Diesel engines are attractive for their energy efficiency, but today they are noisy and they emit unpleasant and possibly noxious particulates. If higher energy prices dramatically shift the product mix toward diesels, in the absence of technical countermeasures a new air-quality and noise crisis might quickly follow. In addition, direct injection of diesel fuel without a prechamber, the most promising technical path to even better diesel energy efficiency, exacerbates both problems. Thus, the path to the future in this area will be decided by a contest between technical imperatives: particulate control plus noise suppression versus direct injection for higher fuel economy.

Fuel economy will continue to be an impetus for technical innovations directed at dealing with a changing operating environment and at gaining competitive advantage in the marketplace. Unlike air quality, noise, and even safety, fuel economy is a high-visibility issue for consumers as well as governments. There are three promising technical paths that may markedly reduce vehicle energy consumption.

The first involves the application of aerodynamic knowledge to auto bodies. The benefits for fuel consumption, especially in highway driving, are great and can often be achieved at low incremental cost to the manufacturer simply by reshaping a fender or smoothing the contour of a rear-view mirror. However, aerodynamics is currently as much an art as a science, requiring lengthy experimentation with mockup vehicles in wind tunnels. Thus, the technologist's task in the short run is to perfect specialized automotive wind tunnels able to model subtle vehicle ground effects and then to minimize drag in existing designs. The longer-run challenge is to develop computer-aided design packages able to calculate aerodynamic drag accurately without the need for expensive wind tunnel testing and then to explore the potential for drag reduction in radically different auto designs.

The distance that can be traveled in this direction is easy to see. The drag coefficient (C_d) of the average vehicle on the road today is around 0.5. The average C_d of new vehicles in dealers' showrooms is about 0.4. The current state of the art in production vehicles, represented by the Audi 100, is 0.3. Ford Motor Company's Probe IV prototype has a C_d of 0.15, and Ford and a number of other designers are working on even more advanced prototypes with C_d values below 0.1.

Some of these prototypes depart too far from current notions of what an automobile ought to look like to find immediate acceptance. There are also practical problems with highly aerodynamic designs. For example, the simple task of getting cooling air into the engine and passenger compartments can greatly increase turbulence and drag. To reach a C_d of 0.15, Probe IV's designers found it necessary to move the radiator to the rear of the car. In aerodynamic terms, this is reflected in the cross-sectional frontal area, which is multiplied by the C_d, the density of the air, and the square of the vehicle's velocity to yield the total drag. Clearly, only the C_d element of the equation is a candidate for major improvement. Nevertheless, it seems possible that within 20 years the average new car could have a C_d of 0.2 or less. Compared with today's average new auto of the same cross-sectional area with its 0.4 C_d, this vehicle would have up to 25 percent better fuel economy at a highway cruising speed of 120 kilometers per hour simply because of its more aerodynamic shape.

A second technical path to improved fuel economy in a vehicle of given carrying capacity is thorough substitution of materials. Already auto designers have incorporated high-strength steels in key body stampings, substituted aluminum and plastic for steel in exterior body panels and bumpers, reduced the thickness of glass, and reduced rolling resistance by switching to radial tires. However, the potential is much greater. The keys to broad use of nonferrous metals, plastics, and fiber composites in most of the vehicle structure are increased knowledge of durability and increased ability to design and fabricate these materials at low cost. As noted earlier, the process-machinery industry is hard at work on low-cost means of producing plastic panels, and the expansion of computer aided design to composites is being pioneered in aircraft (such as the Lear Fan 2100, the British Aerospace/McDonnell-Douglas Harrier AV-8B, and the Beechcraft Starship).

In the mid 1970s, when Ford built a prototype (based on an existing vehicle design) largely out of composites, the company estimated that scale production with that degree of composite use would have tripled the cost of the car—an increase not nearly offset at that time by the fuel savings resulting from a 25 percent reduction in vehicle weight. At some point in the next 20 years, however, as the cost of fuel increases and the cost of body construction in composites decreases, widespread substitution of materials may well occur.

Body materials account for only about half a car's weight. Material substitution is probable in other areas as well. Composite springs are used in the Chevrolet Corvette to obtain a performance advantage by reducing unsprung weight. The new Volkswagen Golf uses a plastic gas tank, which not only weighs less but can be formed in any shape needed to fit compactly into a vehicle. Many suppliers are experimenting with plastic wheels, and tiremakers are well into the testing of all-plastic tires. In addition, technologists are looking hard at material substitutions in the power train, including the use of plastic and magnesium intake manifolds and carburetor bodies. Some materials that save weight, such as ceramics, are doubly attractive because they also increase operating efficiency in such applications as pistons and turbocharger rotors.

The third technical path to fuel efficiency is to improve the power train. Its two main subpaths are material substitution and electronic power train management. Material substitution can play a dual role here by reducing weight while increasing efficiency. At the extreme, extensive substitution of ceramics for metals might permit the introduction of adiabatic engine designs that trap heat within the engine. This would convert a greater proportion of the heat into useful energy, which would in turn increase fuel efficiency. It might also eliminate the weight and complexity of a cooling system.

Similar advances are possible with further refinement of electronic engine controls to gain the greatest benefit from continuously variable transmissions. A bonus is the ability to run many systems off the same microprocessor at little additional manufacturing cost. Other electronic refinements might include the replacement of hydraulic and mechanical devices with electric motors precisely controlled by the microprocessor to supply only as much effort as is needed. Examples include electric water and oil pumps, air-conditioner compressors, and power steering and braking systems. These would accompany and complement the recent and nearly universal transition to electric radiator fans. Each system could be directed by the central processor, which would reduce parasitic losses in power train efficiency as well as demands on the engine during acceleration.

The reader may be struck by the conservatism of these paths to improved fuel efficiency, which seem to assume the continued viability of the internal-combustion engine and of passenger cars with roughly today's carrying capacity. This impression is correct. It reflects the extraordinary potential for wringing fuel efficiency out of relatively "conventional" automobiles.

For example, if a turbocharged, direct-injection diesel engine using some ceramic components in "hot areas" is coupled with a continuously variable transmission and placed in a small passenger car body the size of the Volkswagen Golf/Rabbit, the Ford Escort, or the Toyota Corolla, with a C_d of 0.25 constructed with plastic exterior body panels and a high-strength steel frame, 75 miles per gallon (or about 3 liters per 100 kilometers) on the U.S. EPA city-cycle test is possible with a level of performance about equal to those of today's small diesel passenger cars. The diesel-powered VW Golf I weighs 400 pounds more, has a $C_d \equiv$ of 0.42, and uses a less efficient manual transmission coupled to an indirectly injected, naturally aspirated diesel. It gets 47 mpg on the EPA city cycle.

With the current average fuel consumption of about 25 mpg in the fleet of vehicles in use in the developed countries, it is apparent that a very large increase in fuel prices and a very large cut in petroleum use can be accommodated (over a period of years, of course) by the use of technical innovations already on the shelf in vehicles that the user would consider very similar to those of today. Technical advances beyond the current state of the art, including fiber-composite bodies, fiber-composite/ceramic or ceramic/adiabatic internal-combustion engines, and highly aerodynamic exterior shapes, are also feasible. These could produce important further reductions in fuel consumption. Thus, the "conventional" internal-combustion-powered four-to-five-passenger vehicle will not be threatened in the next 20 years by energy crises or by such alternative power train technologies as turbines or electrics.

How soon will the "conventional" vehicle incorporate the advances described? This is a function of how rapidly energy prices increase, how quickly suppliers of process technology can reduce production costs for the new components, how ardently final assemblers seek competitive advantage by means of superior product technology, how much capital they can raise for the necessary investments in R&D and tools, and how speedily exogenous technology advances. In the last case, the extensive use of composites is just commencing in the civilian aircraft industry. This may speed the introduction of these materials in automobiles, because automakers will face very heavy R&D costs and many technical unknowns if they must introduce composites without being able to draw on substantial experience elsewhere in industry.

On balance, the probable moderate pace of fuel-price increases and the long development time needed to perfect and introduce technologies beyond the present state of the art mean that only a few of the more advanced concepts will find their way into production cars during the next 20 years. However, the potential for rapid introduction is there if conditions demand crash adaptation.

Fuel economy is, of course, only one element of the total purchase and operating cost that consumers keep in mind when shopping for a car. Among the additional paths to lower operating costs are reduced maintenance costs (including crash repair), increased vehicle life, and reduced purchase costs. New technology has a role to play in each of these areas.

Maintenance costs can be reduced by cutting the time needed to find faults and repair them (through self-diagnosis of faults by microprocessors and sensors), by reducing accident-repair costs (through the use of plastic "snap-on" body panels, which reduce body-shop labor), and by increasing service intervals (with electronic engine controls, which do not need tuning, and longer-lived lubricants). Vehicle life can also be extended by the development of better lubricants and corrosion-resistant body materials and coatings. Purchase costs are the most visible costs to the consumer, but they are also the most complex to reduce because far-reaching changes in manufacturing and design technology are needed.

Innovation in Automobile Design

This chapter cannot go deeply into the technology of auto manufacture, nor can it provide a detailed explanation of "how to design a car." However, a brief description of the design and manufacturing process is essential to an understanding of the technological opportunities for cost reduction in the years ahead.

The auto designer's mental conception of a new vehicle must be translated into prototypes for testing, and then into highly detailed instructions that can be passed along to the designers of individual components, to the manufacturers of the necessary process machinery, and to those on the shop floor. Historically, this has required an enormous number of engineering drawings, both to build the prototypes and to guide the manufacture of production vehicles. The process has been very costly, employing literally thousands of junior engineers, model builders, and draftsmen. It has also been time-consuming, responsible in fact for a major portion of the four-year gestation period for a new model.

Technical help now on the way will completely alter the design process during the next twenty years. Computer software specially designed for engineering, design, and drafting tasks will be combined with micro and mini computers in the engineering office and microprocessors on the shop floor to eliminate much of the routine labor in this process, in addition to permitting a reduction in model building and prototyping.

An example was given earlier of the potential time and cost savings of computer-simulated wind tunnel testing. Similar advances will be derived from computer-aided engineering, which assists the engineer in calculating structural loads and choosing appropriate materials, from computer-aided design, which rapidly generates detailed "electronic drawings" of the vehicle and its components, from computer-aided manufacturing, which transfers the design engineer's work directly to the microprocessor-controlled flexible process machinery, and which may eliminate the need for any paper drawings at all.

Advances in Manufacturing Methods

Cost-cutting technological advances are in prospect in auto manufacturing also. In making components for vehicle systems, a large number of pieces (many of them tiny) are fabricated and then assembled into power-steering pumps or alternators or air-conditioning compressors. Microprocessor-controlled flexible machining centers able to perform the first part of this task automatically are now being introduced. These can machine a number of different sizes and types of parts, feed themselves from materials stocks, and change tools as needed for new jobs, all automatically and without operator assistance. (Indeed, in a few demonstration plants the "night shift" is now conducted with no production workers present.) These parts must then be assembled into the completed component. To do this, robotic devices need "sight", "discrimination", and "touch" so they can pick out and properly arrange the dozens or hundreds of pieces in a typical component. Machines with these capabilities are now entering the prototype stage. For many complex components it is possible to imagine, perhaps within 5 years, an unbroken electronic chain between the designer's CRT screen and the finished component—a chain that will eliminate most human mediation and will drastically slash costs.

After the dozens of mechanical components and component systems have been manufactured, the vehicle is ready to be built up by the final assembler from stampings and major mechanicals produced in house. The manufacture of the latter items is also a candidate for new production technology. In the stamping shop, where approximately 300 steel stampings are produced for each model of car, the automated loading equipment and transfer presses already used in the most modern plants will be joined by automated inspection and material-handling equipment. Or the whole operation may be replaced at some point during the next 20 years by automated plastic-molding or composite-fabrication machinery.

Steel stampings are now welded together in the body shop by robots, which are increasingly assisted by automated material handlers. If the change to plastics occurs on a wide scale, the robots may put down their welding guns and pick up adhesive applicators—a relatively simple progression from the current use of robots in some assembly plants to apply sealing compound. Once joined, the parts will generally need protective coatings and final painting. This is the function of the paint shop, which is already fully automated with spraying robots in a number of assembly plants around the world.

Meanwhile, in the engine and transmission plants similar changes will be taking place, particularly in material handling. This will leave only the final assembly of transmissions, of engines, and then of the complete car as processes in need of automation. Final assembly is perhaps the element of auto manufacture most resistant to automation, because of the need to insert and attach components in confined spaces.

One solution could be "design for manufacture," involving the rethinking of the whole vehicle concept. For example, attaching the seats and dashboard to a floor pan that could then be inserted from underneath the vehicle, much as drive trains are now installed, would solve the problem of robot access to final assembly. However, it would also call for a whole new way of thinking about auto bodies, particularly if weight penalties and sealing problems were to be avoided. Design for manufacture is receiving close attention from all car producers and could begin to transform automaking in the 1990s.

Finally, there is the potential for automating quality inspection. Impressive progress has already been made in this area. One example is fully automated engine testing, in which engines are automatically escorted into a dynamometer room, tested through a wide range of operating conditions, and then dispatched to the final assembly building or rerouted for repair in the engine plant. However, the future of quality testing will probably take a different path. If the largely automated part-fabrication and assembly operations incorporate independent-quality checking equipment at every step, also fully automated, the current testing of finished units in the engine and assembly plant, which entails expensive rework beyond the assembly line if problems are found, can be eliminated altogether.

Product quality is, of course, a key competitive factor. Strenuous efforts will be made toward automated quality control, even in the absence of rapid introduction of all the design and manufacturing automation methods that are technically feasible. Other dimensions of competition in products, as suggested earlier, lie in the areas of enhanced utility, performance, and luxury. In each case the pressure of competition is likely to lead to dramatic advances in the years immediately ahead.

Enhanced Vehicle Capabilities

The utility of vehicles can be increased by widening the range of weather and terrain conditions in which they can be operated, expanding the range of loads they can carry, and increasing the ease of use. Four-wheel drive, coupled with electronic traction and skid control, will permit vehicles to operate nearly normally in almost any weather or road condition. The current trend indicates that these options will be offered on a wide range of models within a few years.

It is also apparent that the range of vehicle packages offered to the consumer will expand. This will be encouraged by flexible design and production systems, which will reduce the cost of variants of basic models. For example, manufacturers are now introducing car/vans such as the Honda Civic Wagon and the Nissan Prairie that combine the comfort of passenger cars with the utility of small trucks and can carry 4–8 passengers. Their product technology is conventional (except for the use of reinforcing to maintain the rigidity of the body while installing larger and larger doors) but they would not be producible in such a wide range of sizes tailored to specific user needs without advances in the flexibility of the factory.

Particularly interesting areas in which utility may be enhanced are navigation, trip scheduling, communication, and vehicle control. Interesting experiments have already been carried out in Germany and Japan with route-guidance systems in which the driver specifies a destination. The vehicle's computer, with assistance from a network of traffic sensors and radio transmitters, advises the driver on the best route by indicating where to turn. When this guidance is combined with trip-scheduling computers and cellular telephone contact with clients and headquarters, the efficiency of commercial vehicles may be greatly increased. Similarly, vehicles with "talking" or other types of alternative controls may eventually make it possible for persons with severe physical handicaps to drive motor vehicles.

Far out in this direction lies the self-driving car, the true "auto"-mobile. This idea has been discussed within the industry since the beginning of the computer age. Automated guideway systems under the control of mainframe computers were examined by auto-industry technologists and government transportation planners in the 1950s and the 1960s. Their chief discovery, however, was that such systems would be extraordinarily difficult to operate safely and reliably under centralized guidance.

Rapid and continuing increases in the capabilities of the in-vehicle microcomputer are now making the more advanced idea of a truly self-driving car at least thinkable. However, the technological challenge of a truly autonomous auto—able to start, stop, avoid obstacles and find its destination every time without mishap and without human aid—is truly daunting. In the view of the automotive experts consulted as part of the Auto Program's technology-assessment activities, such automobiles will be feasible only far beyond the time frame of this study.

Nevertheless, the concept remains very much alive as an ultimate step in the long process of automotive development.

Improvements in performance hardly need mentioning. The popular automotive press is filled with concepts for making practically any car more sporty by the use of tuneable suspensions and horsepower boosters such as multiple valves and turbochargers. The challenge here is much less a technological one of perfecting new techniques to enhance performance than a social one of finding the proper balance between individual enjoyment and community safety.

Enhanced luxury is clearly possible in every area from climate control to audio and video entertainment. From the auto producer's perspective, the capacity to think of new and appealing ideas in this area is particularly important. Product planners already note that nearly half of the value added to automobiles is for items not directly connected with getting from point A to point B. They derive this conclusion from the simple observation that the average new car's selling price in the developed countries markets is nearly twice the price of the smallest and most basic automobile available in those markets. Their fear for the future is that the consumer who has a fixed number of dollars to spend will choose to spend less on his automobile and more on items available in other areas, such as home entertainment systems or computers. Thus, the competitive imperative to innovate extends far beyond the contest with other automakers, and in fact across the whole consumer economy.

These, then, are the probable areas of future innovation in the auto industry. Individually, they do not have the spectacular quality often associated in popular discussion with innovation and "high technology." The next 20 years, it should be clear, will not be filled with electric or hydrogen-fueled or self-driving autos, nor will cars pour forth from fully automated factories. Moreover, the primary pattern of innovation will continue to be the incremental one-system-at-a-time, one-market-segment-at-a-time approach described at the beginning of this chapter.

Nevertheless, the effects of a host of incremental innovations are cumulative. Their impact over the next 20 years on the automobile and its use is likely to be very large, particularly in terms of the competitive balance within the world auto industry. One may well ask which producers and which countries are likely to lead in innovation, since this may prove decisive to the future shape of the industry.

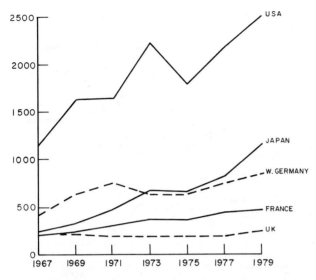

Figure 4.1
Research and development expenditures on motor vehicles (millions of constant dollars, 1975 prices and exchange rates). Expenditures include spending on R&D of new technologies and generic prototypes but not spending on design and tooling for new models. U.S. data are by product rather than by industry; U.K. data are adjusted for comparable years. Source: Estimated by Science Policy Research Unit, University of Sussex, from *Surveys of Resources devoted to R&D by OECD member countries*, Paris: OECD, various years.

Future Leaders in Innovation

The first point to note, and one that is consistent with earlier observations about an upturn in innovative activity during the 1970s, is that everyone is trying to develop new technologies. Spending on research and development is up sharply across the world industry (figure 4.1) and so is patenting activity (figure 4.2).

With regard to the trend in innovation by national industry, it is clear that the Japanese producers have dramatically increased their research activities as manifested in R&D spending and in patenting (figures 4.1, 4.2, and 4.3). This is made even clearer by data on percentage shares of patenting activity by national industry (table 4.1). These data, showing the number of ideas being placed under proprietary control by national industries, do not translate directly into innovations reaching the marketplace.[4] However, they are broadly consistent with the widespread observation within the industry that the Japanese auto-

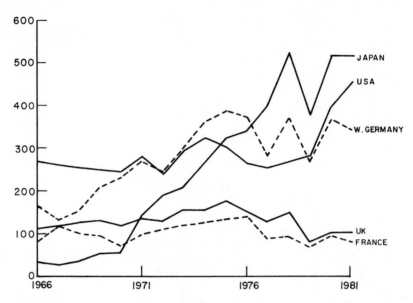

Figure 4.2
The pattern of motor vehicle patenting in the United States [number of patents granted in U.S. under Standard Industrial Classification 371 (motor vehicles)]. For comparability with foreign firms taking out patents in the United States, we have included only those patents taken out by U.S. firms in the United States that are also registered abroad. These patents may be presumed to be those with serious commerical applications and seem to be the relevant measure with which to compare U.S. and foreign patenting. A better measure might be to compare total automotive patenting in all of the auto-producing countries but data for such a comparison are not available. See D. T. Jones, "Technology and Competitiveness in the Automobile Industry," 1982. The granting of patents in 1979 was disrupted by temporary administrative difficulties in the U.S. Patent Office. Source: Estimated by the Science Policy Research Unit, University of Sussex from data supplied by the U.S. Office of Technology Assessment, Washington, D.C.

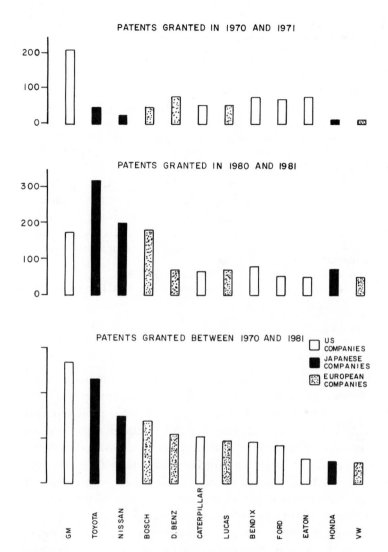

Figure 4.3
Motor-vehicle-related patenting by major firms in the United States [number of patents granted in U.S. under SIC 371 (motor vehicles)]. Toyota includes affiliated companies such as Aishin Seiki and Nippondenso. Source: See figure 4.2

Table 4.1
Percentage shares of patenting activity by auto-producing regions

	1965–66	1970–71	1975–76	1980–81
Total Automotive Patenting[a]				
U.S.	38.5	31.8	22.7	28.7
Japan	4.0	11.9	25.0	34.5
Europe[c]	57.5	56.3	52.3	36.8
Total Patenting by Final Assemblers[b]				
U.S.	n.d.	53.9	34.3	23.9
Japan	n.d.	15.5	35.8	56.4
Europe[c]	n.d.	30.6	29.9	19.7

a. Patents classified under SIC 371 granted to all companies and individuals, some of whom are not formally in the "auto industry."
b. All patents, however classified, granted to final assembler firms.
c. "Europe" in this case includes only Germany, France, and the U.K. because of data limitations.
n.d. = no relevant data available
Source: See figure 4.2.

makers are using the profits they have derived from exports in recent years to establish an independent technological base. This general view is reinforced by the number of new features—such as multivalve engines, electronically tuned suspensions, and electronically controlled automatic transmissions (offering economy and performance modes)—which are appearing on Japanese vehicles. While these are hardly epochal innovations, they are being heavily advertised in an apparent attempt to give the Japanese producers a new image in the marketplace, and this indicates a growing technological orientation.

The European and American producers are by no means dropping out of the race. A strong portfolio of technological know-how has been built up over many years and, in Europe, there is a very strong technological orientation among the suppliers of systems. The Japanese technological challenge will doubtless generate a response, particularly now that North American producers are once more profitable. It is likely that many participants in the world auto industry will strive for technological leadership in the future—both those who now consider themselves leaders and those who wish to join and then lead the pack.

Competition as the Key to Future Technological Advances

This exploration of the nature and future of automotive technology indicates that a major environmental stimulus to innovation, represented by the air-quality and energy crises of the 1970s, received an active response from auto-industry technologists. Indeed, their success in adapting automotive designs to new conditions has been such that the strongest impetuses to innovation in the next 20 years may be the continuing process of invention in areas of science and technology quite outside the automotive world and the need to innovate to be competitive.

Whatever the source of new ideas, it seems clear that the most important determinant of the rate of innovation actually reaching the users in the next 20 years will be the type and intensity of competition in the world auto industry. If competition is very sharp, and if the leading firms adopt a strong technical orientation in choosing the areas in which to compete, the rate of technological advance promises to be very rapid indeed, particularly in comparison with most of the postwar era.

Primitive UFOs

nation will enable women to make a "more informed decision" regarding reproduction, the committee said.

"Ultimately, the woman must decide whether to continue or terminate an existing pregnancy in the face of HIV infection," the panel said.

Of the 154,791 AIDS cases reported in the United States as of the end of November, 15,133 have occurred among women and 2,734 among children, according to the national Centers for Disease Control.

Dangerous Trend

More than 80 percent of the children with AIDS acquired the infection during gestation or at the time of delivery, the panel said. AIDS will become one of the five leading causes of death among

ed," said Dr. Marie C. McCormi committee chair and associate p fessor of pediatrics at the Harva Medical School. "There are gr

EPA Report or

Associated Press

Washington

A scientific advisory bo heard testimony yesterday t challenged research suggestin link between electric power li and cancer.

The draft report on the search by the Environmental I tection Agency has come un fire from the utilities indus which arranged for many of witnesses who appeared bef the EPA panel reviewing the do ment.

TIAA-CR

How Many Cars?

The key finding of chapters 3 and 4 is that automobility will not be significantly constrained over the next 20 or so years by natural-resource shortages, exorbitant energy prices, environmental crises, or stepped-up efforts to deal with the side effects of mass motorization. Higher energy costs and public demands for cleaner air and improved auto safety are indeed likely, along with determined efforts to control motor vehicle use in the most crowded parts of city centers. But the capacity of the world's automakers to deal creatively with the most pressing energy, air-quality, and safety challenges is great, and urban traffic restrictions will not discernibly affect aggregate motor vehicle sales or volumes of travel.

What, then, will determine the level of auto ownership and new-vehicle sales in the years to come? The primary determinants appear to be world economic conditions and population growth. The former are highly uncertain, but we have used the best long-term forecasts available (those by the World Bank); the latter can be estimated with some precision because the driving-age population of the year 2000 has already been born.

Key Considerations

Except in the planned (communist) economies, where governments usually have suppressed automotive demand, national rates of auto ownership around the world correspond very closely to levels of income (table 5.1). There are, of course, threshold effects and differences in the responsiveness of demand to income changes along the income spectrum. Citizens of the very poorest countries cannot support significant automotive markets even if they do achieve some income growth from year to year. Among those countries that are effectively part of

Table 5.1
Selected nations: affluence and motorization 1980

	GDP per capita (dollars)	Automobiles per 1,000 persons
Auto Program countries		
West Germany	13,590	377
Sweden	13,520	347
France	11,730	357
United States	11,360	537
Japan	9,890	203
United Kingdom	7,920	276
Italy	6,480	310
Other OECD countries[a]		
Switzerland	16,440	354
Denmark	12,950	271
Norway	12,650	302
Belgium	12,180	318
Netherlands	11,470	304
Austria	10,230	299
Canada	10,130	428
Australia	9,820	407
Finland	9,720	256
New Zealand	7,090	406
Spain	5,400	202
Ireland	4,880	219
Greece	4,380	93
Yugoslavia	2,620	108
Portugal	2,370	95
Turkey	1,470	16
Centrally Planned Economies		
East Germany	7,180	151
Czechoslovakia	5,820	148
U.S.S.R.	4,550	31
Hungary	4,180	85
Bulgaria	4,150	56
Poland	3,900	67
Rumania	2,340	11
China	290	0.05

Table 5.1 (continued)

	GDP per capita (dollars)	Automobiles per 1,000 persons
Less Developed Countries		
Venezuela	3,630	95
Argentina	2,390	119
South Africa	2,300	84
Mexico	2,090	47
Brazil	2,050	67
South Korea	1,520	6
India	240	1

a. Except Iceland.
The country groupings used in this chapter and in the rest of the volume are the following. Auto Program countries: France, Italy, Japan, Sweden, U.K., U.S., West Germany. Other OECD countries: Australia, Austria, Belgium, Canada, Denmark, Finland, Greece, Iceland, Ireland, Luxembourg, Netherlands, New Zealand, Norway, Portugal, Spain, Switzerland, Turkey. Centrally planned economies: U.S.S.R., Eastern Europe, People's Republic of China. Less developed countries: all countries not in preceding groups.
Sources: GDP per capita from World Bank, *World Development Report 1982*, New York: Oxford University Press, 1982, table 1. Autos per 1,000 population from MVMA, *World Motor Vehicle Data 1982*.

the world auto market, demand tends to be most responsive to income growth in the least affluent. The reason is simply that as countries become more affluent they also approach the stage at which every resident of driving age will already have a car.

In one of the best recent studies, J. C. Tanner of the British Transport and Road Research Laboratory has carefully analyzed all the leading hypotheses about the causes of automotive demand, examining 21 countries for which data were available.[1] Tanner found, surprisingly, that urbanization, population density, and gasoline prices had no apparent impact on the size of national automobile fleets. Gasoline prices did have a dramatic effect on fuel use, but that is another matter. Citizens can save fuel by purchasing smaller, perhaps cheaper cars as fuel prices rise, and they do. Energy shocks, moreover, may cause economic recessions and short-term shifts in consumer spending patterns away from new-car purchases. Over the long run, however, consumers in all developed and newly industrializing countries seem to achieve levels of auto ownership commensurate with their incomes.

The long-run perspective is particularly important, because nations have to adapt their physical infrastructures and even their social attitudes as they adopt the automobile. Tanner noticed in the course of his study that the nations whose levels of auto ownership were lower than one might have expected on the basis of their incomes were those with rapid economic growth. Pursuing this matter, he found that the best predictor of current auto ownership rates was gross domestic product per capita 20 years earlier. In short, countries (such as the United Kindgom) that were already affluent 20 years ago but have had slow growth in the interim have somewhat higher rates of auto ownership today than their current incomes would lead one to expect. Japan's experience is the precise reverse. For countries that have experienced near-average growth in the meantime, of course, this time-lag consideration is irrelevant.

Tanner also sought to estimate for various income levels the degree to which car ownership would rise if income rose by 1 percent. He found that the range was wide and that it varied primarily as a function of existing auto ownership (which in turn varied most closely with income 20 years earlier). In Italy, Spain, and the Netherlands (from 1958–1960 to 1978–1980), the elasticities exceeded 3.0, meaning that a 1 percent growth in income led to a 3 percent increase in ownership. At the other extreme, in the United States and Canada the elasticities were just about 1.0.[2]

Both Tanner and the OECD[3] have recently sought to estimate the levels at which various nations will reach "saturation"—that is, the level of car ownership at which all new-vehicle demand will be for replacement purposes. (These analyses did not consider commercial vehicles.) The OECD staff notes that in most countries 60–63 percent of the population is of age and physically fit to drive a car. Thus, if every individual theoretically eligible to drive had his own car the fleet size would be 600–630 cars per thousand population. At high levels of affluence, however, some individuals choose to have two or more cars for their own exclusive use. Bearing this in mind, the OECD staff estimates that no country should ever have reason to accumulate more than 700 automobiles per thousand population. In actuality, the highest level in the world as of 1980 was 537 in the United States. The OECD staff judges that population densities ultimately will matter, and thus projects that saturation will be reached at different auto densities in different societies. In the Auto Program nations it estimates that saturation will occur at 700 cars per thousand population in the United States, at 600 per thousand in France and Germany, and at 450–500 per thousand in Italy, Japan, Sweden, and the United Kingdom.

Tanner, on the other hand, finds no basis for predicting ultimate saturation levels, given that through 1980 per-capita car ownership in every nation was still rising 1 percent or more for every 1 percent growth of income.[4] This is quite extraordinary, since at saturation ownership growth would be zero no matter how great the rate of income growth. Tanner does not doubt that saturation will occur, of course. He simply cautions that there is no solid basis for predicting when.

It is important to distinguish between levels of auto ownership and levels of new-car sales. The former is a highly stable figure, whereas the latter tends to be quite volatile in response to such phenomena as the business cycle, energy prices, and trends in automotive prices relative to the general rate of inflation. Automobiles are durable consumer goods, and in most of the advanced market economies the typical car is sold three or four times during its life. The purchasers of new cars commonly dispose of them for reasons that have much more to do with fashion and convenience than necessity, and they can easily defer replacement when they feel financially pressed.

During the 1950s and the 1960s, all elements combined in the advanced countries to fuel rapid expansion of the new-car market. Real incomes rose at historically unprecedented rates, fuel costs trended downward, and interest rates were low and stable. The population of automobiles in service soared from 35 million in 1946 to 320 million in 1980. Twice since 1973, however, market variables have simultaneously turned negative in most countries. Moreover, the leading forecasts of economic growth through the remainder of the century suggest that it will be much slower than over the period 1945–1973.

When real income ceases to grow or falls, however, consumers can adjust by holding onto their cars longer. Thus, examining year-to-year changes in auto registrations from 1970 to 1980 in the seven Auto Program countries, one finds 66 "nation-years" of increase, 3 of decrease, and one for which data are unavailable.[5] Even in the United States, where new-car sales have been most volatile, total registrations increased at least 2 percent every year. Moreover, the rate was fairly steady. Against an average 3.7 percent annual rate of increase for the decade, that for the three years of severely depressed new-car sales (1974, 1975, and 1980) was 2.7 percent.

In practice, the average age of passenger cars has recently been increasing after a long period of decline. In the United States, the average age of in-use passenger cars declined from 9 years in 1946 to 5.5 years in 1957, a level around which it hovered through 1973 (when it was 5.7). Since then, however, it climbed steadily back up to 7.2 years (as of 1982). Similarly, a recent study indicates that the median age at which passenger cars are scrapped in Sweden has risen from 9.4 in 1965 to 16.2 years in 1982.[6] These increases have been due partly to technical improvements in car durability, but to a significant degree they have been responses to the slowdown in economic growth.

If these trends were to be extrapolated, one could imagine auto fleets with average ages in excess of 10 years by the year 2000. There is a broad consensus among automotive analysts, however, that the trend will not continue so far. First and mainly, the most significant measures for extending body durability economically seem already to have been exploited. Second, the pace of technical improvement in such areas as engine and transmission efficiency, and in electronics more generally, seem likely to make 10–15-year-old cars seems considerably more obsolete to consumers of the 1990s than cars of similar age seem to consumers today.

Vehicle lifespans will continue to increase in the developed countries, but at a considerably slower rate than during the 1970s. In less developed countries, on the other hand, relatively rapid fleet growth will more than offset the increase in scrappage age of older vehicles, leading to a small decrease in average vehicle age.[7]

Forecasts of Passenger-Car Demand

Our estimates of potential car ownership, based on future population and economic growth, have been derived from a simple model, separately specified for high and low income ranges according to the equation

$$\frac{\log A_n^i}{\log A_b^i} = (x - y\ \log B_b^i)(x - y\ \log B_n^i)^{-1},$$

where A denotes population per car, B denotes GNP per capita, b denotes the base year, n denotes the forecast year, i specifies the nation, and x and y are model parameters. The demographic and economic scenario on which the mid-range estimate is based is described below, along with an indication for each element of the authors' upper- and lower-bound estimates.

Utilizing United Nations forecasts, we have estimated that the world's population will grow 1.7 percent a year, from 4.47 billion in 1983 to 6.10 billion in 2000. Because most of the world's turn-of-the-century population has already been born, the range of potential variation

Table 5.2
Passenger-car ownership (millions), actual and forecast

	1979	1990	2000
Seven Auto Program nations	219.00	255.30	295.30
Other OECD countries	39.90	53.40	67.50
CPEs	15.50	31.40	49.60
LDCs	35.40	66.50	123.60
Total	309.80	406.60	536.00

Sources: MVMA, World Motor Vehicle Data (1979); MIT Auto Program estimates (1990 and 2000).

(barring catastrophe) is quite small, from plus 3 percent to minus 6 percent with respect to the estimated year 2000 total.[8]

Utilizing World Bank forecasts, we estimate that the world's economy will grow by 2.5 percent annually from 1980 through 2000, with regional variations from 1.7 to 3.0 percent.[9] The upper-bound and lower-bound estimates for the world as a whole were 3.0 and 2.0 percent respectively. The global elasticity of demand for auto ownership as a function of income growth has been estimated to be 1.35.

These estimates lead to a mid-range forecast that the world's passenger-car fleet will grow by 2.55 percent annually between 1979 and 1990 and by 2.80 percent annually between 1990 and 2000. In absolute terms, the world's car fleet will grow from its 1979 level of 310 million to 407 million in 1990 and 536 million in 2000. The proportionate growth will vary from 35 percent in the Auto Program nations to 249 percent in the developing countries. Even with such a small proportionate growth rate, however, the Auto Program nations will account for 34 percent of absolute growth and the OECD as a whole for 46 percent (table 5.2).

Aside from the possibility of a major war or economic depression, there are two great uncertainties. The first is whether the communist nations will choose to permit car-ownership levels more closely approximating those prevailing in non-communist countries with similar income levels. Within this category the greatest uncertainty, because of its sheer size, is the People's Republic of China. At present there are fewer passenger cars in China, with its billion people, than in a typical small American city. Should government policy change and permit the car fleet (even if not private ownership, which is today completely prohibited) to rise with personal incomes, the Chinese car fleet could rise to about 10 million by the end of the century. By no means do we expect this to occur, but we estimate that a modest shift toward consumption will occur in the communist world as a whole.

The second great uncertainty is whether the current debt crisis of the developing countries will be resolved in such a way as to permit them to resume rapid growth during the late 1980s and the 1990s. Throughout the 1960s and the 1970s these nations as a group grew considerably more rapidly than the OECD countries, and most forecasts until recently assumed that they would continue to do so. Their growth has been fueled by vast amounts of borrowing, of which roughly $600 billion is currently outstanding. During 1982 and 1983 a series of major repayment crises occurred, with the consequence that the world's financial institutions have become extremely reluctant to lend any more. Unless this crisis is soon resolved in a manner that permits further large-scale economic investment in the Third World, its economic performance and its growth in automotive demand may be far more anemic than today's prevailing forecasts indicate.

Bearing these uncertainties in mind, one can easily imagine the global auto fleet varying in size by 10 percent in either direction from our mid-range forecast. Such variations might have considerably more dramatic effects on the market for new vehicles, moreover. An economic slowdown sufficient to reduce the year-2000 auto fleet by 10 percent would doubtless be associated with intense consumer efforts to stretch out the lives of cars. Thus, it is not implausible that the impact on new-vehicle sales might approach 20 percent. A return to the buoyant economic growth of the 1960s, on the other hand, could conceivably have comparable effects on the up side.

It bears mention that auto-demand analysts focus on two constituent elements of new-vehicle demand: that which simply replaces scrapped vehicles (holding the fleet size constant) and that which entails fleet growth. In nations with relatively mature car populations, replacement demand is dominant. Thus, in the United States the replacement share of the car market has been in the 75–80 percent range for the past two decades. We anticipate that in 1990 and in 2000 the replacement share of global new-car demand will be about 75 percent.

Bearing these caveats in mind, we expect the demand for new passenger cars to be on the order of 37 million units in 1990 and 49 million in the year 2000, in comparison with 30.5 million in 1979 (Table 5.3). These estimates are derived from those reported above on automobile registrations and lifetimes.

Table 5.3
Demand for new passenger cars (millions), actual and forecast

	1979	1990	2000
Seven Auto Program nations	20.50	23.50	26.60
Other OECD countries	4.00	5.50	6.50
CPEs	2.35	2.80	4.20
LDCs	3.65	5.17	11.45
Total	30.50	36.97	48.75

Sources: MVMA (1979); MIT Auto Program estimates (1990 and 2000)

Table 5.4 reports fifteen other forecasts of new-car demand as well as our own. Only two of the others look beyond 1990 (OECD and Arthur D. Little), but all address demand in that year. The Auto Program estimate is at the low end of the range, but it is virtually identical with the two others completed since 1981 (by OECD and General Motors). The main difference between the high and low forecasts lies in their economic-growth estimates; many of the earlier forecasts cited are based on relatively optimistic estimates of world economic growth that were developed in the late 1970s. Additionally, some of the high forecasts neglect to allow for the declining responsiveness of auto demand to income growth at higher levels of affluence.

None of these forecasts is intended to apply to any individual year. Depending on the stage of the business cycle, demand in any particular year may diverge substantially from the long-term trend line. The aim of long-term forecasting, however, is to place the trend line itself accurately.

The short-run sensitivity of new-car demand to economic conditions is a function primarily of two factors. First, sales of durable consumer goods are particularly sensitive to the state of the economy and to the cost and availability of credit. Second, developments like the oil-price increases of the 1970s force consumers to reallocate their household budgets over the short run. (Over the long run, as noted above, they typically find ways to get by with less of the item whose unit cost has risen, for example by purchasing more fuel-efficient cars.) Hence, a decline in the U.S. GNP of less than 3 percent between 1973 and 1975 produced a drop of 24 percent in auto sales, and an economic decline of 1.5 percent from 1978 to the first half of 1980 produced a 19 percent sales decline.[10]

Table 5.4
Comparison of global passenger-car ownership and demand forecasts for 1990 and 2000 (millions)

	1990		2000	
	ownership	demand	ownership	demand
Leach (1975)			524	
Inter Futures (1977)		48.0		
Predicasts (1978)		50.4		
Alfa Romeo (1980)		39.0		
Euro Finance (1980)		43.0		
Industry Projections (1980)		45.4		
Krish Bhaskar (1980)		49.5		
A.D. Little (1980)				47.9
Nomura Research (1980)		43.0		
SMMT (1980)		40.0		
Chase Automotive (1981)		49.1		
Economic Models (1981)		39.5		
J.F. Kain (1981)	414		588	
Gary Shilling (1981)		36.8		
Toyota (1981)		40.6		
General Motors (1982)		37.0		
OECD (1982)	422	38.1	529	46.6
MIT Auto Program	407	37.0	536	48.8

Table 5.5
Commercial-vehicle ownership (millions), actual and forecast

	1979	1990	2000
Seven Auto Program nations	50.0	65.0	75.0
Other OECD countries	13.0	15.0	18.0
CPEs	9.0	13.0	17.5
LDCs	14.4	21.0	32.0
Total	86.4	114.0	142.5

Sources: MVMA (1979); MIT Auto Program estimates (1990 and 2000)

Global demand has historically been much less volatile than U.S. demand. Even so, within the framework of the mid-range scenario, global demand is likely to vary from 5–7 percent above to 5–7 percent below the trend line in any given year (under the assumption that business cycles will be comparable to those experienced between 1973 and 1983).

Forecasts of Commercial-Vehicle Ownership and Demand

Because most of the world's automobile manufacturers also produce trucks and buses, and because these vehicles use the same roadways and draw on the same reservoirs of natural resources for their energy requirements, the Program has also prepared estimates of commercial-vehicle ownership and demand in 1990 and 2000 (tables 5.5 and 5.6).

Generally, the proportion of commercial vehicles is smaller in more compact countries, and with higher levels of passenger-car ownership and well-developed rail systems. Thus, in the Netherlands there are more than 12 passenger cars for every commercial vehicle. In Australia, which is comparably affluent but considerably more auto-reliant, there are 4 passenger cars for every commercial vehicle. At the other extreme, in China, there are 17 commercial vehicles for every passenger car, and in very poor countries generally commercial vehicles tend to out-number passenger cars.

Our forecasting method has been simple: We assume that current relationships of commercial-vehicle demand to passenger-car demand at given national income levels will continue to prevail over the re-maining years of the century, and then we adjust for projected income

Table 5.6
Demand for new commercial vehicles (millions), actual and forecast

	1979	1990	2000
Seven Auto Program nations	5.9	7.5	8.7
Other OECD countries	1.6	1.7	2.1
CPEs	1.6	2.0	2.5
LDCs	1.7	3.0	4.7
Total	10.8	14.2	18.0

Sources: MVMA (1979); MIT Auto Program estimates (1990 and 2000).

growth. The resulting forecast is that the commercial-vehicle fleet as a whole will grow from 86 million in 1979 to 143 million in the year 2000, and that new-vehicle demand will grow from 11 million to 18 million (tables 5.5 and 5.6). These are obviously rough estimates that do not deal with readily apparent changes in the structure of the commercial-vehicle market. For example, in many countries the proportion of very heavy vehicles in the truck fleet has been increasing because of changes in manufacturing and distribution needs and the ability of the vehicle manufacturers to build larger vehicles. At the other end of the spectrum, the boundary between commercial vehicles and passenger cars has become less clear as consumers in the developed countries have used light commercial vehicles for more and more personal travel. In the United States, light trucks and vans are manufactured and sold with performance and comfort standards close to those of passenger cars and have captured a growing share of the combined automobile–light truck market over the past decade.

The Future of Motor-Vehicle Demand: Continuing Moderate Growth

All the credible economic and social scenarios for the world over the next two decades include an expanding role for the automobile in meeting the growing need for transportation. Economic, environmental, and energy factors, as has been shown, will affect the future of the automobile, but none threatens its survival or growth within the next two or three decades.

A composite forecast of automobile demand plus commercial-vehicle demand (table 5.7) indicates a net growth 25.5 million units in total

Table 5.7
Composite vehicle ownership and demand (millions), actual and forecast

	1979		1990		2000	
	ownership	demand	ownership	demand	ownership	demand
Seven Auto Program nations	269.0	26.4	320.3	31.0	370.3	35.3
Other OECD countries	52.9	5.6	68.4	7.2	85.5	8.6
CPEs	24.5	3.95	44.4	4.8	67.1	6.7
LDCs	49.8	5.35	87.5	8.17	155.6	16.15
Total	396.2	41.30	520.6	51.17	678.5	66.75

Sources: tables 5.2, 5.3, 5.5, and 5.6

demand between 1979 and 2000. This 62 percent increase in total output, when translated into broader economic terms, means that the motor-vehicle industry is almost certain to continue as the world's largest manufacturing enterprise. Therefore, the key question about the future of the automobile and its industry (expanded in this reference to include the trucks and buses produced by the same general group of firms) is not whether the future holds security and growth for the industry as a whole but rather which producers at which locations in the world will account for the increases in output. This, in turn, depends on the outcome of the competition between national production systems. The nature of that competition, the long-term competitive trends, and their meaning for the future shape of the world motor vehicle industry are the subject of chapters 6–8.

6   The Nature of Competition

In most countries the buyer of an automobile faces a multitude of choices among body styles, transmissions, upholstery, front or rear drive, number of cylinders, and countless other features over and above the basic questions of the size, the price, and indeed the nationality of the car. There is no better indicator of the intense competition that gives no rest to the world's automakers. They have created the extraordinary diversity of the modern automobile market as a direct result of their relentless search for a competitive advantage. But this visible manifestation of competition in the auto industry tells only part of the story. Competition takes place at many levels among many participants. Before reaching conclusions about the destiny of this industry, we must understand who the competitors are and what they want to achieve.

Actually, the competition is of two kinds. One is intense commercial competition across the world between transnational producers. Although these competitors are only indirectly concerned with where their production takes place, this is the key question for governments involved in the intense political competition to protect or increase national shares of world auto manufacture. It is vital to keep this dual aspect of automotive competition continuously in mind.

Commercial Competition Among Multinational Corporations

Commercial competition in the auto industry is a contest among vast social organizations offering finished automobiles to consumers. Each "producer" is in fact a group of organizations, including a final assembler who organizes the production process, hundreds or thousands of suppliers of components, designs, and production machinery, a distribution network, and a financial network. Even the smallest current production system involves thousands of individuals, and the largest employ more than a million.

A review of the final assemblers with annual volumes of more than 50,000 units (table 6.1) shows that 30 companies account for practically all the world's auto production. The eight largest, all in the non-communist developed countries, account for 72 percent.

A look at the "nationality" of auto production as it is divided among the five main producing blocs shows that the 20 producers headquartered in the seven Auto Program Countries account for more than 92 percent of the world's production. Independent producers in the developing countries (of which there were only two of any size in 1982) and those in the Eastern bloc are scarcely factors in the world industry at present. Therefore, the focus of this review is largely on the 20 multinational producers headquartered in the OECD countries.

This list of 20 producers includes only a fraction of the important players in the world industry, because final assemblers account for less than half the value received by the consumer. The remainder is provided by a vast array of suppliers, distributors, and financing sources. A number of the suppliers, such as Bendix (U.S.), GKN (U.K.), and Nippondenso (Japan), are larger than many of the final assemblers. Similarly, independent technical and design consultants such as Porsche and Ital Design, although tiny alongside the assemblers, play key roles in developing products for the giants. In finance, virtually all the world's largest banks and insurance companies have substantial loans and/or equity positions in final assemblers and suppliers. And in distribution, the number of new-car dealers in the United States, Japan, and Western Europe alone totals more than 50,000.

In addition, for individual product lines there is a growing tendency for final assemblers to purchase major components (including engines and transmissions) from other assemblers and suppliers, and to join other assemblers in co-production ventures. Thus, the "producer" of any given product may be a one-time-only combination of final assembler, designer, suppliers, and distributors. For example, the Ford Sierra to be sold in the United States will be assembled in Germany for Ford by Karmann incorporating a number of modifications to the body design supplied Ital Design of Italy. This combination does not mean that Ford, Karmann, and Ital Design are in the process of merging or even that they will have any commercial relations in the future. Rather, it was a marriage of convenience among an assembler lacking the capacity to take on a special job for the U.S. market, a small specialist assembler for whom the U.S. Sierra is a useful piece of business, and a design house with special know-how in auto-body design and modification.

Another marriage of convenience, this time in the area of distribution, is that of General Motors with Suzuki and Isuzu in Japan to sell certain of their products under General Motors nameplates through GM's worldwide distribution network. Arrangements of this kind promise to become more common in the future.

In listing the larger roster of players it is important not to understate the role of the final assembler at the nerve center of the auto enterprise. The assemblers supply the vital concept, both for individual products and for whole product lines. They then obtain the production financing, coordinate the design and manufacturing process, and integrate the thousands of components needed. Finally, they line up the consumer financing, plan the marketing campaign, and arrange for after-sale service. Thus, it is not by accident that most of the examples of marketing strategies, product innovations, and production-system advances discussed on the following pages focus on the final assembler.

Before we examine the elements of commercial strategy, it is important to remember that businesses fashion their competitive plans to suit a host of constraints imposed by the governments involved in political competition for shares of the world auto industry.

Political Competition among Governments

Two sets of governments make a difference to the future of the world auto industry: those who already have a large auto market with a major domestic industry, and those who have the potential to develop a large auto market during the next 20 years and hope to use this prospect to create a major domestic industry.

The second set includes countries in several subcategories. Mexico and Brazil promise to grow rapidly, bringing automobiles within the reach of millions of citizens. The countries in the Eastern bloc, by contrast, already have high enough per-capita incomes to support a large auto market and might develop one quickly if government policy were to shift in support of this goal. A few countries, including the People's Republic of China, may experience both high growth and a shift in government attitudes toward automobility.

This division of the nations excludes 90 percent of the world's governments from a significant role in the future of the automobile. Cannot a nation desiring an auto industry build one purely on the

Table 6.1
1982 auto production by the 30 largest world producers

	Worldwide automobile production (thousands)	Size or type category	Percent share of 30 producers' auto production	Number of auto product lines	Worldwide commercial-vehicle production (thousands)
Japan					
Toyota	2,386	Full	9.1	12	1,284
Nissan	2,017	Full	7.7	12	941
Honda	860	Medium	3.3	4	160
Toyo Kogyo	824	Medium	3.2	4	286
Mitsubishi	573	Medium	2.2	5	399
Suzuki	114	Small	0.4	1	489
Isuzu	113	Small	0.4	2	292
Subtotal	6,887		26.3	40	3,851
Western Europe					
Renault	1,962	Full	7.5	10	359
Volkswagen	1,828	Full	7.0	7	94
PSA	1,504	Full	5.7	14	182
Fiat	1,468	Full	5.6	8	192
Daimler-Benz	466	Specialist	1.8	2	242
BL	405	Medium	1.5	6	91
BMW	363	Specialist	1.4	3	0
Volvo	302	Specialist	1.2	3	33

Alfa Romeo	189	Specialist	0.7	3	1
Saab	84	Specialist	0.3	2	21
Subtotal	8,571		32.7	58	1,215
United States					
General Motors	4,779	Full	18.3	15	1,107
Ford	2,993	Full	11.4	15	1,146
Chrysler	750	Medium	2.9	3	224
Subtotal	8,522		32.6	33	2,477
Developing Countries					
ZCZ (Zastava) (Yugoslavia)	175	Small	0.7	3	25
Hyundai (Korea)	60	Small	0.2	1	60
Subtotal	235		0.9	4	85
Eastern Bloc					
Vaz (Lada) (U.S.S.R.)	800	Medium	3.1	2	0
FSO (Polski) (Poland)	240	Small	.9	3	0
Azlk (Moskovitch) (U.S.S.R.)	205	Small	.8	1	0
Wartburg/Trabant (E. Germany)	176	Small	.7	2	40
Skoda (Czechoslovakia)	170	Small	.6	1	50
ZAZ (U.S.S.R.)	150	Small	.6	1	0
GAZ (Volga) (U.S.S.R.)	130	Small	.5	1	0
Dacia (Rumania)	91	Small	.3	1	55

Table 6.1 (continued)

Worldwide automobile production (thousands)	Size or type category	Percent share of 30 producers' production	Number of auto product lines	Worldwide commercial-vehicle production (thousands)
Subtotal				
1,962		7.5	12	145
Total for 30 producers				
26,177		100.0	147	7,773

Notes: This table lists automobile and commercial-vehicle production by all of the world's automobile final assemblers who assemble more than 50,000 automobiles annually. Each producer's total includes assemblies by their major foreign subsidiaries with local content above 70 percent (e.g., GM-Opel, GM do Brazil). Thus, the subtotals should not be read as auto production by geographic region but rather as world wide auto production by producers headquartered in a given region. In the table Daihatsu is counted as part of Toyota, American Motors is included with Renault, Fuji Heavy Industries (Subaru) is added in with Nissan, Audi is included with Volkswagen, and Autobianchi, Lancia, and Seat are included with Fiat. In each case the larger firm, as of 1981, either had a controlling equity interest in the smaller firm or supplied all its product designs on license. Because a number of very small producers and some production at low local content are not included, the total production by the 30 largest producers is slightly lower than the world total for 1982 shown in table 2.3. In the case of commercial vehicles the total shown is a considerably smaller portion of world production because this table includes only commercial vehicles produced by firms that are also major auto producers. The term "product line" means a basic body design, commonly called a "platform," including variants such as coupes and station wagons. A number of engine and other mechanical options may be available in the same product line. Only product lines produced in volumes of 20,000 or more units have been counted.

Sources:

Motor Vehicle Manufacturers Association, *World Motor Vehicle Data*; Japan Automobile Manufacturers' Association, *Motor Vehicle Statistics of Japan; L'Argus* (Paris): *Automobile Revue* (Special Annual Issue). Berne, Switzerland (1983); Automobile Club of Italy, *World Cars* 1983, New York: Herald Books, 1983.

basis of exports? Cannot small countries play a key role in the future of the auto industry by exercising controls over access to their markets? Though there may be one or two exceptions, neither development is likely. No nation except Japan has succeeded in the past 40 years in creating an internationally competitive auto industry without the aid of multinational auto producers. Multinational producers, in turn, cannot be enticed into building up a major industry with export potential, except in order to gain access to a major growth market. Thus, those nations with large auto markets, either existing or prospective, are the key players in the game.

If these are the nations participating in the political contest over the future of the industry, what are their aims? In simplest terms, those nations with large, mature auto industries want to increase their share of the world market or at least to protect what they already have. Those nations with little in the way of an industry but with promising market potential would like to use that prospect to create not only a domestic industry but an export earner as well. The latter nations may avail themselves of a number of techniques for promoting their industry. However, the method they most favor is the use of trade policy to control access to their domestic market. Governments use this tool to exert their will on foreign producers and governments and on their domestic industry.

The Strategy of Commercial Competition

How does a producer—by which we mean a group of suppliers, distributors, and financing sources coordinated by a final assembler—go about competing in the world auto industry? Competitive success in this industry, marked by massive investment decisions (billions of dollars) and lengthy gestation periods (5 years before the product reaches the market, 10–15 years before the return on the investment is fully realized), depends on a continuing series of correct actions of three sorts.

First, the producer's products must be competitive in styling, price, image, performance, and reliability. Second, the producer's production system must be competitive in cost, accuracy, and flexibility. This system includes the production hardware, its geographic location, and the social organization of the production process. Together these determine the cost of producing a vehicle of given specification, the accuracy of the production process (e.g., "fits and finishes" and the frequency of defective components), and the speed and flexibility of the system in introducing new products. Third, a producer must be competitive in the range and image of its product line and in the geographic range of markets served, a set of choices collectively termed *market placement*. Included in market placement are decisions on which national markets and which segments within each market should be offered products. The range of models offered is critical to the consumers' image of a producer as well as to its overall production scale. The geographic range of market participation also affects scale, but it often requires, in turn, a willingness to produce locally in many markets. Thus, it is also a measure of the multinationality of a producer.

Because the automobile is probably the most complex consumer good and provides such services for the buyer as status, recreation, entertainment, and comfort in addition to basic transportation, a producer always faces a challenge in successfully combining product designs, production systems, and market placement in a mix that is right for the times. In practice the process is iterative, with producers continually assessing how far they lag or lead the best practice in each area. They strive to close the gap in areas where they trail or to move ahead in areas where they lead. It is important to understand that it is not necessary to be the leader in every area, or even in any area. Rather, it is the combination of products, production systems, and market placement that counts at any point in time, along with not lagging too far behind in any of the three dimensions. Over the long term, success means maintaining a superior combination year after year.

Products

The art of designing automobiles consists of combining technical alternatives with styling elements to yield a distinctive product within a given market class. In addition, careful attention must be paid to the "producibility" of the design: how much labor it requires and how difficult it is to manufacture accurately. The complete design process is a very subtle art in which a producer only gradually accumulates experience and skills.

During much of the postwar period, product designs in national markets were rather stable. In each country producers concentrated on designs and sizes suited to their primary national markets. Very large vehicles with separate-frame construction, such as the Chevrolet Impala, were dominant in the United States and largely unique to that market.

Light and medium-size vehicles such as the Toyota Corolla and the Nissan Bluebird/Maxima accounted for the largest portion of the market in Japan, and a range of dominant national types developed in Europe running from the small Fiat 127 in Italy and Renault 5 in France to the medium-size Ford Cortina in the United Kindgom and the large Mercedes-Benz 200 series in Germany (figure 6.1). Within each national market, a range of product sizes flanked the dominant segment. These tended to vary in a consistent way, with larger models being more luxurious and expensive and smaller models more economical and utilitarian.

As the intra-European and OECD markets were increasingly opened in the 1960s and the early 1970s, "nondominant" types made up the majority of auto exports from Japan and Europe to the United States and most of the auto trade within Europe. This was the situation at the end of a long period of auto-industry growth and energy-price stability in 1973 (figure 6.2). As a marginal phenomenon, these import sales were not directly threatening to the home producers' dominant designs, and they provoked only limited responses in the form of new product initiatives, such as the Chevrolet Corvair and the Ford Falcon (1959) to oppose the Volkswagen Beetle, the Ford Pinto and the Chevrolet Vega (1970) to counter the Toyota Corolla, and the VW Polo and the Ford Fiesta (1974) to compete with French and Italian products in the small-vehicle segment.

After two energy shocks, however, the situation is drastically different (figure 6.3). The American market, which was dominated by "very large" automobiles (all but nonexistent in the rest of the world), has come to resemble more closely the European and Japanese markets.[1] In addition, the Japanese producers' advantage in production systems has increased competition in all market segments. This increases import shares across the board; it also heightens the emphasis on distinctive products, which carmakers in different competitive positions are trying in different ways to create.

Producers with strengths in the production of larger cars are developing a wide range of new product technologies, including diesels, turbocharging, electronic engine controls, and material substitutions in bodies and engines. The objective is to reduce the operating costs of larger cars in order to protect volume in these market segments over the longer term.[2] Producers of small cars have taken note of the fact that market segments are being compressed as large models are "downsized" and have acted accordingly by introducing small "luxury" and

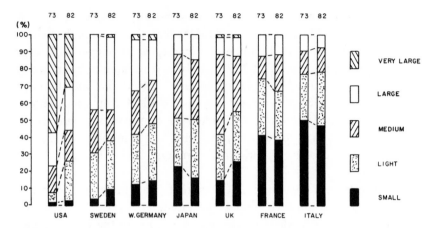

Figure 6.1
Market shares by vehicle size in the Auto Program countries, 1973 and 1982.
The market segments used throughout this volume are based on a combination of the
following:

	Small	Light	Medium	Large	Very Large
Engine size (cc)	up to 1200	1200–1400	1400–1800	1800–2600	2600 & up
Wheelbase (in)	up to 92	92–98	98–102	102–108	108 & up
Weight (lb)	up to 1750	1750–2000	2000–2400	2400–3000	3000 & up

Data on the most popular variants of individual models were gathered and models
were allocated to segments by at least three of four criteria: weight, wheelbase, engine
size, and relative price in the producer's domestic market. For the United States,
engine sizes are one class higher (i.e., a 1500 cc engine would fall in the "light"
rather than the "medium" class) due to emission equipment which reduces power for
a given displacement. Also for the United States, weight classes are 200 lbs. heavier
due to the additional weight of the larger engines, bumpers, etc. compared with the
same models sold in Japan and Europe. In a few cases it was necessary to make
segment judgments on contextual factors. Source: Calculated from Daniel T. Jones,
"SPRU Databank on the Western European Automobile Industry " (1983), *Automotive
News Market Data Book*, Ward's MVMA, *World Motor Data*

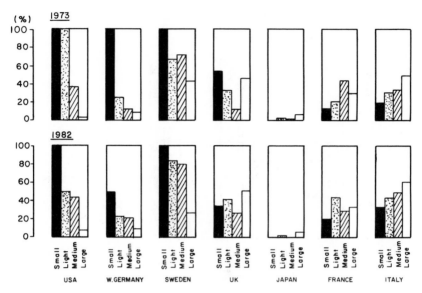

Figure 6.2
Import penetration by market segment in Auto Program countries, 1973 and 1982.
Note: These data represent "apparent" import penetration as perceived by the consumer. Thus, they do not count as imports products built elsewhere by a domesti-
cally-based manufacturer. For example, Granadas and Fiestas built by Ford in
Germany and Spain are not counted in the table as U.K. imports because Ford has a
major manufacturing presence in Britain and Ford products are generally perceived as
"British." The "large" category combines the "large" and "very large" categories used
in figure 6.1. Source: See figure 6.1

"sporty" packages, such as the Honda Accord and CRX, which blur
the traditional relationship between a vehicle's size and its attributes.
The effect is to differentiate the car market not just along the dimension
of size but also along entirely independent dimensions of luxury, utility,
economy, and performance. Producers with a production-cost disadvantage are seeking to move "upmarket" by means of unique designs
and product technologies that can be manufactured at a somewhat
higher cost and sold at a much higher price.

  New approaches are not solely of interest to producers with weaknesses in other areas. All producers have observed the maturity of the
OECD auto market and are showing interest in new product concepts,
including minivans, minipickup trucks, a host of high-performance
versions of their more sedate models in all market segments, and four-
wheel drive applied to all of the above. High-cost producers hope to
create new market segments, or at least find niches, where direct com-

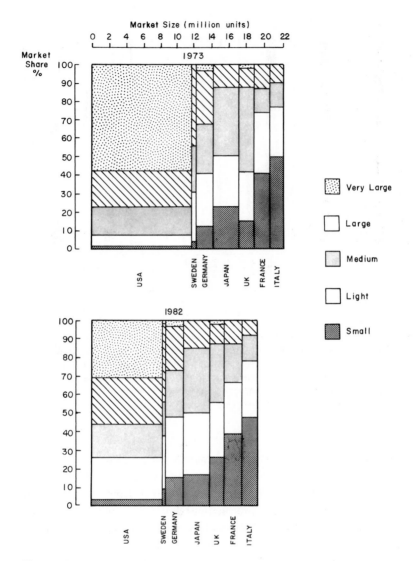

Figure 6.3
Structure of car demand in Auto Program countries, 1973 and 1982. Source: See figure 6.1

petition on the basis of price can be avoided. And producers will try to enlarge the total automotive market by "making markets" with such sharply different vehicles as the Honda City and the Nissan Prairie. Finally, all producers, including those with advantages in production cost and accuracy, are pursuing innovations in product design that facilitate automated manufacturing.

The mere fact that producers are keenly interested in developing new and distinctive products does not mean that this is easy to do. As illustrated in chapter 4, building passenger cars for new market segments with new technologies is not so simple as it appears to outside observers who are deceived by the superficial similarity of vehicles of all sizes and the apparent maturity of the auto industry's technology. Though the individual technologies in today's (and tomorrow's) automobiles are not exotic, and though small cars do have many similarities with big cars, the real challenge lies in putting the whole package together harmoniously. This is particularly so because an automobile is a highly complex set of systems and subsystems whose smooth functioning in combination, rather than virtuosity in any particular function, is the prime concern of the buyer.

Getting a vehicle right therefore requires much experimentation— including feedback from users, which can only be gained over time. Thus, we may speak of generations of product learning in the auto business. This is well illustrated by the experience of the Japanese automakers since the end of World War II and the experience of the American automakers since the beginning of serious import competition (that is to say, the point at which the Japanese learning process began to pay off in export markets).

The Japanese automakers have progressed steadily through stage after stage, with each generation of vehicles an improvement on the last and a step closer to the best practice of the American and European producers. Their initial postwar products were based on outdated European models produced under license.[3] Several generations of improvement followed until the two largest Japanese producers, Toyota and Nissan, believed they were ready to export cars of their own design to the United States (1959–1964). This initiative was a failure, however, because the vehicles were not mechanically suited to the demands of American use, such as prolonged operation at high speeds.[4] The next Japanese generation, exported in the mid to late 1960s, was able to stand up to American conditions but competed in only a small segment of the market as a basic and cheap product. The generation after that, born around 1973, dropped the emphasis on low price and converted production cost advantages plus growing skill in vehicle design and packaging into a quality image. Although still sold as economy cars, the Japanese vehicles gained an image of craftsmanship and even luxury in a small package. The next leap for the Japanese producers is into the "large"-car market segment (as defined in figure 6.1) with successors to the current Nissan Maxima/Bluebird and Toyota Cressida as well as the all-new Project XX car to be built by Honda in cooperation with BL. Although the existing Nissan and Toyota models in this class are creditable efforts, they are essentially the first export generation of large Japanese products. They are rather heavy for their interior space and not up to the level of large European models in handling or performance. However, they provide an experience base and vital consumer feedback that will no doubt make the next iteration more competitive.

The Americans, by contrast, have been working down from the large-car end of the market. After generations of accumulating learning about the very large models known as "standard-sized" cars, the North American industry faced the necessity after 1973 to become competitive in all sizes of products, at least down to the light class. To the outside observer, this did not appear difficult. To the auto producers, however, a rapid shift from large cars to highly competitive small cars was an awesome challenge. General Motor's experience with its X-body cars is illustrative. The 1979 models were GM's first venture into mass-market front-wheel-drive vehicles. Though they were creditable and necessary pioneers, the X-body cars were too complex to manufacture cheaply and reliably and did not achieve the efficient packaging of space for vehicle weight that is possible in state-of-the-art front-wheel-drive designs. The company's J-body models, which followed only 2 years later, achieved a big advance in manufacturability and packaging in a slightly smaller size class. The new A/X-body line GM is preparing for introduction in 1986 will doubtless advance still further.

The lesson is clear: building a first-rate car requires iterative learning for even the most competent company. The marketplace deals harshly with producers who fall behind or who find the market shifting beneath them, demanding that they suddenly offer products in market segments they have not served. The same holds—and even more so—for new entrants, who must generally get the vehicle right the first time or fail. This goes far toward explaining why no successful new entrants to the auto business have appeared in the developing countries, despite lower labor costs, and why no company in the developed countries has made a successful entrance to volume auto production in the past 20 years.

Production Systems

Even the simplest automobile is constructed from thousands of parts and incorporates many technologies.[5] The parts must be manufactured and assembled at a competitive cost and in such a manner as to provide high reliability. Failure to devise a production system suited to the product may cause even a very fine product concept, such as the Jaguar sedan of the mid 1970s, to fail in the marketplace. A deficient production system is even more damaging for a producer concentrating on the economy segments of the market and therefore competing largely on price. The complexity of the automobile requires intricate production systems with thousands of suppliers of components, manufacturing machinery, and technical services. These systems' most critical task is to successfully integrate a broad set of production technologies with a complex social organization.

In the realm of production technology, it is clear that the auto industry has just emerged from the situation described in William Abernathy's *Productivity Dilemma.*[6] The product technology of the automobile was stable for most of the postwar era; in consequence, production systems were able to use higher and higher levels of automation for mechanical components (such as engines and transmissions) that did not change for many years. By contrast, large amounts of semi-skilled labor were used in the body plant and the final assembly line to accommodate the year-to-year changes in the product. Under this system, the heavy capital investment in automation constrained innovation in engines and other mechanical components because the production machinery was quite inflexible. Even a small change in a product could make enormously expensive machines obsolete. It also built considerable scale-economy advantages into high-volume production, because the lowest cost per unit of engine production was achieved at rates of several hundred thousand identical engines annually. In the body plant the producer faced a choice between inflexible automation, with very high production volumes and long unchanged product runs to justify its cost, and flexible manual systems with higher labor content.

The Volkswagen Beetle production system at Wolfsburg was the apotheosis of the former approach. By concentrating on high volume with a single model available in one body style for many years, VW could justify the industry's highest level of dedicated automation in its stamping, body, and paint shops. This meant low labor content, and it was suited to the labor shortage in postwar Germany. The alternative system, as developed by most of the other world producers, involved greater use of semi-skilled labor for practically all operations in the stamping, body, paint, and final assembly operations and was suited to frequent model changes and simultaneous production of many body styles and accessory combinations.

Both these traditional approaches are now obsolete. They have been outpaced by the ability of the microprocessor to make manufacturing equipment much more flexible. For example, the multiwelders introduced in the 1950s automatically joined major subassemblies into a complete body and were a major advance over the hand welding used previously. However, they were enormously expensive and could handle only a single body style. The new robot welding systems, by contrast, can be programmed to weld a wide range of models and body styles as they proceed through the production system in random order.

Volkswagen's new production system for its Golf II model illustrates how different the two production techniques can be, even when installed on the same shop floor. The new VW system has a fully automated and flexible body-welding line, a robotized paint shop, and high levels of automation in material transfer. In addition, it takes the first steps along the path to automated final assembly, with robots installing the engine, brake lines, battery, and wheels. This system is able to produce not only Golfs in several body styles but also Jettas without changing tools or stopping production. In addition, Volkswagen and other producers are experimenting with more flexible tooling and automated material handling in engine and transmission plants to permit, for example, machining of a whole family of engines on the same transfer lines. The result may be the best of both worlds from the manufacturer's standpoint: an increase in flexibility and manufacturing accuracy with a decrease in production labor. The flexibility will permit rapid adjustments in product mix as market demand shifts and will speed up introduction of new models. The reduction in labor will permit cost savings. Simultaneously, however, it will create a need for a more technically skilled work force to work on the assembly machinery instead of performing assembly.

The new technologies are not limited to the shop floor. An even greater change has been making its way through the design and engineering offices of world automakers. Computer-aided design, engineering, and manufacturing make it possible to design, engineer, and tool new models and model variants much more rapidly and with much less engineering manpower.

The rate of this shift in production technology, which is well underway in the assembler plants and beginning in the supplier plants, will depend on the financial situation of the industry, on acceptance by the work force, and on the way in which competition develops. However, it seems clear that the new production technologies will rapidly work their way through the world's production systems even if the auto market is sluggish and current OECD auto competition is dampened.

The social organization of production—the other element in the production equation, and probably the more important—includes the system of human organization within the final assembler and the component companies, and also the relations among the final assembler, the component suppliers, the distributors, and the financing sources. Here, as with production technology, a seemingly mature system, thought to have been perfected in the United States by Henry Ford and Alfred Sloan in the 1920s, is now recognized to be in the process of transformation. Within the plant the Ford principles, worked out in Detroit in the early days of the auto industry, called for assembly workers, machine feeders, and material handlers with very limited skills and little knowledge about the total production operation. A second set of workers maintained the machinery. A third set supervised the line and maintenance workers, checked on product quality, and fed information on shop-floor conditions back to senior management. It was assumed under this system that the assembly workers would not report on problems, would not repair their own machines, and would take no initiative in spotting or correcting faults. It seemed to follow that large inventories would be needed as buffers so that parts of the system could continue to operate while problems in other parts were being diagnosed and repaired. It was also assumed that quality could be maintained only by careful inspection of parts by supervisors, and that improvements in the production process could be devised only by yet another set of specialists, the industrial engineers.

A new approach, pioneered by the Japanese auto producers, has turned all these propositions on their heads. It starts with the fundamental assumption that if production workers are treated as professionals and given the skills and responsibility to diagnose problems, repair equipment, and spot defects, then the ranks of supervisors and machine repairmen can be greatly thinned even as quality is improved.

This approach asserts that large supply buffers hide problems rather than ameliorate them and that elimination of buffers makes it possible to identify and eliminate production bottlenecks in their order of priority.

The new approach also asserts that defect prevention by line workers is far superior to defect detection by inspectors, and holds that ideas for improving the production process can and should come largely from the front-line workers, who know the system best. A further result of this approach is an increase in process yield (i.e., percentage of "up" time for the whole system) and a significant reduction of human effort in a given product compared with an identical item produced under the Fordist system using identical process technology.[7]

Beyond the shop floor, a higher level of production organization is required to coordinate designers, final assembly operations, components suppliers, and financing sources. In the United States this evolved in the 1920s as managers struggled to guide the giant organizations brought into being by the Fordist system of mass production. The American approach achieved a high degree of vertical integration where possible, but otherwise employed "arms-length" relations between the suppliers, the assemblers, and the financing sources. Competitive bidding for orders and dual or triple sourcing of many components were felt to increase incentives for lowering costs and to prevent stoppages if a supplier failed to deliver. Financing was internal when possible or arranged directly between suppliers and bankers when necessary. R&D was largely self-contained within individual assembler or supplier firms, and planning for new products and technologies was conducted in secret.

In recent years alternatives to this system have been created, sometimes with striking results. The Japanese producers have pioneered the concept of operational coordination without financial and legal integration through their industrial and conglomerate groups. Many of the European producers have developed joint ventures to make major mechanical components that could not be produced at sufficient scale by a single manufacturer. These new approaches, in combination, suggest a new definition of integration in the industry. Greater significance is attached to mutual cooperation, information flow, and product cross-flow among the members of a system than to the level of financial and legal integration. A particular advantage of the new arrangements is that competitive checks can be maintained because at each stage of production the cost of the products and services being traded is fully known. Another advantage of cooperative networks seem to be that innovations in technology and management diffuse more quickly through a production chain and across the industry.

Market Placement

Market placement is a matter of choosing which national markets and segments of those markets to serve. The conventional wisdom of segment strategy was that there was no viable position between the full-line producer and the specialist: "Be a GM or a BMW, but nothing in between." Full-line producers were to compete on low prices for standard products and the presence of their badge across the whole auto market. Thus, a company could attract a buyer for life by offering an economy car to the first-time buyer and then "trading him up" from one segment to the next. The great scale of the full-line producer, with cost savings extending to general corporate overheads and the distribution network, would permit low production costs. Specialists, by contrast, were to compete on the basis of unique product attributes, sometimes in niches not fiercely contested, and thus were obliged to worry less about production costs and high volume.

Recently this wisdom has been questioned. The American downsizing and the Japanese and European success in developing smaller luxury cars have blurred size segments. In addition, new four-wheel-drive vehicles of many sizes, personal-use pickups and vans (including mini-pickups and mini-vans), and a proliferation of high-performance versions of otherwise sedate models have made it clear that there is considerable latitude for creating distinctive products for special niches.

Furthermore, a number of new organizational arrangements have been created to permit specialist or narrow-line producers to cooperate to offer a full line at the point of distribution. Saab is selling Lancias under its own nameplate in Scandinavia, protecting the lower end of its range. Volvo is selling small Renaults through its Scandinavian dealer network, and continues to market the product of a Dutch-owned car company as its 300-series autos. Chrysler was able to fill the gap in the bottom of its line with Mitsubishi's Colt and Champ. BL obtained a desperately needed product from Honda, produced under license as the Acclaim, to keep its dealer network alive until BL could develop new models of its own.

At the same time, full-line producers are feeling pressure to develop products for specialized market segments but are discovering how difficult this task can be for a very large, high-volume enterprise. In the

United States, both GM and Ford have worked hard at devising new Cadillac and Lincoln products to stem the growth of European specialists in the luxury segments of the American market; however, the image of their American products as mass-market offerings has thus far undermined attempts to create an aura of exclusivity. Similarly, Ford's efforts to tap a two-seater market with the EXP and LN7 variants of its high-volume Ford Escort and Mercury Lynx models were unsuccessful. General Motors seems recently to have made a breakthrough with its Pontiac Fiero two-seater. However, it was necessary to develop an entirely new product and new construction technique to give the Fiero the desired sense of uniqueness. In Europe, attempts by Volkswagen, Renault, and Fiat to enter the luxury segment, which generally offers higher profitability, have proceeded at a very slow pace. (Volkswagen, of course, has had considerable success with its separate Audi line.) Several generations of expensive product development seem to be necessary to change a full-line producer's image, if this can be done at all.

It is becoming easier for a medium-sized producer to use computer-aided design and flexible manufacturing to bring out variants of a few basic lines at relatively low cost and give the appearance of being a full-line producer. The revitalization of the Chrysler Corporation since 1979 offers a dramatic demonstration of this capability. Chrysler actually makes two basic vehicles with one basic engine: the Omni/Horizon in the light market segment and the Aries/Reliant in the medium segment, both of which offer Chrysler's 2.2-liter four-cylinder engine as standard equipment. But by clever reuse of basic mechanicals, purchase of optional engines from European and Japanese suppliers, and minor modifications to major stampings, the company has introduced a host of new products serving almost as many market segments as the full-line producers with six or seven distinct models.

The other aspect of market placement is the choice of national markets. In general, serving a large number of markets with a wide range of products makes a producer less vulnerable to dramatic demand shifts in individual markets or to disasters in individual economies. However, achieving broad market access in the future will almost certainly involve willingness to produce in many markets, partly because of trade restrictions. It will also involve delicate balancing between the advantages of market access gained through local manufacturing and the advantages of concentrating production in the producer's home country, and exporting wherever possible. On the latter point, it is important to note that the Japanese producers are not the only ones to have had doubts about the advantages of manufacturing abroad. Neither the Americans nor the Europeans have found great economic incentives to do so, except to acquire access to major markets that would otherwise be closed. Some producers have had immediate success, notably Ford in Europe, VW in Brazil, and Mitsubishi in Australia. The experience of many others has been disappointing. Chrysler's European adventure in the 1960s was very costly. VW has had continuing problems in the United States. Renault, which needed a dealer network more than local production but purchased the latter (by buying into American Motors) to get the former, is now facing the high cost of entering a mature market in North America. And no producer seems to have succeeded in producing a vehicle in any of the non-OECD countries at a cost *and* a level of quality superior to the best-practice standard of OECD production sites.

The key to success in adding national market coverage—particularly in the growth markets of the next 20 years, such as Mexico, Brazil, and Korea—seems to lie in early entry (VW in Brazil) or the transfer of superior systems of production organization to new locales (Mitsubishi in Australia). In the future it may also be necessary to agree to export production from new locations in return for market access, but this will raise many problems with the newly emergent notions of concentrating production in one geographic location. The large in-transit inventories and quality problems associated with this approach run directly counter to the emerging best production practice of geographic concentration.

Constraints on Competitors

Life for the automakers would be complicated enough if competition only involved bundling up combinations of products, production systems and market placements. In practice, the assemblers must devise their competitive strategies while also taking into account financial, work-force, and social constraints on their freedom to act.

Financial limits constrain the funding that can be obtained to endure demand cycles, to recover from miscalculations, and to adjust to market discontinuities. These financing needs are not trivial. Developing an entirely new model with a new engine and other mechanical components may cost $3 billion. Nor is the need for funds short-term. Four to five years pass between the first spending on a new model and its introduction in the market, the first point at which any revenues are generated.

In stable circumstances a producer can and does generate the needed funds from its existing automotive activities. However, when the financing requirement is prompted by a drastic shift in the market, the appearance of a new competitor with a better product or a superior production process, or a miscalculation on a recently introduced model, the producer will almost certainly have to turn to external sources of finance. Over the very long run, as practically all producers make expensive mistakes or fall victim to rapidly changing markets, access to external financing is vital to the ability of any producer to remain competitive. What determines whether a producer can obtain the funds needed to turn one of these adverse situations around?

Partly, it depends on the diversity of the producer's activities and the cash-generating capacity of its nonautomotive businesses. The 20 final assemblers headquartered in the Auto Program countries vary greatly in their reliance on automobile manufacture as their primary activity, in the portion of their output made and sold in a single national market, and in the size of their related businesses. Eighteen of the 20 produce commercial vehicles in substantial volume, although the contribution of these vehicles to total revenues varies widely. Chrysler, at one extreme, makes and sells practically all of its output in the North American market, while Ford covers the world, building and selling more cars abroad than in the United States. A number of firms have entirely separate businesses, such as Saab, Nissan, and Ford in aerospace. Finally, many of the Japanese producers have group affiliations with conglomerations of companies in other sectors who may provide forms of financial assistance in times of need. Because these other activities and market outlets will rarely encounter sales slumps or heightened competitive threats at the same time, the diversified auto producer is more likely to find funds internally to deal with a setback in its auto business.[8]

The ability of an auto producer to obtain external funds also depends on the nature of the national financial system in its headquarters country. National financial systems vary greatly in their ability to form useful judgments about the situation of a producer and to interpret feedback from the marketplace when trying to decide whether to provide backing. If the finance sources understand the industry and have some power to demand early action by the producer to rectify poor performance, they are likely to increase their lending. Even when bankers and other financial sources are not accurate in assessing the future profitability of a producer, their willingness to lend to that producer may yield a long-term advantage in world competition.

Producers must also cope with work-force constraints on the acceptance of new technologies, new work procedures, wage adjustments and layoffs, and limitations imposed by skill and educational levels. Planners within firms and in the financial community are often ready to respond to problems more quickly than the industry's work force. In addition, the cost and timing of response vary considerably among production locations. For example, producers are now facing constraints caused by the mismatch between the skills of their current work force and the skills demanded by flexible manufacturing systems. In some countries government assistance with retraining is available, but these are also generally the countries where layoffs are most difficult and expensive. A similar constraint is imposed by work force acceptance of the new practices and technologies needed to attain best practice in production organization.

Far beyond the production system are social constraints of many kinds. Some are expressed in the form of government vetos of options attractive to auto producers, such as access to markets, mergers, or large-scale plant closings. That this is so is understandable in light of the central importance of the auto industry in modern economies, including its frequently assigned though seldom sought role as a diffusion agent for new best practices in production technology and social organization across all the heavy manufacturing industries. However, the effect is that auto producers do not have and have never had the luxury of behaving as if their decisions on products and production locations did not have major consequences for entire economies and societies.

Assessing Overall Competitiveness

As noted earlier, success in the auto industry may come from brilliance along one competitive dimension. Most often, however, a balance of competitive competence is needed, assisted by creative approaches to constraints. For example, Honda has made rapid strides in the automotive world since its very late entry in 1957. The company's success has derived in part from a series of highly imaginative new models that have continuously expanded Honda's product range and sometimes created whole new market segments. In addition, Honda's manufacturing system has consistently provided high quality, and recently the company has seized the initiative in surmounting trade restraints by manufacturing in the United States.

Without question a producer must sustain a coherent strategy over a period of many years, because the interval between the conception of a new product or production system and its reward in the marketplace may be a decade or more. This not only makes a competitive advantage a challenge for the producer to sustain; it also makes an assessment of competitiveness very difficult for outside observers to assess.

I need a head shot that will fax well.

BUSI

What War

Analysts believe that Dow will fall additional 100 to 200 points

WA

War

1.15

OLLAR
5.15 yen
from
4:00 yen

The world auto industry entered a period of major competitive imbalance among producing regions during the 1970s. Such an imbalance must be resolved in some way, whether by convergence of competitiveness among national industries, by protection of uncompetitive producers in their home markets, or by elimination of the least competitive production locations. Whatever the resolution, it is bound to have sharp consequences for national economies, individual producers, employees of the auto industry, and the world economic community.

This chapter will assess the current competitive status of the auto industries of Japan, the United States, the various Western European nations, the less developed countries, and the Eastern bloc, pointing to the nature and causes of competitive imbalance. In addition, it will review the competitive status of different types of producers, from the full-line giant to the single-line specialist.

In such an analysis there is a danger of confusing a nation's inherent characteristics, advantages, and limitations as a production location, including resource availability and average wage levels, with the performance of the producers operating there. The former are not easily changeable; the latter may be. Indeed, whether or not there is a potential for transferring competitive advantage from one nation to another without major changes in prevailing national wage levels, capital costs, and raw-materials prices is one of the most interesting questions about the future of commercial competition and production location in the auto industry.

Similar confusion may arise in assessing the competitiveness of types of production organizations. Our objective is not to pass judgment on any particular producer but to assess the general competitive prospects of different organizational approaches to competition in the auto industry.

The Competitiveness of Japanese Manufacturers

Over a period of some 15 years, beginning around 1960, the Japanese auto producers evolved a production system based on a new approach to the social organization of the factory and the production chain. Different producers have taken somewhat different approaches, and it is an error to overlook these variations; however, it is clear that on average the Japanese auto industry requires fewer hours of labor by factory workers, designers, technicians, and managers at all levels of the production chain to make a vehicle of any given description than any other nation's auto industry. In addition, the Japanese auto industry on average has a very high level (perhaps the highest level) of manufacturing accuracy, a wage level nearly the lowest among the Auto Program countries, a lower level of in-process inventories, and greater versatility in shifting model mix and in developing new products. This contributes to lower production costs, high product quality, and flexibility in meeting changing market conditions. Producers operating in other locations are now taking steps to catch up, but it is clear that at present the Japanese production system confers a considerable competitive advantage.

As outlined in the previous chapter, this new system utilizes several key concepts that turn old ideas about production organization upside down. The notion that quality costs more has been reversed. Defect prevention turns out to cost less. Similarly, the traditional assumption that large inventory buffers are needed for high process yield has been turned around. High yield, defined as a large number of good parts per unit of operating time, seems most likely to be obtained with very low buffers. Yet another notion that has been reversed is that output can be increased and information about factory conditions can be obtained only through an independent system of supervision and information reporting. Instead of sending manufacturing orders from the top down and bringing information from the bottom up, the Japanese producers have learned that moving knowledge, skills, and decision making down the system into the hands of the primary work force makes the old supervision and information-gathering systems redundant. Between the assemblers and suppliers the Japanese have also pioneered new techniques. The old ideas that financial integration, top-down decision making with tight control of product information, multiple sourcing, and geographic dispersion are the keys to production efficiency have given way to operational coordination combined with financial disaggregation, increased single sourcing, and geographic concentration.

The key to the successful implementation of this new Japanese system is the industrial group. This consists of as many as several hundred legally separate but operationally coordinated companies surrounding each of the major assembler firms.[1] The Toyota and Nissan groups provide examples. Each consists of several core companies surrounded by a number of affiliates who are considered independent under Japanese financial reporting requirements but who would be considered consolidated subsidiaries in many other countries. However, this is only the tip of the iceberg. If the supplier associations surrounding the affiliated suppliers are considered, one can find more than 100 companies in each group responding to operational coordination.

The working of this system can be illustrated by a specific case. Aishin Keikinzoku is a Toyota group affiliate financially reporting as an independent company. More than eighty percent of the firm's output goes to the Toyota group; 40 percent of the firm's equity is owned by Toyota Motor Company and 40 percent by Aishin Seiki. Furthermore, Toyota Motor Company and Toyoda Automatic Loom, two senior Toyota group companies, own substantial equity in Aishin Seiki. Because no firm has explicit majority ownership the supplier firm is independent for purposes of financial reporting. Thus, it is financially and legally separate, but clearly resides within a multilayered, tightly held equity structure. This equity pattern is the rule rather than the exception, and it runs deep into the supplier chains of Japanese auto groups where still smaller companies are linked in a similar fashion to component suppliers such as Aishin Keikinzoku. In addition, a number of major supplier firms are jointly owned by two or more of the final assembler firms. The two leading shareholders of Press Kogyo, a major producer of metal stampings for auto bodies, are Isuzu and Nissan.

The traditional Western concept of vertical integration has mixed implications for the competitive stance of auto companies. In the past it was often assumed that high degrees of vertical integration led to lower capital cost per unit produced, more operating control over the production system, and greater protection of proprietary technology. However, many of these objectives seem less achievable in a rapidly changing international market. A high degree of vertical integration may drive up costs in component manufacturing if the high pay scales for workers and managers typical of final assembler firms are adopted in supplier subsidiaries. Also, a vertically integrated organization may tend to favor sunk capital investments in production equipment over purchases of new technology from outside suppliers. Similarly, it may be difficult for a final assembler to refuse parts supplied by a subsidiary even if cheaper or better parts could be obtained outside the organization.

Although the Japanese auto groups are more operationally coordinated, perhaps encompassing 70 or 80 percent of components in some cases, than many of the production systems in the United States and Europe, the evidence is that without sophisticated coordination systems and the ability to set different compensation scales between assembler and supplier firms this degree of coordination would be a disadvantage if achieved through traditional vertical integration. Indeed, the pattern of the American producers and some European producers in the troubled period since 1979 has been to disintegrate, purchasing even major mechanical components from independent suppliers (including other final assemblers).

The Japanese practice of group coordination, by contrast, clearly offers a competitive plus. It simultaneously attains the scale and coordination advantages of Western-style vertical integration and the flexibility of decentralization. Its aim is cooperation and mutual information flow between the parts rather than rigid top-down hierarchy. Its distinctive capabilities are tight production scheduling, cooperation on research and product design, and sharing of staff and production capacity, all while the independence of supplier firms in general management and in the setting of wage levels is maintained.

The Japanese system makes it possible for the final assembler to design all elements of the vehicle with full knowledge of the capabilities and needs of the supplier system. Because the tooling inventory, the work-force skills, and the financial situation of the supplier who will be asked to make each part are well known, and because the assembler's design team and the supplier have worked together on many parts over many years, they are able to coordinate not only the technology of the design but also the labor content, the job characteristics, and the quality-control measures that are essential to a superior product. Suppliers and assemblers in the United States and Europe also cooperate extensively. Control over suppliers is much weaker, however. Relationships may be for one product at a time, and the financial goals of the supplier may be very different from those of the assembler. The process is often adversarial, structured in terms of multiple sourcing and continuous competition between suppliers. As a result, much less information flows, and the agenda of items that can be coordinated is necessarily much shorter.

In research and development, staffing, and capacity utilization the Japanese system shows further advantages. Because the members of an industrial group are coordinated through their equity links and management working groups, they are able to share research facilities, support staff (such as accountants and marketing representatives), and production capacity. The process of sharing increases the effective knowledge in the organization, increases the collective capacity of the group's equipment, and reduces the total staff needed through elimination of such functions as marketing by supplier representatives and complex purchasing systems in the final assembler. Thus, the Japanese system delivers the commonly cited advantages of vertical integration while adding flexibility by encouraging information flow up and down the system as required by the independent financial reporting of the member firms. In addition, the system does not incur the cost penalty of high compensation levels in the supplier chain that typifies integrated production systems in the West.

Finally, the Japanese have developed relationships among the automotive industrial groups, their financing sources, and industrial groups in other sectors that seem to carry competitive advantages over typical arrangements in the United States and some of the European Auto Program countries. This is the system of conglomerate grouping (keiretsu) that links an auto producer to a major bank and a host of other industrial enterprises.[2]

The keiretsu structure grew up after World War II when funds for industrial investment were in short supply and could most easily be obtained through one of the major "city" banks. These commercial banks, such as Mitsui, Sumitomo, and Mitsubishi, were under the "window guidance" of the Bank of Japan which loaned funds to the banks for re-loan to industry. The city banks also obtained funds for industrial loans from the Japan Development Bank, the Export and Import Bank, and the Japan Industrial Bank. Producers wishing to expand realized that a strong affiliation with one of the city banks was vital in obtaining needed funds. In the Japanese system it was also considered natural for the enterprises affiliated with each bank to share common viewpoints and interests.

In the early postwar reconstruction period, the government and the banks tolerated and indeed encouraged remarkably high debt/equity ratios. As the postwar economic boom continued, these gradually fell (to the point that several of the Japanese automakers today are practically debt-free), but were supplanted by another type of group affiliation in the form of cross-equity holdings.

Although Japanese laws do not permit banks to hold more than 5 percent of the equity of an industrial enterprise, there are no rules against cross-equity holdings within a group. Thus, a pattern has emerged in which the group's lead bank will hold 5 percent or less of the equity in each of the group enterprises and each of the enterprises will hold a small share of the equity in each of the other group enterprises, including the bank. The net result is that the group members collectively hold a controlling interest in each others' enterprises. Foreign ownership is effectively blocked, assuaging a primary fear that arose among the Japanese as their industries became successful and began to threaten the markets of larger foreign corporations, including car companies. In addition, to the benefit of each group member, a system of group cross-checks of producer performance has evolved.

The contrasting experiences of Toyo Kogyo (Mazda) and Chrysler during recent periods of financial crisis illustrate the unusual features of this Japanese system and the competitive advantage it carries over American and much European financial practice.[3]

In 1973, Toyo Kogyo was a successful producer of light and medium-sized cars. It had risen rapidly in the Japanese automotive world after a late entry into the automobile business, in 1960. The company had created an image as the "high-tech" Japanese carmaker by perfecting the Wankel rotary engine for mass production. This permitted the company to charge somewhat more for what was otherwise a very conventional line of cars and thereby to offset the higher production costs that were incurred by its lower volume and its earlier position on the production learning curve compared with the larger Japanese producers.

The energy crisis of 1974 precipitated a crisis at TK because the fuel consumption of the rotary-engine Wankel powered Mazda models was much higher than that of competing models in the light-automobile market segment. TK's automobile production slumped 19 percent from 1973 to 1974. Sales in the vital North American market declined a calamitous 40 percent by 1975.

Despite its short-term problems, Toyo Kogyo was still marginally profitable. In another country it might have weathered the crisis by cutting back its product offerings, laying off workers, and accepting a more modest position in the automotive world. TK, however, was part of the giant Sumitomo group of companies, and its problems and deteriorating performance quickly became a concern of the group as a whole. From the group's perspective, the car busines was still attractive, because market growth was expected to be higher than average over the next 10–20 years. However, it was also apparent that Toyo Kogyo was in a difficult position. A cutback on product offerings to weather a crisis might lead to a permanent downward ratcheting of the auto producer's size and market share. To avoid such a cutback, massive borrowing would be needed to underwrite rapid development of a new and distinctive product line and a better production system.

The Sumitomo group had the resources to rescue Toyo Kogyo. However, the group and the lead bank were deeply concerned about the adequacy of TK's management and were determined to completely understand the true condition of the company before proceeding with massive lending. Their solution was to remove the senior management, headed by the grandson of the firm's founder and its largest private stockholder. In their stead the group installed nine senior executives from the Sumitomo Bank and other group companies.

With its own representatives in charge of Toyo Kogyo, the group proceeded with sufficient lending to finance the simultaneous development of three new models and to completely overhaul the production system. In addition, an injection of capital was obtained by an investment from the Ford Motor Company, which purchased a 25 percent holding in Toyo Kogyo. The Ford link gave TK direct connections to world component markets that it had lacked.

The new models were highly successful, and labor productivity in the revamped production system grew by 118 percent over 7 years. By 1980, Toyo Kogyo not only was profitable (having shown a loss in only one year of the turnaround), but had expanded its product offerings and increased its market share, particularly in Europe and the United States.

Several elements of the Toyo Kogyo turnaround shed light on the strength of the Japanese financial system as a factor in the long-term success of the Japanese auto industry. First, the Sumitomo group took a long-term perspective. It calculated that TK's product offerings and marketing network had to be expanded, even at the expense of short-term losses and very high debt/equity ratios, if TK was to remain in the world auto contest. As witness of their determination the group publicly declared that it would not allow TK to fail, thereby avoiding the "orphan car" phobia that plagued Chrysler for several years and BL for nearly a decade. Second, the Sumitomo group, with annual revenues of nearly $200 billion (about 3 times the revenues of General Motors), had tremendous financial resources. Perhaps most important, the group had thorough knowledge and competence with regard to Toyo Kogyo's operations. This made it possible to reinforce the feedback from the market instead of providing funds to allow the company to ignore market signals, as banks sometimes do. The group's collective expertise facilitated the rapid replacement of senior management, the development of a new product strategy, and the improvements in production efficiency essential to the success of the product strategy.

The Toyo Kogyo case is not an isolated example. Although the groups and bankers are not always successful in turning around companies, the basic approach to a crisis seems to be pursued by all the major conglomerate groups, and all the Japanese auto producers have links to such groups.

By contrast, at Chrysler (the case of BL would serve equally well) the relationships with lenders and stockholders were distant. Although Chrysler was founded with the assistance of the Chase Bank, its equity had become so widely dispersed that no individual or corporation held more than 1 percent. The firm's leading banker was only one of 400 banks around the world involved in Chrysler's syndicated loans by the time of the company's near collapse in 1979.

Although Chrysler's performance had been quite poor since the end of the great postwar sellers' market, the American financial system had no effective mechanisms to seek remedies. When the firm lost a substantial sum in the 1958 recession, no action was taken by the stockholders or lenders beyond the offer of loans, which were not large enough to renew the product line. Despite the activities of a dissident stockholder group and the misgivings of a few financial institutions, the company continued under a self-perpetuating management into the 1970s.

In the auto recession and crisis of 1974 the lenders were again faced with requests for large-scale assistance to Chrysler. Once again the existing management was retained and provided only enough funds for the most pressing capital spending. With government-imposed fuel-economy mandates facing the firm after 1975, it was possible to predict (as did several independent analysts) that any downturn in the auto market or unanticipated shift in the type of car demanded during the period between 1975 and 1985 would cause Chrysler insurmountable problems.

When the crisis came in 1979, with the 400 bankers and the widely scattered stockholders unwilling to advance additional funds or purchase additional stock, the financial community had none of the Japanese methods available. Sumitomo Bank had installed its own employees as the new controller and treasurer at Toyo Kogyo at the very start of the crisis in order to gain a complete understanding of the company's financial situation. The American banks had an incomplete understanding of Chrysler's plight and an even less thorough grasp of the situation of Chrysler's suppliers. Worse still, they had no way to obtain all the essential information. Even if they had, American banks did not have analysts with detailed operational knowledge of borrowers' businesses and could hardly have sent in the same type of rescue team.

In the end, Chrysler fell into the hands of the American government, which pursued a conservative strategy by offering loan guarantees sufficient for survival of the company at about half its former size. Subsequently, Chrysler has made creative use of this financial assistance to become fully competitive once more with its North American rivals. This is turn has permitted it to repay its government loans and access the private financial system for $5 billion in additional equity and debt financing. However, Chrysler's competitive weaknesses against many foreign rivals remain to be fully remedied and, over the long term, if American and some European firms continue to receive this kind of support and guidance from their national financial systems, Japanese firms such as Toyo Kogyo will have a competitive advantage. This is generally labeled superior "cycle endurance"; however, as the examples show, there is much more involved in an active financial system that is able to spot long-term problems early and to devise creative remedies.

One additional point about the financial situation of the Japanese industry must be mentioned. The five largest producers, by virtue of their recent success in export markets, are so strong financially that they face few financial constraints. The debt/equity ratios of Toyota, Nissan, and Honda have fallen steadily for the past decade (table 7.1). The Toyota Motor Company's long-term debt is now zero—an extraordinary reversal from the early days of the Japanese industry, when debt/equity ratios were far higher than financial sources ever permit in the West.

A consequence of the 1979–1982 slump in the U.S. auto market was that the domestic producers, who historically had very limited needs for external funds, financed an entire product-replacement cycle with borrowing. Although the industry's cash flow turned strongly positive

Table 7.1
Long-term debt as a percent of long-term capital for leading Japanese and American auto companies, 1971–1982

	1971	1972	1973	1974	1975	1976	1977	1978	1979	1980	1981	1982
Honda	57.8	54.6	51.4	46.3	52.9	51.8	39.5	28.9	32. 3	26.0	19.7	25.1
Nissan	37.7	27.3	24.5	29.4	25.4	18.4	15.5	12.4	14 .2	11.1	16.1	n.d.
Toyota	11.0	7.9	5.0	3.6	2.1	0.8	0.0	0.0	0.0	0.0	0.0	0.0
GM	5.1	6.3	5.7	6.5	8.5	6.8	6.3	5.3	4.4	9.6	17.7	19.6
Ford	12.6	14.3	13.2	19.1	19.4	16.6	13.8	10.6	10.9	19.4	26.9	26.4

Ratios = long-term debt/(long-term debt + equity). n.d = no relevant data available.
Long-term debt for Japanese companies excludes severance and pension liabilities.
Sources:
Martin L. Anderson, "Financial Restructuring of the World Auto Industry," paper prepared for International Automobile Program International Policy Forum, Hakone, Japan, May 1982, and calculations by the authors based on corporate annual reports.

in 1983, the $15.7 billion in cumulative negative cash flow at GM and Ford for the years 1979–1982 (table 7.2) marked a historic transfer in financial strength from the American industry to the Japanese. The Americans and several European producers must hope for prolonged stability in the marketplace, because the 1979–1982 slump has all but exhausted their ability to obtain external financing for new-product development.

When all the parts of the Japanese system of production organization—within the plant, between plants, and within the group financial planning system—are tied together, they yield cost advantages quite independent of factor costs. They also provide higher product quality through manufacturing accuracy at all levels, greater system flexibility to develop new products and to shift the mix, robust cycle endurance, and guidance mechanisms in the financial system that provide intense feedback on producer performance.

An American-European-Japanese Cost Comparison

The cost advantages of the Japanese system are worthy of special comment, not only because of the attention they have attracted in other auto-producing nations but also because of the need to assess carefully the role of production cost in overall competitiveness. However, assessing comparative costs is a complex task made more difficult by problems of product comparability, differing degrees of capacity utilization, exchange-rate fluctuations, and the proprietary nature of much of the information that is useful for cost estimation. Nevertheless, we estimate that the U.S.-Japan production cost difference on a typical smaller car exceeds $1,500 (at 215 yen $= \$1$) and that some recent estimates of the U.S.-Japan cost gap, setting it lower than $1,000 on a typical small car, are impossible to support given the evidence at hand. With regard to the European producers, we estimate that although costs vary considerably among producers, the Japanese have a substantial, although lesser, cost advantage.

The simplest approach to estimation of cost differentials is to compare the average automotive value per unit as found in manufacturers' financial statements. This has been done in table 7.3, which compares automotive revenue, including parts sales, per unit exported by Toyota with the same measure for all production at Volkswagen, Ford of Germany, Ford North America, General Motors North America, and Ford and GM world wide. Toyota exports primarily it higher-value vehicles

Table 7.2
Primary operating cash flow of leading Japanese and American auto companies, 1973–1982 (millions of dollars)

	1973	1974	1975	1976	1977	1978	1979	1980	1981	1982
Honda	22	−42	−47	−57	20	−38	1122	9	167	−143
Nissan	nr	nr	nr	209	194	96	249	108	−5	n.d.
GM	2278	−173	1102	2831	2070	1179	−409	−4345	−5002	−699
Ford	368	−200	385	949	1026	360	−667	−2342	−1042	−1151

Notes:
n.r. = not reported in translation; n.d. = no relevant data available; "primary operating cash flow" = (net profit + depreciation) − capital spending. Yen have been converted to dollars at $1 = 215 yen.
Sources: Martin L. Anderson, "Financial Restrucuturing of the World Auto Industry," table 3; and calculations by the authors based on corporate annual reports.

Table 7.3
Estimated revenue per unit produced (vehicle and parts revenue divided by units produced), in current dollars

	1970	1971	1972	1973	1974	1975	1976	1977	1978	1979	1980	1981	1982
Toyota (export vehicles)	2,245	2,377	2,472	2,434	2,567	3,270	3,814	4,049	4,235	4,238	4,688	4,823	nr
VW (excludes Audi)	2,450	2,745	2,944	3,326	3,775	3,492	4,513	4,899	5,322	5,859	6,427	7,030	7,363
Ford Germany	2,841	2,970	3,389	3,392	4,439	4,180	4,438	4,820	5,151	5,279	5,620	5,984	6,138
General Motors worldwide	3,107	nr	nr	nr	nr	nr	nr	5,672	6,221	6,895	7,488	8,634	9,077
General Motors N.A.	3,429	3,556	3,821	3,936	4,432	4,961	5,353	5,897	6,399	6,967	7,717	9,032	9,981
Ford worldwide	2,839	3,040	3,311	3,584	4,094	4,738	4,996	5,461	6,196	6,867	7,694	8,039	7,916
Ford North America	nr	nr	3,633	3,848	4,223	4,867	5,202	5,782	6,360	6,934	7,695	8,514	9,000
Production revenue per car, West Germany (VDA)	n.d.	n.d.	n.d.	n.d.	n.d.	n.d.	n.d.	4,640	4,927	5,379	5,848	n.d.	n.d.
Average retail-transaction price of U.S.-produced cars sold in U.S. (BEA)	3,708	3,919	4,034	4,180	4,523	5,083	5,504	5,985	6,481	6,906	7,630	8,940	9,880

Notes: The revenues reported in this table are total motor-vehicle revenues, including revenues for replacement parts, divided by the total number of motor vehicles produced. For General Motors worldwide, Ford worldwide, Volkswagen, and Toyota's exported motor vehicles, these revenues are routinely reported in corporate annual reports (except that Toyota stopped this practice in 1982). In the case of GM's and Ford's North American operations these data are reported in some years but in other years only total corporate revenues (including aerospace and other non-motor-vehicle activities) are reported. To develop a continuous data series, the average ratio of motor vehicle revenues to total revenues in the years in which these figures are reported was multiplied by total corporate revenues in the years in which only this figure was available. Marks and yen were converted to dollars at $1 = 215 yen and $1 = 2.4 marks. The VDA data showing the average producer revenues per unit for the entire German industry are shown to provide a cross-check on the corporate data. Similarly, average retail-transaction prices for U.S.-produced cars sold in the U.S., as determined by the Bureau of Economic Analysis of the U.S. Department of Commerce, are shown as a cross-check on North American producers' revenues as reported in corporate statements. n.r. = not reported; n.d. = no relevant data available.
Sources: Corporate annual reports; VDA; BEA.

with high levels of trim and options, a mix which closely approximates the overall luxury level of vehicles sold in Europe and North America.

The results are striking, and make it difficult to argue that the U.S.-Japan cost differential is below $2,000 per unit or that the Europe-Japan cost difference is less than $500–700 per unit. These figures do not translate directly to a delivered cost comparison because Toyota incurs some distribution costs above the level in table 7.3 and because adjustments must be made for the small proportion of trucks in the GM and Ford North American production mix. However, these adjustments are quite small in comparison to the wide value differences reported in the financial statements.

There is, of course, much disagreement in the automotive world about the precise size of these differences in national production costs. However, one position advanced by a number of auto producers and unions is that, whatever the precise level of the cost difference, a major factor is improperly aligned currencies (particularly an overvalued dollar).[4] Therefore, it is important to ask whether currency values tend to outweigh other factors in determining the cost competitiveness of national auto industries.

Our belief is that they do not. The exchange rate used to convert the Japanese and German costs estimated in table 7.3 into dollars was 215 yen and 2.4 marks to the dollar. The mark/yen rate is roughly the level of the past two years, but the yen/dollar rate indicates a yen about 10 percent stronger than in the recent past, when the yen has hovered around 240. Thus, we have already made an adjustment to bring the yen/dollar rate closer to what we believe is a realistic long-term value, and this makes our estimate of the cost gap smaller than if it were calculated at the recent yen rate.

But what if the yen should strengthen to a level of around 185, which some observers in the auto industry have suggested is its proper long-term value? A simple reworking of the U.S.-Japan cost comparison in table 7.3 indicates that there would still be a substantial cost gap. With a yen at 185 to the dollar, Toyota's value in table 7.3 might rise by about $700 dollars. However, Toyota's factory prices are unlikely to rise to that extent because many items needed in Japanese production (including process energy to run the factory, practically all the raw materials in the vehicle, and a number of components manufactured by Toyota affiliates in East Asia) can be purchased by Toyota with non-yen currencies earned in profitable export sales. These transactions could largely mitigate the effects of a strengthening yen. Thus, the increase in export prices is likely to be much less than directly proportional to the rate of yen appreciation. In short, it appears that restoring the competitive balance in the world auto industry would require a much stronger yen than any analyst of exchange rates has suggested is feasible.

If not primarily misaligned currencies, what is the basis of these cost differences? Unfortunately, a full cost accounting conducted by product line requires data that even auto producers lack in many cases and such data, when collected, are closely held proprietary information. However, it is apparent that a very large part of the cost of producing a car is accounted for by employment practices and compensation at all levels of the assembler and supplier firms. Government data make it possible to calculate an approximate Japanese-German-American comparison of these costs. The first step is to calculate the number of hours of effort by managers, designers, engineers, and production workers in the assembler and supplier firms needed to produce a roughly comparable vehicle (figure 7.1). The differences, as with total cost, are striking. The Japanese industry seems to have steadily reduced the amount of human effort needed to produce a car since 1970, even as the complexity of the vehicles being produced has risen. The Americans, in contrast, have been at roughly the same level of labor content per vehicle for many years if adjustments are made for the period after 1979 when volume fell off dramatically, increasing hours per unit in the short term. (These numbers must not be taken to mean, however, that productivity has not grown over time in the American industry. In fact, it has increased substantially because the vehicles being produced in 1981 were much more complex than the vehicles being produced in 1970.) In the early 1980s the Japanese producers needed only about 65 percent of the labor required in the American industry to produce a comparable product and about 30 percent fewer labor hours than the German auto producers on average. Like the cost data, these estimates incorporate assumptions—about vehicle mix, capacity utilization, and the comparability of government labor surveys—that rest on informed judgment rather than absolute knowledge. However, in general we believe that our assumptions produce conservative estimates of the difference in labor content between the Western and Japanese producers.

The second step in estimating employment cost per vehicle, which involves the multiplication of the average hours of labor per vehicle by the average cost per hour of compensation in the Japanese, German,

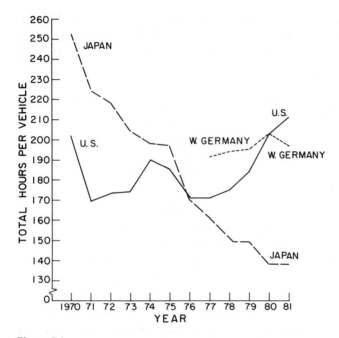

Figure 7.1
Total hours of employment to produce a motor vehicle, including management and production labor in the final assembler and supplier firms, in the American, Japanese, and German motor vehicle industries, 1970–1981.

The Japanese data include workers producing 6 million motorcycles and 400,000 automobile and light-truck export kits. Because these units are not included in the production total, the figure overstates Japanese employment hours per vehicle. The U.S. data include only workers in Standard Industrial Classification 371. Approximately 100,000 workers employed in automotive stamping operations are not included. Thus, the figure understates the employment hours in an American vehicle. The West German data include some workers producing exported parts which are assembled into finished vehicles in other countries. Because these vehicles are not included in the German production total, the figure tends to overstate employment hours in a German vehicle.

Sources: Japan, employment from Ministry of International Trade and Industry, *MITI Industrial Census*, Tokyo: MITI, various years; working hours per employee from Ministry of Labor, *Survey of Labor Statistics*; Germany, *Tatsachen und Zahlen aus der Kraftverkehrswirtschaft*, Verbank der Automobilindustrie (VDA), Frankfurt; United States, U.S. Department of Labor, Bureau of Labor Statistics

and American industries, is much more difficult. This is owing to differing forms of social compensation and the different combinations of management, technical, and production labor used in each industry. The employment hours in figure 7.1 are not comparable to the cost of production labor reported in table 9.6 because the hours in figure 7.1 include clerical employees not included in the hourly compensation cost estimates. Despite this difficulty, it is apparent that the difference in total employee cost per vehicle is large. Use of approximate hourly compensation estimates (based on table 9.6) indicates a U.S.-Japan employment cost difference per vehicle approaching $2000 and a German-Japanese difference roughly half as large. These employment cost differences roughly equal the total cost differentials estimated above. We believe, however, that there are other sources of comparative cost advantage for the Japanese in the area of processed materials such as steel and in lower capital costs per vehicle. The latter is not due primarily to lower capital costs in Japan but to the fact that Japanese producers seem to require much less plant and equipment per unit produced and to have much lower in-process inventories than the American and German producers.

As we have noted, these estimates are not precise, and we doubt that any comparative cost estimates can ever be developed for the world auto industry that do not have some margin of error. Nevertheless, the cost and labor-content gaps indicated are so large that different estimating techniques and assumptions are unlikely to change either the general magnitude or the trend.

With regard to the rest of Europe, we have found it difficult to make precise comparisons because of differences in national labor statistics and the financial reporting practices of producers. Our general belief, however, is that most European producers with relatively lower wage levels require larger amounts of labor per vehicle produced, with the result that their total employment costs do not differ substantially from the German averages. One or two lower-wage European producers may currently enjoy lower employment costs per vehicle, largely because of recent improvements in small car manufacturing technology and depressed national currency values, but these differences do not indicate long-term differences in cost of a fundamental nature.[5]

Thus, the Japanese approach to production organization establishes a new standard of best practice for the world. It supplants the old Ford system in the plant and the Sloan formula for coordinating the production chain as the recipe for competitive success. What is more, the

Japanese approach has applications not just in the auto industry but in all of mass manufacturing, as is illustrated by Japan's success in exporting motorcycles, consumer electronics, photographic equipment, construction machinery, and a host of other products.

Production Costs and Competition

What does this production-system advantage, expressed as a cost differential, mean in terms of competition among Japanese, American, and European auto producers? First, it is important to note that the estimates in table 7.3 cover only a small sample of producers. The gap between the most efficient American and European producers and the least efficient Japanese producers is far less than the gap between the least efficient American and European producers and the most efficient Japanese producers, which is truly enormous. Thus, the competitive implications differ for different producers.

Second, the Japanese producers have had a very large cost advantage over American and some European producers since at least the early 1970s and probably since the late 1960s. Their growth in world market share, however, has been a function of their range of product offerings, their production capacity, and the mix demanded by the market, as well as of production cost differences. In the U.S. market, the Japanese share jumped sharply during 1974–75 but then was reasonably stable until 1979, when it jumped again. The Japanese cost advantage seems to have widened only slowly during this period, indicating that market demand and product availability must be synchronized with production cost for a national industry to expand its world share. This suggests that in the future a cost gap of the present magnitude, especially when combined with high production accuracy and low delivered defects, will continue to convey a considerable competitive advantage. However, it can only be converted into increased market share if the model mix and specification demanded in the marketplace continue to correspond with the capability of the Japanese production system.

The effects of the Japanese cost advantage will vary with the type of producer. Specialist producers in Europe who offer products with unique performance or image may succeed in the world auto business, at least for the next decade, without having to match the Japanese in the area of production systems. The Western mass-market producers cannot take this position. They urgently need to improve their production systems.

With regard to products, the competitive status of the Japanese industry is less clear. As explained in chapter 6, the development of automotive products is an art as well as a science that evolves over generations of vehicles. Until recently the Japanese producers devoted most of their export energy to light vehicles such as the Toyota Corolla and the Nissan Sentra. After three to four product generations, Japanese cars in this class have reached a very high standard of sophistication.

Because the Japanese makers are now facing unit limitations on their access to a number of important export markets, all have stepped up work on new medium and large cars, such as the Honda-BL Project XX, Toyota's Camry and next-generation Cressida, and the new, front-wheel drive Nissan Maxima/Bluebird. In addition, to cope with the intense domestic competition and the approaching saturation of the Japanese market, Japanese producers are attempting to differentiate their offerings within the light and small-car market segments with products such as the Honda City and CRX and the Nissan Prairie which shift competition from price to the special attributes of the product and which have the potential to increase the total size of the auto market as well. The consequence of this may be a shift by the Japanese producers from market followers to market definers in many classes. This would complete a historic shift in their image from lowest-cost producers to producers of high-specification products in every market segment. Such a transition by the Japanese would pose a special competitive problem for the European specialist producers, whose particular strength in the postwar era has been the development of distinctive products aimed at particular market niches.

Thus, the Japanese producers are strong in production systems and becoming stronger in products. Paradoxically, this has led to both a growing penetration of foreign markets and a growing vulnerability in market placement, the latter caused by restrictions on market access for fully built-up units. Japanese makers have concentrated on the export of built-up vehicles because the transfer of their production techniques to foreign sites is a major challenge in view of the great importance of physical concentration of the production process to facilitate just-in-time supply and tight system coordination.

Recently a move to foreign production has commenced in earnest. Honda and Nissan are now assembling cars and light trucks in the United States and increasing their percentage of domestic content. Nissan has agreed to build an assembly facility in Britain, eventually increasing the level of European content in the vehicles produced there to 80 percent. Toyota has agreed to a joint venture with General Motors to assemble cars in California. The other Japanese producers are likely to establish manufacturing facilities in the United States and Europe to protect their competitive position, particularly if it appears that trade restraints will persist.

There is a large difference, however, between establishing a manufacturing facility in another country and returning a profit with that facility. It will be a decade or more before the success of these foreign ventures in producing superior products at competitive costs can be assessed.

Competitiveness of Western European Manufacturers

European auto designers in the postwar period have had a considerable advantage over the Americans and the Japanese with regard to products. In the United States a dominant very large design developed, while the Japanese specialized in light and medium cars (typified respectively by the Toyota Corolla and the Nissan Bluebird/Maxima). In addition, a single firm in the United States (GM) and two in Japan (Toyota and Nissan) were, until recently, the styling and design leaders in their respective industries. In Europe, by contrast, each national market emphasized (and continues to emphasize) a different dominant size of vehicle, ranging from small in Italy and France to large in Germany. In addition, there are many producers of roughly the same size and market power. The result has been that no single design philosophy or producer could dominate the market.

The different national market mixes were the result of isolation among the European markets before the late 1960s. There were sharp differences in vehicle taxation, degree of population concentration, purchasing traditions (fleet versus individual), driving conditions, and income levels. These factors led to four distinct dominant designs.

In France and Italy, high registration taxes on large cars and the concentration of population in large cities encouraged a very small dominant design. Initially very utilitarian (Citroen 2CV, Fiat 500), it gradually evolved into the standard small hatchback with the introduction of the Fiat 127 in 1971 and the Renault 5 in 1972. In Germany, taxation was neutral on vehicle size, but the dispersion of major population centers created a demand for intercity travel, aided by the autobahn system. The upper-income portion of the market settled on a dominant design in the Mercedes-Benz and BMW touring sedans, while the lower-income market was defined by the VW Beetle. The Beetle was succeeded by the Golf in 1974, which prompted responses from Opel (Kadett, 1979) and Ford (Escort, 1980). In the United Kingdom the exemption of employee perquisites from personal income taxes created a company-car segment accounting for at least 45 percent of the market. Because these vehicles were justified by their business use, the dominant type became the medium-size "salesman's car." Ford Cortina designs from 1961 on typified this vehicle, now in its fifth generation with the Sierra (1982). Thus, each European nation's market developed around one or two dominant designs, and each national producer specialized in a dominant national type: Renault and Fiat in small cars, Volkswagen in light cars, Ford U.K. in the medium-size cars, and BMW and Mercedes-Benz in large touring cars. Figures 6.1 and 7.2 together show this tendency.

By the mid 1970s, formal trade barriers in the European market were eliminated. However, market integration has not altered the conditions that produced differences in national demand patterns. Differing designs are still dominant in each national market. The trend is for each major producer to offer a full range of models in all four segments, to specialize in the segment dominant in its home market, and to work very hard at maintaining its share in that market (figure 7.2).

Of particular importance has been the almost even division of the European market among six producers with market shares in the 10–15 percent range and a host of specialist producers in the 1–3 percent range (table 7.4). It has been quite impossible for a single producer to dominate the European market or for a single design philosophy to prevail. And at any given time, a wide range of models and national preferences protects the mass-market producers from dramatic demand shifts and presents a diffuse target for the Japanese volume producers.

An additional benefit to the European automakers of the lack of dominant producers has been the intensity of continuing experimentation with vehicle technologies in search of a competitive advantage. The smaller size of the specialist firms might have presented a problem, since they have limited resources to spend on research and development; however, this gap has been filled by independent supplier, design, and engineering companies (e.g., Bosch in complex componentry such as fuel injection, Bertone in design, and Porsche in engineering). The result has been the long-standing European competitive strength in product technology.

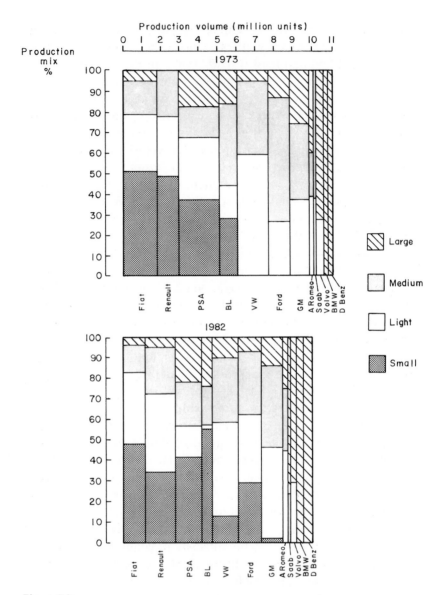

Figure 7.2
Production by European automakers by market segment, 1973 and 1982. Source:
Jones, "SPRU Databank of the Western European Auto Industry."

Table 7.4
Producer market shares in Western Europe, 1979 and 1982

	1979	1982	Home-market sales/ European sales (1982)
GM	9.6	10.4	41.4
Ford	12.0	12.4	39.0
Volkswagen	12.1	11.8	52.4
Renault	13.4	14.7	55.7
PSA	17.3	12.4	51.0
Fiat	10.3	12.5	70.8
BL	4.1	3.7	75.9
Daimler Benz	3.0	3.2	72.1
BMW	2.5	2.8	46.7
Volvo	2.0	2.0	28.9
Alfa Romeo	1.8	1.8	58.9
Saab	0.6	0.6	49.2

Note: The "home market" is the country in which a producer is headquartered and makes the largest portion of its sales. In the case of General Motors (Opel) this is West Germany; in the case of Ford of Europe this is the U.K.
Source: SPRU Databank of the Western European Auto Industry

Whether the European technological edge can be kept sharp in the future is less certain. The Japanese producers have large financial resources, which they may invest in new product technology. Their new models are being marketed heavily on the basis of their technical attributes, such as Toyota's four-valve engine in the Supra and Mazda's electronically tunable suspension in the 626. Recent patent data, reviewed in another context in chapter 4, indicate an extraordinary upturn in Japanese patenting. In addition, Japanese producers are making use of the independent European design and engineering firms that have contributed to specialist technology in the past. For example, Toyota has bought an equity interest in Lotus, one of the most innovative automotive engineering firms.

Thus, the European lead in products may be challenged. It no longer resides in technical know-how protected by patents (since most of this knowledge is for sale to any producer), but rather in the art of putting advanced packages together harmoniously. If the Japanese were able to build automobiles with characteristics similar or identical to those of European specialist producers, they would probably be able to do it at much lower cost. However, to move successfully into the Audi

100 size segment and above represents a major leap from smaller ve-hicles, one that would probably take several product generations for the Japanese producers to accomplish. In addition, because the European producers realize the nature and importance of their advantage in this area, it seems certain that they will continue to invest heavily in R&D and product development, presenting foreign competitors with a moving target.

It is clear that product distinctiveness is the major competitive ad-vantage of the European producers and that they will lose it only at great risk. In the small-car segment of the market (Fiat Panda, BL Metro, Ford Fiesta) and even more so in medium- and large-car segments, the lead has been retained and Japanese penetration has been low, even in open national markets. In the Golf/Escort/Kadett light-vehicle seg-ment, however, the European product lead is gone; this is precisely where the Japanese producers have scored their greatest market suc-cesses. In the future, one strategy for the European producers will lie in stressing the diversity (even the nationalism) of their design phi-losophies and refusing to present a unified target to Japanese product designers.

The situation of the European-based producers is not only weaker with regard to market placement but also more complex to analyze because of the different situation of each producer in each of the national markets. Because the European national markets show little tendency to converge, are now mature in all but the southern countries, and permit exclusive dealing practices within the distribution network, it is apparent that intra-European shifts of market share will be very expensive to obtain. The market is saturated, with many producers offering products in each segment. Producers can expand into new territory only by establishing a new and independent sales network, because exclusive franchising prevents the "dualing" with established dealers which Japanese and European producers have used to advantage in entering the American market. Many products still retain a national flavor that endears them to home-country purchasers but repels export consumers. Therefore, dramatic shifts in the European producers' shares are unlikely. The stability of market shares has been high in the period since 1973; BL, PSA (the merger of Citroen, Peugeot, and Chrysler Europe), and Fiat have been the exceptions but they show strong signs of stabilizing.

It is evident that the Japanese automakers' share in Europe has now been stabilized by government pressures. The Japanese producers can hope to grow mainly by increasing volume in periods of ebullient auto sales, by increasing revenue through sale of more luxurious models, or through local production with very high local content. Their future in Europe is therefore largely subject to political rather than commercial considerations.

In non-European markets the placement of European mass-market producers is generally poor. Finished-unit export volume has been severely eroded by the Japanese, and the efforts of various national producers to become multinational manufacturers on the GM/Ford model have so far been a cash drain rather than a source of strength.

Volkswagen has the most comprehensive world strategy. It supplies the less developed countries with kits from Brazil, serves Europe and the American "up market" from Germany, and goes after the American "down market" with U.S. assembly of components from Germany, Brazil, and Mexico. Although the prolonged economic slump in Brazil and Mexico and special problems in the United States have put the VW multinationalization program under pressure, in the longer run VW's very strong position in Brazil and Mexico may generate sufficient profits to make it one of the strongest multinational companies.

Renault has been the other European full-line producer with an energetic multinational strategy. Its foreign manufacturing operations are based in Spain, in Mexico, and in the United States through its buy-in to American Motors. The company's strategy, planned for the long run, will require heavy additional investments to produce a wider range of automobiles in the United States and integrate its Spanish operations into a European production network if Spain joins the EEC. Thus, it will be a number of years before the competitive consequences are known.

Otherwise the story of the European multinational automakers is one of failure. BL retrenched from its foreign commitments in the 1970s. Peugeot has never really left home. Fiat has ventured the most and lost the most, having failed at rationalizing SEAT (its licensee in Spain), at buying into Citroen, at producing profitably in Brazil, at establishing a continuing presence in Eastern Europe, and at developing a North American distribution system. Thus, except for VW and Renault, the European full-line producers are for the period under study just that: European producers.

The European specialists, by contrast, have had remarkable success in capturing top-of-the-line markets across the world through sales of finished units shipped from their domestic production bases. They have even had some success in Japan. Daimler-Benz, BMW, Volvo, and Saab (soon to be joined by Jaguar as it is split off from BL) are currently claiming substantial price premiums in most export markets outside of Europe. This strengthens them competitively within Europe as well. Eventually, however, they are certain to face a strong Japanese challenge and an American counterchallenge for these lucrative markets. This is particularly so in the case of the Japanese, because the typical current practice of expressing trade restrictions in units gives Japanese producers a strong incentive to shift their product mix to garner more revenues per unit and perhaps larger profit margins.

With regard to production systems, the European producers divide into three categories. One group of mass-market producers, consisting of BL, PSA and Fiat, is in the process of catching up with European best practice in production systems. They must still complete the rationalization of their production systems and deal with overmanning in some facilities. PSA and BL mostly need additional rationalization in the components sector, where large numbers of small suppliers must be realigned to match the rationalization of the final assembly operations now nearly completed after a long period of mergers. In the case of Fiat and BL, labor-relations deadlocks have recently been broken to permit manning at levels much nearer, although still above, the European average.

A second group of full-line producers—Ford, GM, VW, and Renault—have attained the best production practice in Europe, including a high level of production reliability and accuracy as well as integrated trans-European production systems, but lag behind the Japanese in manning levels and in-process inventories per unit of production. Only if this gap is closed will these makers be competitive in export markets outside of Europe and in the European fringe markets, which remain relatively open to the Japanese producers. This process requires a very large amount of organizational learning, which will take a number of years.

The third group of European producers, the five specialists, have generally attained a high level of production reliability and accuracy after some lapses in the 1970s. They do not for the moment have to match Japanese manning and inventory levels, because they are competing more on product attributes than on price.

In view of the social constraints on European producers in workforce reductions and wage levels, as illustrated in chapter 9 and appendix C, it is not surprising that they look to flexible manufacturing technologies to close the productivity gap. Volkswagen, Renault, and Fiat are world leaders in flexible manufacturing technology and hope to develop profitable businesses by serving other auto producers with products developed initially for their own needs.

The Competitiveness of American Manufacturers

Auto production in the United States was severely threatened by the combination of the extreme slump in the auto market during 1979–1982 and a shift in product demand that caught the American producers out of phase while Japanese and European rivals were well positioned. More ominous, the U.S. production system was shown to be broadly deficient in cost and precision, even with the return of a strong market and with an improved mix of product sizes.

Perhaps the key competitive strength of the American industry lies in market placement. The traditional size difference between North American cars and those of the rest of the world continues. Nearly one third of 1982 car sales in North American were in the very large size class which the rest of the world's producers (except Rolls-Royce and Daimler-Benz) do not serve.

The "very large" class will remain a source of competitive strength for U.S.-based production, because the Japanese in particular would be taking an unacceptable risk in developing large production capacity in Japan for a product that could be sold only in North America. In addition, it would take several product generations to reach the American level of sophistication in this class, where the American product is truly distinctive after more than 30 years of development. After 1979, many observers of the industry wrote off this segment as a casualty of higher energy prices. However, the American manufacturers, after a trip to the technology shelf, applied a number of short-term technical fixes for excessive fuel consumption to subtly downsized but still very large automobiles. In 1983 and 1984, North American sales of these more economical "very large" cars have been strong.

Because the American-based manufacturers are continuing to refine fuel-efficient drive trains and bodies and have the ability to quickly shift the drive train mix toward increased fuel efficiency, they should be able to defend volume in this segment if energy prices rise again. Also, they have not yet taken full advantage of the technologies available, such as diesels with turbochargers and lock-up torque converters combined with lighter front-wheel-drive layouts of the same general external dimensions. Thus, the unexpected durability of the "very large" market segment gives the North American producers some breathing room in meeting the extreme challenges presented them at the small-car end of the market.

A second aspect of American market placement that confers a competitive advantage (although not to the extent that many observers believed prior to 1979) is the location of American-owned production around the world and the existence of a broad range of products at these other production locations. In two previous crises in the North American industry—the market slump and European import surge of 1958–59 and the initial Japanese success in the American market at the end of the 1960s—the American producers were able to import products from Europe while new domestic designs were being readied. This plugged gaps in their product lines, maintained their market share, sustained cash flow, and discouraged their dealers from taking on import franchises. However, this path was blocked in the 1979–1982 crisis by the lack of extra production capacity in Europe, the lack of a Japanese production base, and regulatory complications in the United States.

There are two major regulatory impediments to substitution of foreign-built products in response to demand shifts in the United States toward market segments not adequately covered by domestic products or production capacity. One is the need to "federalize" vehicles for the U.S. market in terms of emissions and safety. The other is the need to meet the Corporate Average Fuel Economy (CAFE) standards, which calculate a producer's fuel-economy average for domestic and import production separately. Because federalizing vehicles for safety adds about 200 pounds and considerable cost, producers are reluctant to federalize foreign products for the remote contingency that they may be demanded in the United States at some point. Similiarly, developing an engine able to meet the U.S. emission standards is an expensive process that adds cost to the base engine even if the catalysts and other bolt-on items are left off products produced for other markets. In consequence, when foreign products were needed in the United States after 1979, many potential entrants were disqualified by high conversion costs. Just as serious was the fact that the models most demanded were in the small- and light-car segments. American manufacturers reasoned that their fuel-efficient imports would partially displace their fuel-efficient domestic products, leaving the manufacturer's U.S. output with too high an average fuel consumption to meet the government's fuel-economy regulations.

The main benefit the American multinational automakers gained from their worldwide production organizations, therefore, was financial. Foreign sales did not slump nearly as much as American sales, so the foreign subsidiaries were able to provide substantial financial assistance to their parent companies. For example, Ford of Europe loaned its North American parent more than $1.0 billion dollars. Without this aid the American producers would have had to slow the pace of new product introductions and this would have had serious longer-term consequences for domestic sales.

The rest of the market placement of the American industry is, on balance, a weakness, even with the naturally protected very-large-car segment because of the peculiarities of the North American market. Because this is the world's most mature and volatile market, it is risky for any producer to have it as a primary market. In addition, it is the world's easiest market for foreign producers to enter because of the organization of the American retail distribution system. In Europe and Japan retailers are either owned by the final assembler or tied tightly through "exclusive dealing" agreements which stipulate that a dealer may sell only the manufacturer's products or face the loss of his franchise. In the United States, court decisions in the late 1940s outlawed exclusive dealing clauses in franchises. Since that time a simple strategy for foreign producers wishing to enter the U.S. market has been to sign up established dealers who wish to expand and cannot obtain additional franchises from domestic producers or who are experiencing trouble in maintaining sales volumes with their existing lines. For example, Isuzu and Mitsubishi were recently able to establish dealer networks in the United States mostly by "dualing" with Ford, GM, and Chrysler dealers worried about declining sales of domestic products. They did this in a very short period of time and without major investments.

Yet another market placement problem for North American producers involves the introduction of new products. Any new product from any world manufacturer will experience some unanticipated problems in its first months of consumer use. However, the North American producers release new products directly into their primary market where they must compete against European and Japanese products which invariably have undergone a period of "consumer proving" in their home market before the commencement of exports. This situation obviously magnifies any quality problems the North American producers may have and works to the benefit of Japanese producers in particular, who face little foreign competition in their home market during the "proving period" and who then export more than half of their total output.

The competitive situation of the American manufacturers in regard to products is precarious outside the "very large" segment. Historically, the entire industry was vulnerable to the weakness, often ascribed to Henry Ford and Volkswagen, of sticking with a dominant design past its time. The designs in the "very large" segment proved difficult to scale down quickly or to reconstitute as competitors to European luxury models. They carried an image of retrograde technology: rear drive, separate chassis and body, and simple suspensions adequate to the very soft "boulevard" ride Americans once preferred. With such vehicles it was easy, as product demand shifted, for the American producers to lose not only volume but, perhaps more important, image leadership that also affected the "light," "medium," and "large" market segments.

American producers are now imitating the Europeans in designs for sporty and touring/luxury versions of mass-market models and imitating the Japanese in designs emphasizing economy and utility. The result is that the traditional American domination not only of the volume but also of the spirit and style of the domestic market is now greatly weakened.

The American production systems are also an area of competitive disadvantage. The differences from the Japanese system are apparent in labor relations, production organization, supplier relations, and financial resources.

Financial constraints pose a particular problem because a long time is required for social learning in organizations the size of auto-production systems. As discussed in chapter 6, these large organizations are collections of innumerable skills, ways of conceptualizing problems, and accommodations for working collectively. When old approaches are suddenly inadequate to new conditions, the initial response of denial of the problem is often followed by chaos as different solutions and programs of action vie for supremacy. This characterizes the response of the American producers since 1979. First they needed to get new models into production because of the mismatch between the pre-1980 models and the post-1979 market. Only when this was well in hand did it become apparent that the new models had no technical or design superiority over the imports that would allow them to compete on attributes other than price. It also became apparent that American production organization, manufacturing costs, and assembly accuracy, after decades of effective market isolation by virtue of cheap energy, had developed without reference to world trends and were well out of line with the Japanese and in some cases with the Europeans.

Substantial reforms are underway, encouraged by the initiation of production in the United States by Honda and Nissan and by the General Motors–Toyota joint venture. Developments within the established domestic production organizations, such as the "Buick City" complex and the new manufacturing system for the Pontiac Fiero, are encouraging as well. However, a full reworking of the production system cannot be achieved in a short period. The whole work force (including middle managers, engineers, and production workers) must be retrained in new organizational approaches, and production facilities must be concentrated in a few geographic areas to permit full use of the just-in-time method and other improved methods of inventory and quality control. The Japanese, it must be remembered, needed nearly 20 years to create their present system.

Revitalization of the industry on this scale requires enormous financial resources over a long period of time and, no less important, a capacity in the financial system for independent and informed criticism. The American financial system is not well suited to either task, and American government intervenes only as a financial source of last resort after companies have already sustained a great deal of damage. Thus, the outlook for the American industry to reestablish a competitive balance is uncertain.

The Competitiveness of Locales Outside the OECD Countries

The Less Developed Countries

The evidence is that there is a marked competitive imbalance among the seven Auto Program countries. But does a more important competitive imbalance lie outside the developed world? Product-cycle theories suggest that, because the auto industry is now mature in many market segments, with competition largely on price, and because production techniques are well understood and at least potentially transferrable, auto production ought to be shifting to less-developed countries where wages are low. Is it possible, particularly if competitive pressures push the multinational auto producers in this direction, to build automobiles for many developed-country markets more cheaply in the LDCs?

A wholesale transfer is not possible now and is unlikely to occur soon. The main obstacles are the complexity of the motor vehicle as a consumer good and the vast scale of the world industry. Producing a simple item in moderate volume in an LDC for its domestic market is one matter; making millions of units of a complex product in an LDC for shipment halfway around the world to a sophisticated OECD market is another. So far, none of the multinational auto producers has been able to do this and no indigenous producers have arisen or seem likely to arise in the LDCs to do it in their stead.

But what about components? If the complex process of putting all the parts together is best done in the OECD countries, where design activities and overall production coordination take place, is it possible that most components could be produced more efficiently and with adequate quality in the LDCs?

Auto components can be divided into three types in terms of their suitability for production in LDCs.[6] Major mechanical components, notably engines and transmissions, require heavy initial investments and are highly automated with low amounts of direct labor. "Finish" parts, such as exterior body stampings, seats, and dashboard moldings, are bulky to ship and must fit very precisely. In addition, it is critical that their finish quality and color precisely meet specifications. Minor mechanical components, including starters, radiators, springs, and wiring harnesses, require much simpler manufacturing techniques.

Major mechanicals require technically skilled labor to run the complex plant equipment. In addition, the size of the investment and the importance of uninterrupted supply make political and economic stability, often termed "country risk", an important factor in location. Thus, only a few sites in low-wage areas are suitable. In Korea, the most favorable of these areas, a cost saving of about 20 percent could be achieved on engines (as of 1980) by American-based producers after shipping and additional inventory costs are taken into account. This is a significant saving, to be sure, although not nearly so large as one might have expected. However, the more important fact about Korean production costs is that they are probably above Japanese costs and it is not apparent that any low-wage site can now produce major mechanicals more cheaply than Japan. This is because the Japanese producers have made such progress in reducing the total labor hours needed for engine and transmission manufacture that their higher wage costs per hour are more than offset.

"Finish" parts are expensive to ship because of their bulk, and producing them at remote locations creates great quality control problems. Indeed, the remote sourcing of these parts runs against the strong desire of most automakers to centralize production at the point of final manufacture.

Minor mechanicals are the components best suited to low-wage sourcing. As of 1980, starter motors could be manufactured in Korea and delivered to Detroit for 35 percent less than they would cost to manufacture in Detroit. The saving on wiring harnesses made in Mexico was 25 percent. (Mexico was the lowest-cost site for delivery to Detroit because of the relative bulk of harnesses and the greater shipping cost from Korea or Taiwan.) However, LDC costs are currently no lower than Japanese costs except for a few items, and minor mechanicals are also the components most suited to automated manufacture as flexible manufacturing systems achieve the "seeing and feeling" capabilities needed for automated machining and assembly of parts.

In sum (see table 7.5), only a small advantage can be gained at present through sourcing in low-wage areas and the number of components on which costs can be saved is likely to decline as OECD factories are more highly automated and OECD production systems are more tightly centralized. This does not mean that the LDCs have no potential for automotive exports to the OECD countries, but rather that their often-assumed competitive advantage, based on low unit labor cost, does not shift the competitive balance away from the developed countries. The need to achieve scale economies in developing countries with high local-content requirments, coupled with the feasibility of building highly automated plants in those countries which can produce at an adequate standard of quality, means that some OECD production is being transferred from the United States and Europe to developing countries such as Mexico, Brazil, and Korea. For different reasons, some Japanese production may be transferred also. For example, General Motors is reportedly considering a plan to assemble Japanese components into finished units in Korea for sale in the United States. This arrangement would preserve most of the Japanese advantage in production cost while skirting the present U.S. unit limitation on Japanese imports. Ford and Toyo Kogyo have recently announced a similar plan for a new assembly plant in Mexico which will send its output to the United States. Clearly, the main aim of such transfers is not to produce cost savings for multinational producers in the OECD markets; rather, it is to gain access to developing and developed markets. Fur-

Table 7.5
Cost savings in U.S. auto manufacture from remote sourcing of auto components in low-wage countries (1980)

Component	Labor cost saving	Additional shipping cost	Net saving	Net saving/ value added	Cheapest country
Engine	$89.00	$44.00	$45.00	20%	Korea[a]
Transmission	55.00	21.00	34.00	29%	Korea[a]
Body stampings (set)	90.00	64.00	26.00	12%	Mexico
Starter motor	3.03	1.65	1.38	35%	Korea
Radiator	.97	1.14	−.17	—	Mexico
Coil spring	1.61	1.41	.20	6%	Mexico
Wiring harness	1.00	.59	.41	25%	Mexico

Notes:
a. These components are cheaper when sourced in Korea than in the United States but not necessarily cheaper than when sourced in Japan. Japanese wages are much higher than Korean, but total labor (direct plus indirect) is probably much lower.
Source:
Derived from published and unpublished data including Rath and Strong, Harbour and Associates, U.S. Department of Transportation, Transportation Systems Center, and company data.

thermore, the magnitude of these transfers, though it has grown in recent years, is tiny as a fraction of total world production.

The Eastern Bloc

A different situation is presented by the Eastern bloc, where governments are able to set wage and exchange rates to produce an industry that seems "competitive" in some OECD markets. The Eastern Europeans attracted attention in the late 1960s and the early 1970s with plans to enter world auto competition by buying the previous generation of auto tooling from Western producers and using it to export vehicles aimed at the lowest-cost, basic transportation segment of the European and North American auto markets. The program ran according to plan initially, after Fiat's sale to the Russians of production technology for its 124 line. Eastern bloc exports to the West rose from 60,000 per year in 1973 (mostly Skodas and other indigenous East European designs) to 149,000 in 1979.

Prospects for further growth of these exports have been dealt a heavy blow by the poor recent performance of the Eastern economies and the fact that they have reached the upper limit of borrowing from Western bankers. In consequence, the only way the Eastern European industry can pay for the next generation of auto technology is through the barter of finished vehicles or components.

Fiat is receiving some cars and components as partial payment for transfers of technology, but the failure of the Oltcit venture with Citroen in Rumania has cast doubt on the barter principle. Citroen offered designs and tooling for a current-generation model to Rumania's state-owned motor company in the hopes of recouping its investment in a model no longer needed after its merger with Peugeot and developing an Eastern European foothold at the same time. Payment was to be in the form of 30,000 finished vehicles, which PSA would retail in Western Europe. The exchange has been blocked, however, by the inability of the Rumanian firm to produce vehicles to PSA's minimum standard of quality. (The same problem was mentioned earlier in connection with LDC production of fully built-up automobiles.)

With PSA unpaid, the idea of bartering auto technology for finished cars is understandably receiving a critical reexamination in the West. As a result, the Eastern Europeans are being forced to sell increasingly outdated products at lower and lower prices, particularly since they must now compete against low-priced Japanese products of very high quality in the low end of the European market.

Only the Russians are going ahead with a new auto generation aimed at export markets, a front-drive Lada successor designed by Porsche in return for cash payment. However, the ability of the Russians to go forward rapidly in vehicle production seems to be constrained by operating problems at the Kama River truck plant. The familiar Russian difficulty with running massive industrial complexes on the Leninist industrial model seems in this case to be soaking up the whole of available spending for the vehicle sector, delaying the new Lada into the next plan, which commences in 1985. Some additional export success can be expected for Lada's four-wheel-drive Niva model, which is tailored to cold climates. In general, however, the Eastern Europeans are not likely to offer a competitive threat in the OECD marketplace during the next 20 years.

A Major Competitive Imbalance Among the Developed Countries

What may be concluded about the state of competition within the automotive world? First, there is a competitive imbalance between the developed countries and the rest of the world, but it favors the most competitive among the developed countries. Second, the major competitive imbalances among the Auto Program countries, favoring the Japanese producers, are currently very large in many market segments. They create extreme pressures for restructuring and rebalancing, which will be the major force driving the development of the world auto industry over the next 20 years.

The Future Shape of the World Auto Industry

When the Auto Program was launched, a conventional wisdom prevailed about the future of the auto industry, a view the authors largely shared. The main elements of this view are worthy of listing, not because they are valuable as guidelines to the future but rather because we have found them to be far off the mark.

One common belief was that intense pressure for energy conservation and environmental protection would make the small or light car the standard-size vehicle in all the world's auto markets. This would allow this type of car to become increasingly commoditized; all cars would be small and all would look pretty much alike, yielding the "world car."

A second assumption was that marketplace competition in this commoditized product would be based increasingly on price and that high manufacturing volume would be the key to low cost. Perhaps six "mega-producers" were to coalesce out of the 20 final assemblers in the Western world in a race to keep ahead in economies of scale. This would lead to a tight oligopoly for the entire automotive world similar to the former oligopoly of the "big three" in the United States.

Finally, manufacturing would shift from the developed countries to the less developed countries as automakers took advantage of lower wages to reduce manufacturing costs.

In the course of the Auto Program we have identified four factors that alter this vision of the future. These are the introduction of microprocessor-controlled flexible production methods, the ready availability of new product technologies, the perfection of a new system of social organization for the production process, and the failure of the world's auto purchasers to demand a single size and type of car.

Four Factors Shaping the Future

• New production hardware is already lowering the minimum efficient annual manufacturing scale for individual product lines in the auto industry and will lower it further in the future. For example, final-assembly plants were formerly most efficient when producing one model on a two-shift work schedule at a total volume of about 240,000 units per year. In the future, however, the increasing use of flexible automation able to assemble a wide range of products on the same line will mean that a plant may be highly efficient if the cumulative volume spread over several models is around 240,000. Thus, a producer with modest volume in several individual lines can offer these at a competitive cost, whereas until recently it appeared that a medium-sized or specialist producer's volume could support competition only on the basis of unique product attributes, since costs would inevitably be high. In addition, the new hardware on the plant floor, in combination with computer-aided design, engineering, and tooling, is reducing the total number of units of a given model that must be produced over its production life in order to recoup development costs. This dimension of receding scale economies also works to the benefit of the smaller producer. Volumes in the range of a half million units per year may continue to be essential in some mechanical components, such as engines, and smaller producers may have to team up with other assemblers to achieve the necessary volume of these items. However, scale requirements in general are no longer the driving force for industry concentration they have been in the past.

• New product technologies will mean not only that the automobile as the prime means of personal transport is not endangered but also that the range of automobiles that will seem "sensible" is much wider than was thought only a few years ago. Large fuel-efficient models will exist side by side with small fuel-efficient models, economical high-performance vehicles with utilitarian vehicles, and so forth. In addition, technical advances will permit greater safety and reduced emissions to meet society's requirements without requiring the repackaging of autos as small, uniform, Spartan boxes. Thus, commoditization is neither evident nor inevitable. In fact, the trend of the 1980s is in the opposite direction, toward many new product concepts and a proliferation of models.

• The social organization of the production process, long thought to be fully perfected and "rationalized" along classical Ford and Sloan lines, is now in dramatic flux in response to the Japanese innovations on the shop floor, in the supplier chain, and in the financial system. American and European responses to this challenge, as well as Japanese efforts to adapt their methods to production at foreign locations, are generating further organizational innovations and new ways of combining the elements of production that significantly reduce labor content and interim financing needs.

• The world's automotive markets are not demanding the same types of vehicles, as was widely predicted only recently. As shown in chapter 6, the European, North American, and Japanese markets continue to demand very different vehicle mixes even after two energy shocks. In addition, there is a continuing demand for differing design philosophies and product aesthetics, and consumers' interest in new product concepts is strong.

What these four factors create in combination is a new shape for the world auto industry that is quite different from the one widely forecast. "Shape" in this context means both the future structure of the industry— the number of producers and their internal organization—and the future geographic distribution of production.

The Future Structure of the Industry

Because of strong restraints on entry and exit, there are likely to be about as many automakers 20 years from now as today. Departures from the industry will be minimal for several reasons. The declining minimum efficient scale in manufacturing will give the medium-size and specialist producers a more level field on which to compete. The growing emphasis on product differentiation may even afford a competitive advantage to specialist producers who can achieve dominance in one or several of the many market niches that seem likely to develop. In addition, new forms of cooperation being developed among final assemblers will increase the survivability of specialists and medium-line producers.

Further, the present auto industry is the product of a rigorous selection process. All members of the industry today are "survivors" who were reasonably competitive before the late 1970s, who have recently rationalized their operations (BL and Chrysler), or who are proceeding with rationalizations (PSA and Fiat). Although some facilities may change ownership and other, obsolete facilities may be scrapped, the remaining assemblers are unlikely to simply disappear even if they make serious product errors or encounter more vigorous competition.

Most of the present competitors will be protected from precipitate collapse by their national governments or national financial systems. Only the General Motors and Ford operations in Europe are without a clear government or banker patron, and even in these cases European governments are likely to provide aid if large production cutbacks seem imminent. Though aid from governments and major financial institutions does not ensure long-term survival, it buys time for producers to adjust to new competitive threats and it blocks the opportunity for competitors to target faltering firms for quick elimination.

In addition, the support of automakers by governments and the financial system in the future is likely to be more sophisticated. It will look toward improving the operating performance of the troubled producer, perhaps by means of thoroughgoing rationalization or collaboration with another producer. This contrasts with the past tendency of bankers to seek a partner for a defensive merger (as in BL's many mergers during the 1960s and the PSA consolidation of Peugeot, Citroen, and Chrysler Europe) without demanding true rationalization and with the tendency of governments to buy time with loans to troubled producers without facing up to the hard realities of their situation (as in the case of the British government's dealings with BL between 1968 and 1978).

A declining minimum production scale, the small number of remaining merger candidates within each nation, political obstacles to transnational mergers, and cooperation between producers with offsetting competitive weaknesses will combine to keep the existing players in the game. A few mergers of the very weakest final assemblers with stronger firms are possible, but most of today's "household names" in the auto industry will be in business 20 years hence. GM may initiate new collaborations with a number of Japanese producers in different product lines and market segments; Ford may widen its collaboration with Toyo Kogyo; Chrysler may develop wide-ranging links with Mitsubishi or some other Japanese producer; BL may be more closely affiliated with Honda; Alfa Romeo and Volkswagen may broaden their contacts with Nissan; and so forth; however, these will continue to be independent firms cooperating on some ventures while competing in other markets.

Few if any new names will be added to the end-of-century list of assemblers. One reason is the very large initial investment, a figure swollen in recent years by the cost of regulatory and type certifications needed to market vehicles in each country. However, a much more important reason for a lack of entrants is the extreme difficulty of auto design and manufacture. The automobile is now so complicated that getting a new vehicle right generally takes several generations of product learning, even for an established manufacturer.

If entry were only a matter of lining up an adequate array of component suppliers, as in the 1920s, it might actually be much easier to break into the industry in the coming years, because suppliers are expected to become even more proficient at supporting the assemblers. However, the history of the auto industry over the past quarter-century is littered with the remains of would-be entrants who tried and failed at this approach even when they were able to offer distinctive products in relatively uncontested specialty niches. In each case the challenge of developing an adequate product backed up by an adequate sales-and-service network proved too difficult.

The entry challenge is also daunting for would-be entrants in the less developed countries and the Eastern bloc who are independent of the established multinational automakers. There have, of course, been a number of new entrants during the past 20 years in completely protected domestic markets where it would hardly be possible to fail. However, the real test of entry "success" is whether a new producer can also export, and practically all entrants have failed at this during the past 25 years. Examples include Hyundai in Korea and the many indigenous Eastern European producers such as Skoda in Czechoslovakia. They have experienced immense difficulties in developing an independent product (even when using components from established assemblers) and in updating their product line to meet changing market demands.

If they aim to participate in the auto industry outside their borders, automakers in the LDCs and Eastern bloc will need to affiliate with the established multinational assemblers, who can perform the role of systems integrator as well as orchestrate worldwide marketing and distribution. In return, of course, the multinational company will desire access to the home market for its manufacturing equipment, components, or finished units. This approach has recently been implemented in the Mitsubishi tie-up with Hyundai in Korea and the Suzuki collaboration with a small Indian producer, both of which call for the multinational company to promote exports of locally manufactured vehicles and also provide for use of the multinational's componentry and tooling in the production system and the vehicles of the domestic producer.

This is not to say that it is impossible for new entrants to join the world's assemblers during the next 20 years. However, any new assembler will almost certainly enter the industry as a supplier of a radical new component technology. It might then move up to assembly if its technology so redefines the product or the production system that it offers a competitive opening. Such an entrant could be the developer of techniques for fabricating bodies out of composites, or the perfecter of a new drive-train technology such as a new electric motor and battery combination or an internal-combustion engine fashioned out of ceramics or plastics. There is, however, only a low probability that this will occur.

Within the roster of the industry's familiar names today, the specialist and medium-line producers may well improve their positions. They will not need to merge to survive and would gain no advantage in doing so. Joint ventures and collaborations with other final assemblers on some components and product lines will, however, be essential.

The specialists' share of the total car market, especially on a value basis rather than a unit basis, may actually increase over the next 20 years at the expense of the current full-line producers, for several reasons. First, the minimum manufacturing scale for single body types is declining. Also, the development of many new product and process technologies is occurring in supplier firms who are eager and willing to sell to any assembler. This means that medium-line and specialist firms need not suffer production-cost penalties if they work out purchase or co-production arrangements for components still requiring high volume, and that they can keep up in both product and process technology. Second, a highly differentiated auto market offers specialist and medium-line producers an opportunity to find market niches where they can compete on the basis of a unique product or company image and where the mass-market producers may have difficulty competing precisely because they have a mass-market image. The mass-market producers are already aware of this problem and are attempting to give their lines more distinct images. For example, General Motors authorized the Pontiac Division to develop its Fiero sports car for exclusive divisional use. This was a departure from the GM practice of sharing body types across most of the five divisions. Pontiac hopes that the Fiero will help give its other products a distinctive, sporty image, perhaps making Pontiac the "Audi of General Motors."

It may be very difficult for highly centralized companies such as Ford, Toyota, and Renault to create truly distinctive products in their separate divisions to avoid the mass-market image that is so stigmatizing in a highly differentiated market. Today's mass-market producer may be pushed to become in effect a group of specialist companies with separate and more autonomous divisions for different kinds of cars.

Medium-line and specialist producers will also be helped in the years ahead by the arrangements recently developed to allow smaller producers to "buy in" major mechanical components to create a range of derivatives from a few basic models. Volvo, for example, has sufficient sales volume for economical in-house production of only a single engine family, an in-line 4-cylinder gasoline model. However, the growing popularity of diesels and the company's desire to offer a higher-performance version of what had been a rather staid product created a need for additional drive trains. In the past these might not have been available, since final assemblers typically did not sell engines to each other. However, in the mid 1970s Volvo joined a venture with Renault and PSA to manufacture and share the production of a higher-performance V-6 engine. Another arrangement with Volkswagen secures limited quantities of a 6-cylinder diesel. These arrangements have given Volvo a wide range of performance and fuel-efficiency options in exchange for only moderate direct investment and risk.

Cross-purchases of major components are not limited to the smaller producers. Nor will future commercial links between competitors stop with purchases of components. Indeed, it appears that new patterns of interaction among competitors will transform commercial strategies in the auto industry. This will be one of the most significant changes in the structure of the auto industry; the other will be the reorganization of the entire production chain.

A New Competitive Dynamic: Cooperation in the Context of Competition

Final assemblers cooperating on individual projects and product lines seem certain to remain strong competitors in other areas. This is because all companies will have competitive strengths, provided in some instances by their nationalities and production locations. They will also have competitive weaknesses. No competitor will be uniquely strong along every dimension, including products, production systems, and market placement and access. Therefore, there will be many new opportunities for competitors to bargain strengths and weaknesses.

New models, technologies, and core components will be developed jointly when such activities are marginal for several companies but make sense collectively, when no single company has the financial resources to undertake the project alone, and when no producer can gain sufficient scale in solo manufacture to make the project profitable. Early examples of this trend are the BL-Honda collaboration on the Project XX sedan (set for mid-1985 introduction), the PSA-Fiat collaboration on a new 4-cylinder gasoline engine, and the Volkswagen-Renault joint venture for a new 4-speed automatic gearbox.

Trade between producers in marginal product lines will increase. This will include license production and the "buying in" of fully built-up models and components in order to fill out product lines. Recent examples of trade in product lines include BL's purchase of tooling and licenses from Honda to produce the Triumph Acclaim, Chrysler's "buying in" the Mitsubishi Colt to fill out the bottom of its model line, Toyo Kogyo's manufacture of "Ford" cars for Far Eastern markets, and the Nissan–Alfa Romeo joint venture on the Arna car, which gives Nissan additional access to Europe and Alfa a broadened product range at low investment.

Current trading in core components includes Ford's purchase of diesel engines from BMW's venture in Austria and Chrysler's purchases of engines from Mitsubishi.

A broader cooperative trade will emerge in other areas of strength and weakness, such as the exchange of manufacturing know-how for market access and/or a broadened distribution system. Examples include the GM-Toyota joint venture at Fremont, California, the BL-Honda Project XX, and the production under license of the Volkswagen Santana by Nissan in Japan. Though the focus of each collaboration is a particular product, the objective for both parties is to obtain something of greater long-term use. For example, at Fremont Toyota wants to learn about manufacturing under American conditions while gaining broader access to the American market in case the import-restraint agreement of recent years becomes permanent. The joint venture permits Toyota to do this with a modest initial investment (because the car to be produced is an existing Toyota design) and at low risk since the cars produced at Fremont will carry a GM label and cannot harm Toyota's quality image if production problems develop. GM also has long-term aims: a demonstration plant for new manufacturing techniques to transplant to its other North American production facilities, and new products in the "light" market segment to sustain its market share and dealer network while the company works on new light cars of its own.

To reiterate, the pattern emerging from these sometimes confusing trades is cooperation between assemblers on individual projects or product lines in the context of continuing competition over the longer run and in the auto marketplace generally. Indeed, such cooperation in the short term will make continuing competition among a large number of final assemblers possible in the long term.

New Approaches to Organizing the Production Chain

As noted previously, auto production involves much more than the final assembler. Each product delivered to the consumer is a joint effort by thousands of suppliers, distributors, and financing sources whose actions must be tightly coordinated. This aspect of the industry's structure is also set for dramatic reorganization in the coming years. It will lead to less formal vertical integration but closer operational coordination among members of the production chain, with greater geographic concentration of production at the point of final assembly. This process will have several aspects.

For the final assembler, a new role is emerging. Traditionally, final assemblers in the United States and the full-line producers in Europe designed the product, manufactured nearly all the necessary core components such as engines and transmissions, and coordinated production. About half the value of the product was added in house, and the balance was provided by suppliers on an "arms length" basis. This meant that suppliers bid on individual parts from assemblers' drawings, contracted for their supply over short time periods, and were more or less on their own in handling financing, production engineering, and quality assurance. The final assembler's job was to select best bids and demand timely delivery at an acceptable level of quality.

The evolving role for the final assembler is as the coordinator of the increasingly intricate production system and the manager of large distribution systems. Final assemblers are now purchasing more core componentry, reducing vertical integration. At the same time they are working more closely with component suppliers to ensure that problems of financing, design, quality, and cost are tackled at the earliest opportunity and resolved cooperatively. In the past the attitude of the final assembler toward the supplier was often "Don't tell me about your problems, just deliver on time." Now, increasingly, the final assembler's posture is "Tell me about your problems at the outset so we can find solutions together."

This new approach among Western assemblers derives many of its features from the Japanese model. Typical elements are a smaller number of suppliers for each assembler, a striving to obtain specific parts from single sources, the development of longer-term and even open-ended associations with suppliers, and an effort to bring much of the production operation as close as possible to the point of final assembly to reduce inventories and identify quality problems immediately. The future structure of the supplier industry, as it will evolve in response to these trends, is visible when the types of components are assessed in terms of their probable sources (table 8.1).

Final assemblers will emerge as major suppliers of engines, drive trains, and even unassembled kits for complete cars to other final assemblers. These components will be manufactured adjacent to the final assembly point when used for the assembler's own finished products, and at a mutually convenient location when produced as a joint venture or bought in by another assembler. However, because these trends apply to new investment in an industry with a tremendous amount of sunk investment arranged in a very different pattern, the industry as a whole will assume the character described slowly.

Suppliers of vehicle systems will come increasingly to the fore. These companies specialize in pushing ahead technical frontiers in individual systems for increasingly modularized vehicle designs. Some current leaders in this area are Robert Bosch (West Germany), Nippondenso (Japan), and Bendix (U.S.), in such systems as fuel injection, engine management, and braking. These suppliers will serve many or all of the world's final assemblers, and will have close relationships with each of them in developing the dedicated systems needed for individual product lines. Production will be located near the point of final assembly when possible, though scale considerations may cause some system suppliers to continue with centralized manufacturing facilities. The lure of low-wage areas will not be great for these suppliers, because of the complex technology of the product and the production hardware.

Dedicated suppliers, tightly linked to though not necessarily legally integrated with a single final assembler, will increasingly emerge to supply minor and finish parts at the point of final assembly. Because many minor parts are made with relatively simple process technologies and high labor content, they are prime candidates for sourcing in low-

Table 8.1
Emerging structure of the automotive supplier industry by type of component

Type of component	Example	Emerging pattern of supply	Emerging pattern of production location
Major mechanicals	Engine, drive train	In house or joint venture with other final assemblers for basic engines; joint ventured or "bought in" in from other final assemblers for marginal engine lines	At point of final assembly when produced in house; at mutually convenient location when joint-ventured
Vehicle systems	Fuel/engine management, lighting, braking, suspension, steering, instrumentation	Specialist systems suppliers in the case of new technology components; in-house or bought from systems suppliers in the case of traditional-technology components	At supplier's centralized production location in the case of new-technology components where scale economies are important; at point of final assembly when supplier's scale economies permit and when no advantage is gained from low-wage production
Finish parts	Seats, dashboards, major stampings	In house or in close collaboration with suppliers	At point of final assembly
Minor parts	Fasteners, minor trim, glass, tires	"Bought in" from suppliers	At point of final assembly when production technology does not require very high scale or favor low-wage sites

wage countries. However, over the next 20 years, as flexible manufacturing is extended to these parts and the entire industry shifts toward a philosophy of manufacture at integrated final-assembly sites, it seems likely that minor parts suppliers will be closely linked to their assembler, as in the Japanese system, and will operate at the final assembly point. This is even more true of finish parts, whose fit and appearance is crucial. To ensure adequate quality, it seems certain that almost all of these parts will be made near the final-assembly plant.

As this grouping of suppliers develops, the supply system as a whole will exhibit a trait described earlier for relationships between the final assemblers: cooperation in the context of competition. Formal integration in the total production chain will decline (the more so under conditions of intense competition and rapid introduction of new technologies), yet operational coordination and cooperation within the production systems of the major assemblers will rise.

Final assemblers will themselves become major suppliers of components to other final assemblers, cooperating on component design and supply with many of the same firms they compete with for sales of finished units. A recent example is the agreement for BMW to supply Ford with 6-cylinder diesel engines for Lincoln models. Although Ford and BMW are competitors in the U.S. luxury market, Ford believed it could not sell enough diesels to justify producing them for internal use only. BMW lacked both a diesel model and the volume to justify the cost of designing and tooling for one on a solo basis. By signing a long-term agreement on engine supply, both Ford and BWM feel they have strengthened themselves against other competitors in the luxury segment.

The Future Geography of the World Auto Industry

A more concentrated and coordinated process of auto production does not imply any particular pattern of geographic distribution of production around the world. Production may well become more tightly concentrated at the point of final assembly. But where will final assembly occur?

Chapter 7 concluded that if decisions on production location are based on overall economic considerations, a very high proportion of auto production for all markets will continue to occur in the OECD countries. The advantages of low wages in the less developed countries do not offset the quality and coordination handicaps, the "country risk," and the use of many more hours of labor for most production steps. However, in practice, politics rather than economics will rule. LDCs with the prospect of rapid growth in their auto markets will require domestic manufacture at high local content or with a manufacturing trade balance in return for market access by the multinational producers. Many multinational companies have accepted and will accept these terms. Thus, auto production for much of the less developed world will occur in the individual LDCs. The trade-balancing or local-content needs of the multinational producers will produce substantial flows of components to the OECD countries as these LDC markets grow, but the LDC markets will also represent component-export opportunities for the OECD production locations.

Mexico provides an example of this process. Stringent trade-balancing requirements for each multinational producer, promulgated by Mexico in 1980, prompted several multinational assemblers to construct engine plants there. In addition, Ford has announced plans to construct a Mexican assembly plant for a new model in collaboration with Toyo Kogyo. In each case the output is principally earmarked for the North American market. In return, Ford and the other multinational automakers may increase their shipments to Mexico of other components.

The multinational assemblers in Mexico seem intent on meeting rather than exceeding their trade-balance requirements. This is only logical, since there is little economic advantage to Mexican production except in the cases of a few minor parts with high labor content. Thus, the net loss to the OECD countries so far is their relatively small export surplus in components to a number of LDC markets. For the future it is clear that the leverage LDC governments have in negotiating with the assemblers will depend on the size and growth prospects of their domestic markets. In particular, any demands that the multinational producers run large trade surpluses in finished automobiles and parts will quickly lead to an impasse in the absence of production cost savings.

A second type of impasse may develop, between governments in OECD countries with auto industries and LDC governments with automotive export ambitions. Thus far the developed countries have been receptive to increased automotive exports from Brazil, Mexico, and Korea, partly because auto exports help these countries manage their foreign debt burden. As the export volumes grow, however, OECD governments will balance progress in debt repayment against the effects of these exports on the health of OECD auto industries. The acceptable limit on LDC automotive imports may be reached rather quickly, particularly if export success in the LDCs is based largely on export incentives from governments.

Over the very long term, it seems certain that the collective auto markets of the nations currently classed as "less developed" will at some point exceed the size of the OECD auto market. If production for the LDC markets is required by their governments to be carried out within those markets, it follows that the majority of world auto production will at some point take place outside the OECD countries. However, as illustrated in chapter 5, this point is far beyond the time limits of this study. In the more immediate future, the pressing question is the location of production within the OECD countries.

Chapter 7 presented striking evidence of competitive imbalances within the OECD auto industry—imbalances that are closely associated with production location. Production systems in Japan were found to have large cost advantages and smaller quality advantages over other OECD production locations. The advantages are so great as to require rebalancing. One means of achieving this would be a massive relocation of productive capacity from the least to the most competitive locales, a catastrophic uprooting that would probably cause the elimination of a number of final assemblers and suppliers.

The evident need for a new balance and the dramatic consequences for nations, producers, and employees if it were to be achieved through production relocation has caused us to pay more attention to this issue than to any other concerning the future of the automobile and the auto industry. Logically, the OECD auto industry can be rebalanced in three ways. The least efficient producers at the least efficient production locations can be eliminated and their output transferred to the most competitive locations, or the OECD market can be divided by trade barriers so that less efficient producers will only compete with producers at the same or similarly competitive production locations, or national auto industries with competitive disadvantages can adapt and learn to catch up with the state of the art in competitive practice and reestablish a relative stability of market shares for the competing production locations.

The current imbalance will probably not be resolved through pure forms of any of these approaches. It is apparent from the recent behavior of governments in the Auto Program countries that nations with major auto industries will not, despite occasional vacillation, allow their rapid transfer over the short term to foreign locales. It is equally apparent that over the longer term the degree of structural integration of the

OECD economies makes it difficult for governments, even if they so desire, to hermetically insulate their auto industries from competitive threats by superior foreign-based producers. In addition, there is no reason why auto production in each of the current OECD production centers is inherently unviable in the long term. Considerable amounts of organizational knowledge must be transferred, considerable restructuring must occur, and in some cases wages and other social costs must be adjusted. However, it is clear that adjustment has already begun.

Thus, it seems most likely that a rebalancing of competitiveness in the OECD auto industry will occur but that the process will be gradual, as it has been during past periods of competitive imbalance. The consequences for the location of auto production will depend mainly on the speed with which the less competitive producers adapt and learn. If they adapt slowly or stagnate they will lose all their export markets. Quite possibly they will cede a slowly growing share of their domestic market as well, as they come under increasing pressure from domestic critics and superior foreign producers to change their techniques in the direction of best practice (often by use of foreign components). If they adapt quickly, a rough competitive balance will be restored with limited loss of world market share. The critical question, therefore, is how, and how rapidly, national industries with competitive disadvantages can catch up.

How National Industries Can Catch Up

There are three principal means by which a national auto industry with competitive weaknesses can regain lost ground. Put simply, these are copying, collaboration, and substitution.

Copying the best-practice techniques of the leaders is the most obvious way to catch up. When this involves only installing comparable production machinery, introducing of a new model range, or adjusting wage levels, it can, in principle, be accomplished rapidly. However, as shown in chapter 7, the current competitive imbalance has little to do with differences in production hardware or the available model mix. It involves a productivity gap so great that wage adjustments alone cannot eliminate the differences in production cost and product quality. What is needed is an entirely new approach to the overall production system.

Other production systems may be very difficult to copy quickly by observation from a distance, particularly when those being copied refuse to freeze their own pace of innovation. Thus, it is not surprising that many collaborations between final assemblers have been announced since the current imbalance became visible in 1979. The BL–Honda venture, perhaps the pacesetter, shows the bartering of strengths and weaknesses that is the essence of this approach. BL needed new models to fill out its product line. It also needed to obtain them without enormous capital expenditure and to undergo an intense learning exercise in the fine points of production engineering and manufacturing systems. Honda was in an excellent position to provide these things. In return, the venture addressed Honda's key weakness in market access, because the jointly developed and produced vehicles could gain entry to European markets in which Japanese home-based exports were capped.

Although many casual observers have assumed that such collaborative efforts are logically the first steps toward a merger or a buyout, this is not true. BL, for example, has made great progress in strengthening its product line and improving its overall production system. As the company grows stronger, it is less rather than more interested in seeking a merger partner. As competitors across the world auto industry progressively bargain strengths for weaknesses, the viability of each of the existing producers may increase.

An alternative or supplement to copying and collaboration is substitution, the direct investment by more efficient producers in new production facilities in the home markets of weaker producers. Many initiatives of this type are also underway. To the extent that producers with superior production systems can replicate their advantages in new locales, this has a double effect: It substitutes superior systems for some existing production capacity, and it has a dramatic demonstration effect on existing production systems.

The Nissan plant at Smyrna, Tennessee, and the Honda plant at Marysville, Ohio, demonstrate both effects. Honda and Nissan believe that with a new approach to auto production at a new site, they can dramatically reduce the labor content and improve the quality of American automotive production. To the extent that they succeed, they will increase their market shares at the expense of other domestic producers. At the same time, the example of Nissan and Honda in developing an entire production system with adjacent supplier plants organized for just-in-time delivery produces a vivid demonstration effect for the rest of U.S. auto industry. When and if successfully implemented, such plants will vitiate the familar arguments among managers and workers in existing facilities that the success of foreign automakers is based on cultural or site-specific factors.

The Prospect for a New Equilibrium

There is ample evidence that a vast process of copying, collaboration, and substitution is under way. General Motors, at its Buick City complex in Flint, Michigan, is consciously copying Toyota City in Nagoya by placing many elements of the auto-production system in close physical proximity. Ford and Toyo Kogyo, General Motors and Toyota, Volkswagen and Nissan, Alfa Romeo and Nissan, and BL and Honda are collaborating on new models and production facilities. Honda and Nissan have taken the bold step of direct investment in new production facilities in the United States. Nissan is also investing in the United Kingdom, where it has promised to increase local content to 80 percent by 1991.

As shown above and in chapter 7, there is nothing inherent in the present imbalance that bars the attainment of a new competitive equilibrium in the OECD auto industry at very nearly the present distribution of national shares of total production. However, it is too soon to tell whether the trend is in this direction. The most interesting copying, the most thoroughgoing collaborations, and the most dramatic direct investments, such as those of Nissan in the United Kindgom, either are still in the planning stage or have been commenced so recently that no results are in.

Because the present competitive gap between the best Japanese producers and the weakest Western producers is so great, and because the process of adjustment by its nature will require many years to complete, it is evident that the potential for dramatic shifts in share among national auto industries and for disaster for individual producers will persist for many years. To make matters worse, the adjustment process will proceed in a macroeconomic environment that is likely to be only marginally better than that of the period since 1973. Thus, it seems certain that the process of adjustment will continue to provoke trade tensions between the OECD governments even if learning and adaptation by the weaker companies and countries is rapid. In addition, the simultaneous introduction of new process technologies will create continuing dilemmas for the automotive work force, even in the most competitive national auto industries.

Labor Relations and Employment Adjustments

In each of the Auto Program countries the automobile industry employs a significant share of the national work force. The dramatic worldwide changes in the industry will affect these workers in coming decades. The many changes the industry is undergoing will also affect the structures and roles of automobile trade unions and may bring about far-reaching changes in industrial-relations systems. Conversely, trade union action inside and outside existing industrial-relations institutions will have an important effect on the course and the results of restructuring in the auto industry. These circumstances require us to look at automobile industrial relations from two perspectives: as a conditioner of industrial change and as a system that must respond and adapt to industrial change.

Output and Employment, 1970–1981

The importance of the motor vehicle industry as a major employer is even greater when the "multiplier effect" of this employment is taken into account, as illustrated in chapter 1. Moreover, auto-industry jobs have paid well historically in comparison with other industrial jobs in the Auto Program countries. Will the automobile industry continue to be the provider of a significant number of well-paying jobs? Our answer to this question is a qualified yes. Employment projections, discussed in more detail later, suggest that the auto industry will remain a major source of employment in the seven countries. Furthermore, these jobs are likely to continue to pay better than national mean earnings. The qualifications are twofold. First, it appears that the auto industry's historical role over the postwar period as a provider of new jobs is ended. Sales and productivity trends imply that total auto-industry employment in the Auto Program countries in the 1990s will be significantly below recent levels. Second, declining employment and strong international competition will press the industry to moderate the growth in compensation of auto-industry employees. As a result, in the 1990s auto workers' earnings will probably be much closer to the earnings received by workers in other industries.

To get some perspective on future trends in auto-industry employment, it is useful to look back at changes in employment over the 1970s (table 9.1). Differences between countries in the amount of secondary employment in the supplier sectors included in these figures keep them from being strictly comparable across countries but they are useful for tracking employment trends over time. Combined blue-collar and white-collar employment in the motor vehicle industries of the seven Auto Program countries did not change much from 1970 to 1981 even though total motor vehicle production in 1981 was 19 percent higher than in 1970.[1] During this period there was modest general growth in employment between 1970 and 1973, a 12 percent general decline during the recession of 1973–1975, further modest growth during 1976–1978, and sharp employment declines in Britain and the United States after 1979.

By 1981, employment in the British and American motor vehicle industries stood at 68 percent and 91 percent of 1970 levels, respectively. These trend figures, however, understate the enormous magnitude of the employment declines that occurred in these countries after 1979. From 1979 to 1981, auto employment in the two countries declined, respectively, 23 and 26 percent. The decline steepened from 1981 through mid 1983, followed by a moderate upturn. This suggests that it is important to distinguish between the early to mid 1970s and the late 1970s to the early 1980s. In the first period, even in the face of sharp cyclical movements, employment levels and shares across the seven countries remained remarkably stable (tables 9.1 and 9.2). In the late 1970s and the early 1980s, however, this stability seemed to end as international competition intensified and certain countries (Britain and the United States in particular) faced heavy competitive challenges.

The Japanese auto industry's share of total auto-sector employment in the Auto Program countries was stable through the 1970s in spite of the steady advance in Japan's share of auto production (table 9.3). This growth in market share, unaccompanied by growth in employment share, signals Japan's enormous relative advance in productivity.

Output and employment data can be combined to indicate trends in output per employee. The figures in table 9.4 are not adjusted for

Table 9.1
Employment in the motor vehicle and equipment industry in Auto Program countries (thousands)

	1970	1973	1975	1978	1979	1980	1981
U.S.	799.0	976.0	792.0	977.1	982.2	773.8	723.2
Japan	580.0	634.4	601.2	637.8	651.3	682.8	704.3
European Auto Program countries	1899.5	2007.5	1844.2	2000.1	2008.9	1963.3	1853.1
W. Ger.	605.7	625.4	566.3	650.2	673.3	684.1	670.0
France	476.4	528.5	507.4	534.1	523.5	503.0	505.2
U.K.	512.4	510.0	457.1	471.3	456.7	424.0	347.7
Italy	(258.8)	290.1	252.6	282.2	289.3	285.1	269.5
Sweden	46.2	53.5	60.8	62.3	66.1	67.1	60.7
Auto Program total	3278.5	3617.9	3237.4	3615.0	3642.4	3419.9	3280.6

Notes:
These figures include blue- and white-collar employment in the component industry and correspond to NACE 35 (OECD classification) and SIC 371 in the U.S. The series for W. Germany, France, and Italy are not strictly comparable over time. In Italy, component production was not included before 1972 in reported statistics. The 1970 and 1971 figures for Italy were estimated from available data.
Sources:
Some of the European data are from *Tatsachen und Zahlen aus der Kraftverkehrswirtschaft*, Verbank der Automobilindustrie (VDA), Frankfurt, West Germany. Additional European data and data for Japan are from the country reports in "Industrial Relations in the World Automobile Industry—The Experience of the 1970s", Wolfgang Streeck and Andreas Hoff, eds., Science Center, Berlin, 1982. The U.S. data are from *Employment and Earnings*, Bureau of Labor Statistics, U.S. Department of Labor, various years.

Table 9.2
Shares of total motor vehicle employment of each Auto Program country, in percent

	1970	1973	1975	1978	1979	1980	1981
U.S.	24.4	27.0	24.5	27.0	27.0	22.6	22.0
Japan	17.7	17.5	18.6	17.7	17.9	20.0	21.5
Europe	57.9	55.5	57.0	55.3	55.1	57.4	56.5
W. Ger.	18.5	17.3	17.5	18.0	18.5	20.0	20.4
France	14.5	14.6	15.7	14.8	14.4	14.7	15.4
U.K.	15.6	14.1	14.1	13.0	12.5	12.4	10.6
Italy	7.9	8.0	7.8	7.8	7.9	8.3	8.2
Sweden	1.4	1.5	1.9	1.7	1.8	2.0	1.9
Auto Program total	100.0	100.0	100.0	100.0	100.0	100.0	100.0

Source:
Table 9.1

Table 9.3
Shares of total motor vehicle unit output of each Auto Program country, in percent

	1970	1973	1975	1978	1979	1980	1981
U.S.	34.4	40.3	35.3	39.0	35.4	27.1	27.4
Japan	21.9	22.6	27.3	27.0	29.7	37.3	38.6
Europe	43.7	37.1	37.4	34.0	35.0	35.6	34.0
W. Ger.	15.9	12.6	12.6	12.6	13.1	13.1	13.5
France	10.4	10.2	11.2	10.6	11.1	11.4	10.4
U.K.	8.5	6.9	6.5	4.9	4.6	4.6	4.1
Italy	7.6	6.2	5.7	5.0	5.0	5.4	5.0
Sweden	1.3	1.2	1.4	0.9	1.1	1.0	1.1
Total	100.0	100.0	100.0	100.0	100.0	100.0	100.0

Source:
VDA

Table 9.4
Growth in units producted per hour worked 1970–72 to 1980–81

	Index
United States	91
Japan	166
West Germany	104
France	124
United Kingdom	84
Italy	84
Sweden	81

Notes:
These figures are indices of units produced per hour worked in the years 1980–1981 compared with 1970–1972. Average values for a span of years are used in these calculations to reduce the effect of cyclical fluctuations and statistical errors. The figures measure growth in each country over the period and do not provide a basis for cross-country comparisons. At any point in time, the countries differed in how close to full capacity auto producers were operating. By measuring vehicle output, these figures also ignore changes in value added per vehicle, which may be significant. Nonetheless, the figures are consistent with the data reported in chapter 7 and provide further indications that sizable relative improvements in productivity occurred in Japan in the 1970s.
Sources: The indices were derived from data in the sources described in the notes to table 9.1.

changes in vehicle mix or complexity, which may explain the poor standing of Sweden where value added per vehicle increased significantly over the 1970s. Thus, they should not be interpreted as measures of productivity in the traditional sense. Nonetheless, the figures illustrate that Japan's growth of 66 percent in units produced per hour worked from 1970 to 1980 significantly exceeded the growth in all other countries. Furthermore, evidence that Japan has gained relatively in product quality and value per car suggests that these figures understate Japan's true productivity growth.

Forecasting Future Auto-Industry Employment

The crucial ingredients needed to derive employment projections for the auto industry are predictions of changes in motor vehicle demand and productivity. Our employment forecasts are based on the demand projections in chapter 5. The employment projections (table 9.5) assume

Table 9.5
Employment, actual and projected (thousands)

	1979	1990	2000
United States	982.2	778.1	596.4
European Auto Program countries	2008.9	1591.4	1219.9
Japan	651.3	525.4	463.3
Auto Program Country Total	3642.4	2894.9	2279.6

Notes:
The employment figures represent blue- and white-collar employment, using the 1979 figures reported in Table 9.1. The following additional assumptions were utilized:
• 4% annual growth in labor productivity;
• Japan's home market grows at 1% per year;
• Japan's market share in North America and Europe rises from 11.5% in 1979 to 13.0% in 1980 and beyond;
• Japan's market share in LDCs rises from 26.6% in 1979 to 28.0% in 1980 and beyond;
• There is no change in the market shares between the U.S. and European MHNs;
• A total world output volume of 41.3 million units is assumed for 1979. Production in Japan, U.S. and Europe in 1979 is 32.0 million (the difference is CPE and LDC production). The 1990 and 2000 employment projections utilize the Auto Program production estimates of total world car and truck output of 51.2 million units in 1990 and 66.8 million units in 2000 (table 5.7).

labor productivity will grow 4 percent per year. This rate may prove to be conservative because of the production advances discussed in chapter 6. Higher productivity growth in any one country will lead to improved international competitiveness, increased sales, and stable or higher employment in that country. Higher productivity growth across all the Auto Program countries will have complex net effects on total employment. Fewer labor hours per vehicle will be offset to a modest extent by increased automobile sales due to lower prices.

Assumptions about future market shares (table 9.5) were also required. Although changes in these assumptions affect the specific magnitude of the employment projections, the general size and course of employment will not be strongly altered by reasonable alternative assumptions. In these calculations the assumed 1979 blue-collar and white-collar employment figures are taken from table 9.1 and include parts production as well as assembly operations. Of course, a broader definition including the total labor input into materials (such as steel) plus energy inputs would yield larger employment estimates.

The figures suggest that employment in the motor vehicle industry in the Auto Program countries is likely to decline significantly in the long run from the peak reached in the late 1970s. In our forecast employment drops 21 percent below 1979 levels by 1990 and a further 21 percent between 1990 and 2000. Thus employment is likely to decline by 37 percent, a total of 1,362,800 jobs, between 1979 and the year 2000. This is likely to occur even as auto demand in the seven countries grows by 30 percent (table 5.3). Such gloomy employment forecasts inevitably provoke questions about the influence of industrial relations on industry competitiveness. One question is whether the successful conduct of labor relations can and will confer a competitive advantage that countries will be able to use to expand their shares of the world auto market. Another question is whether and how industrial-relations systems can adjust to declining employment levels.

Contributions of Industrial-Relations Systems to International Competitiveness

Labor-relations systems have only recently been recognized as powerful contributors to the efficiency and competitiveness of national auto industries. In times of growth, attention was focused on other aspects of the auto-production system. The second oil shock, however, highlighted advantages of the Japanese labor-relations system and raised doubts about the structural soundness of some of the Western automobile industries—particularly about their conduct of labor-management relations. In addition, industrial-relations systems came under pressure in some countries when companies responding to the crisis attempted to push back the influence of organized labor.

What is the structure of the Japanese industrial-relations system, and how does it compare with those in the West? What is it about the Japanese industrial relations system that facilitates flexible manpower deployment and adjustment? The striking success of the Japanese production system has thrust these questions to center stage.

The Japanese Labor-Relations System

In Japan's automobile industry, lifetime employment commitments are made to the permanent employees of the major producers. Fluctuations in factory output are compensated through the heavy use of overtime, adjustments in temporary or secondary employment, and the reassignment of permanent workers to new jobs, work areas, or corporate affiliates.[2] Extensive career planning and guidance are provided to workers as part of this system.

Although lifetime employment is a principle that companies try to adhere to, no explicit legal or contractual guarantees are provided. Severe financial reverses have caused some companies outside the auto industry that were previously dedicated to lifetime employment to dismiss workers, and this could presumably happen in the auto industry if export markets were to be cut off and one or more producers faced a financial crisis. During the only auto industry crisis of recent years, however, at Toyo Kogyo in the mid 1970s, the company maintained the lifetime employment principle even while reducing its workforce from 37,000 to 27,000 over several years. It did this through attrition and transfer of workers to other jobs, particularly in its auto sales network. No workers were involuntarily terminated, indicating that a very severe crisis would be needed to force abandonment of the lifetime employment principle. Thus far the Japanese motor vehicle industry as a whole has had a relatively high cyclical correspondence between output and employment. Employment in the primary companies has not been threatened, however, because cyclical fluctuations have been small and shifts in output have been buffered by reduction of overtime and the adjustment of temporary or seasonal employment.

Wages are influenced strongly by seniority, modified by consideration of individual skill levels. In addition, significant annual bonuses are tied to the company's performance and partially to individual merit evaluations. In this way workers are paid chiefly on the basis of who they are rather than what they do. Payment systems are not used as a mechanism to motivate job performance; for this, other social controls (mostly informal) are used. Wage setting at the company level is linked through pattern following to the "spring offensive" national wage negotiations.

Generous training is provided to workers, and internal promotion is used as a chief source of skill generation. Japanese employers make large investments in on-the-job training, and workers are expected to learn more than the job they are performing at a given time. Provisions are made for job rotation, the learning of multiple skills, and lifelong learning. The tremendous on-the-job human-capital investment made in workers in the primary firms is tied to the lifetime employment principle, which helps keep workers in the firm after they receive valuable training.

Extensive consultation occurs through labor-management committees and shop-floor quality circles. By Western standards this consultation is extremely informal, though there are some contractually defined mechanisms. Relatively little recourse is made to written or judicial procedures to resolve labor-management disagreements.

Union representation in Japan is enterprise-based and linked to an industrywide federation of unions. Both white-collar and blue-collar workers belong to the same enterprise unions.

From a Western point of view many of these features might appear inefficient and "pre-modern." For example, Western economists might see employment commitments as creating costly rigidities that make adaptation to changing external conditions difficult if not impossible. Yet the Japanese experience suggests that such commitments ease workers' fears that efficiency will bring redundancy. In combination with intensive training and more flexible work rules, employment commitments also appear to facilitate flexible production arrangements such as making several models on the same line, speedy rescheduling and retooling, and attention to quality.

Similarly, in isolation a seniority-based wage system might appear to be poorly suited to motivating workers. However, because it reduces the need to reevaluate jobs or renegotiate pay rates when technology changes or workers are temporarily reassigned, this wage system contributes to high performance and adaptability.

In summary, the elements of the Japanese industrial-relations system fit together in a remarkably efficient and adaptive way. Furthermore, part of this efficiency appears to derive from the fact that Japanese workers are ready to accept technological innovations, retraining, and redeployment while maintaining a strong commitment to quality.

Clearly, the superior competitiveness of the Japanese auto industry is not accounted for by these institutional factors alone. Relatively low compensation costs also make an important contribution (table 9.6).[3] In 1981, Japan's hourly compensation costs were 44 percent of those in the United States and significantly below those of Germany, Sweden, and France. Although Japan's costs moved a bit closer to those in the West between 1975 and 1981 and reached those in Italy and the United Kingdom, the ranking of the countries was constant between the two periods.

When addressing compensation issues it is important to consider the standing of auto workers' compensation with respect to the earnings of other industrial workers within each country (table 9.7). In all the

Table 9.6
Hourly compensation costs for production workers in motor-vehicle and equipment industry

	1975			1981		
	U.S. dollars	Index (U.S. = 100)	National currency units per U.S. dollar	U.S. dollars	Index (U.S. = 100)	National currency units per U.S. dollar
United States	9.44	100	—	17.55	100	—
West Germany	7.68	81	2.46	12.89	73	2.25
Sweden	7.44	79	4.14	11.50	66	5.04
France	5.22	55	4.28	9.20	52	5.41
Italy	5.10	54	652.4	7.86	45	1,131
United Kingdom	3.96	42	0.45	7.83	45	0.49
Japan	3.56	38	296.7	7.74	44	220.1

Note:
These figures include an assessment of the cost of fringe benefits as well as wages, bonuses, and deferred compensation. The figures are from an unpublished series prepared by the Office of Productivity and Technology, U.S. Department of Labor, B.L.S. These figures cover the industry as a whole and not just the main assemblers, though the degree of vertical integration covered is not identical in each country.

Table 9.7
Ratio of average hourly earnings in motor-vehicle industry versus average hourly earnings in all private industry (for production workers), 1970 and 1980

	1970	1980
United States	1.310	1.485
West Germany	1.198	1.208
France	1.248	1.157
Italy	1.323	1.005
United Kingdom	1.339	1.086
Japan	1.130	1.231
Sweden	1.190	1.050

The data for France, West Germany, Italy, and the U.K. come from Eurostat's harmonized series of hourly earnings. The authors are grateful to David Marsden for assisting in the interpretation of these data. U.S. data are from *Employment and Earnings*, U.S. Department of Labor, B.L.S. (calculated).
The data for Japan compare average earnings of production workers in the auto industry to earnings in all manufacturing industries (and not *all* private industry).

Auto Program countries, auto workers earn more on average than other production workers. However, the relative earnings of auto workers in Italy and the United Kindgom fell markedly in the 1970s, fell moderately in France and Sweden, remained constant in West Germany, rose moderately in Japan, and rose signficantly in the United States. The declines in Italy and the United Kingdom are quite significant, especially since interindustry earnings in Western countries were stable generally in the postwar years.[4] The relative wage declines in the United Kingdom were associated with significant employment declines (table 9.1), although in Italy relative wages fell over the 1970s even though there was no employment decline until the early 1980s.

The rise in the earnings of U.S. auto workers relative to other U.S. industrial workers over the 1970s can be attributed in part to the cost-of-living escalator in the United Auto Workers' contracts. This formula shielded auto workers from the real wage declines imposed on many U.S. workers in the 1970s as a result of higher energy prices prices and inflation. The wage concessions at Chrysler, GM and Ford in the early 1980s (detailed in Appendix C) produced a fall in relative pay for auto workers of a few percentage points but did not significantly alter the high relative standing of their earnings.

The broad implication of these figures is that Japan's compensation costs continue to pose a severe challenge to certain of the Western

producing nations. Because of labor's large contribution to auto production costs, significant productivity differentials would be needed to
outweigh Japan's labor cost advantage. At the same time, data presented
earlier in this chapter and in chapter 7 suggest that Japan has been
achieving relative productivity advances that make the compensation-
cost differentials even more troublesome for many Western producers.

The Western Labor-Relations Systems

The Western industrial-relations systems differ greatly. Each is a particular blend of culture, formal law, organizational structure, and substantive policies (both public and private). Each is called upon to deal
with a range of issues: the determination of wages and working conditions, shop-floor arrangements, skill development, and the terms and
extent of worker and union involvement in decision making.

A critical feature of each industrial-relations system is the structure
of union representation. Three general patterns of representation exist
in the motor vehicle industries within the major Western auto-producing
nations. The first is that found in the United States, where only one
union (the UAW) organizes auto workers (although in recent years
there is an increasing non-union sector). Bargaining takes place with
individual companies at the national level. Supplementary bargaining
at the plant level covers seniority systems and some work rules. However, the national offices of both the UAW and the auto companies try
to keep variations between plants within close limits. Differences between companies in wages and work rules also have been limited by
the established system of pattern bargaining.

A second system is found in West Germany and Sweden, where auto
workers are represented by industrial unions that cover the entire
metalworking industry. Their sectoral interests are mediated through
internal compromises, although auto workers generally hold a strong
position in these unions. Collective bargaining takes place at the national
level in Sweden. In West Germany bargaining is formally at the regional
level, but in fact it is controlled and coordinated by the national executives of the union and the employers association. Volkswagen, which
as a semipublic enterprise is not eligible to join an employers association,
has an independent company agreement. In West German companies
there are also legally constituted works councils that are formally independent of the union. They carry out day-to-day discussions and
bargaining with management on work-force deployment and other

personnel policies. The rights of the works councils were expanded considerably in 1972. In Sweden, committees on working conditions, safety, and similar subjects are set up jointly by employers and unions; their number was increased considerably during the 1970s. In some respects they perform functions similar to those of the German works councils. In both countries, there is also trade-union representation on the boards of big companies.

The third industrial-relations pattern is followed in France, Italy, and Great Britain, where auto workers in the same plant are organized by more than one union. In France and Italy, unions are split along political or ideological lines and some include workers not only from the auto industry but from other metalworking industries. In Great Britain a variety of unions exist. Some are very narrowly based craft unions, while others extend even outside the metalworking sector. There is extensive interunion competition in France and Britain. In France, where union representation at the workplace traditionally has been weak, there is no supplementary shop-floor bargaining. In Britain and Italy, shop stewards are (or used to be) at the core of union power, so company and workplace bargaining play a much more important role in these countries. This decentralization of bargaining in Britain and Italy has led to a high incidence of industrial conflicts and stoppages, often unofficial. At British Leyland, where bargaining historically took place at individual plants and workshops, management succeeded during the 1970s in shifting collective bargaining to the company level.

Institutional rules governing employment also vary widely. In countries such as Germany and Sweden, accommodation to output variations is commonly made by reduction of hours or by reassignment. The institutional system of worker participation in these countries, encouraged by federal co-determination laws, plays an integral role in the negotiations that achieve these adjustments. In contrast, the seniority and unemployment-insurance systems in the United States are institutional structures that facilitate the use of layoffs in response to changes in output.

The differences between countries in comparative compensation costs should not be allowed to mask a common attribute of wage systems in the West. In contrast with Japan, wages in the Western systems are closely tied to specific jobs by piece-rate systems and scientific management techniques such as job evaluation. The actual negotiation of wage levels in each country, however, is linked to union representation and jurisdiction patterns. Sweden, the United States, and Germany provide examples of highly centralized wage agreements. In Britain, wages traditionally have been heavily influenced by shop-floor negotiations, though recently there has been a shift to more bargaining at the company level.

Related to the close tie that exists between wages and job content is the fact that skill development is much less career-oriented in the West than it is in Japan. In the West, greater use is made of external recruitment and less emphasis is given to the development of skills through on-the-job training and career planning.

The extent and form of worker participation in decision making varies extensively in the West, from the German system of co-determination to the American practice of very limited direct employee participation. Some of these variations among countries arise from differences in the ways governments regulate labor relations. For example, in the United States federal labor laws emphasize procedural rather than substantive regulation, leaving it to labor and management to decide labor's role in decision making; in Germany, on the other hand, federal legislation has encouraged the development of a co-determination system that has markedly increased labor's involvement in corporate decision making.

The varied industrial-relations systems of the Western auto industries have come under strong pressure in recent years. Western auto producers are facing a number of significant challenges with important consequences for the design of work-rule and compensation systems and the conduct of labor relations.

One challenge is posed by the new manufacturing technologies, which require greater coordination across work groups and more flexibility in labor allocation. The new production technology has altered and eventually may abolish traditional distinctions between occupations and jobs, most notably between skilled maintenance workers (such as fitters and electricians) and direct production workers. The new technology also requires more mobility of workers between different jobs. Both labor and management are challenged to develop compensation and work-rule systems that suit the new technologies in a manner that avoids costly industrial conflict.

Another challenge arises from the vital role that quality now plays in the competition among automobile producers. Quality in automobiles is partly a function of production hardware. Yet there is a limit to what technology alone can achieve if the workers do not play an active role in quality improvement. Labor and management must create incentives and motivational systems that encourage this heightened quality consciousness.

This transition to new compensation and work-rule systems is made particularly difficult by the environment of employment contraction forecast above. The existing work force will resist outside recruitment as a source of skill generation and will push for greatly expanded and intensified internal training.

Other problems result from the parallel changes in the industry's structure. In earlier chapters it was argued that vertical integration of assembler firms will decline and that joint production arrangements between producers and across national boundaries will grow. But these shifts in the industry's structure may conflict with the needed changes in labor systems caused by the new technologies and the need for heightened quality consciousness. For example, increased internal training may be hampered by the simultaneous need for organizational and industry restructuring which cuts across established union jurisdictions.

On the positive side, the new corporate entities created by these changes may be useful development and testing grounds for new labor-relations practices. Innovative organizational practices often gestate in such new businesses. But will labor and management view these entities as testing grounds? And how can a healthy interaction between in-novative and traditional areas of the industry be encouraged?

The structural differences among Western industrial-relations systems seem to bear on their responsiveness to industrial change. The two indicative factors seem to be the presence of worker participation in decision making at the company level and the existence of industrial unionism at the higher sectoral level.

Company-level worker participation permits the expression and rep-resentation of the interests of the work force of a given company as a whole; in this respect, it serves some of the functions of the enterprise union in Japan. It is important to note that worker participation at the company level and workers' control on the shop floor tend to be in-compatible; where one exists, the other is likely to be absent (consider Sweden and Germany on the one hand, the United Kindgom and Italy on the other). This is not surprising, since shop-floor control tends to emphasize the specific interests of individual sections of the work force at the expense of the company's long-term economic viability.

The second factor that distinguishes between more or less cooperative systems of industrial relations is whether there is only one trade union for the metalworking industries representing all workers regardless of sector, skill, and occupation. Such unions (which exist in Sweden and Germany) are as a rule less antagonistic toward industrial change because they represent other industries besides auto manufacturing. They are not bound to the interests of particular skills and occupations, and since they have no competitors they can safely trade off the short-term interests of specific groups of members for the conservation of broader gains.

Where metalworking-industry unionism and institutionalized worker participation at the company level come together, one would expect the labor-relations system to be more responsive to the need for change. There should also be relatively strong identification of workers with their company, resulting in high acceptance of technological change and flexible work organization, and a high commitment to quality. This describes the circumstances in Sweden and West Germany, which have been the most successful Western automobile-producing countries in international competition.

Resistance to change should be strongest in systems that combine competitive multi-unionism with "sectional" shop-floor autonomy and effective challenges to management's "right to manage." The principal example here, at least for most of the 1960s and the 1970s, was the United Kingdom. Italy also had considerable shop-floor autonomy after 1969, little or no institutionalized participation at the company level, a union structure that was only somewhat more unified than that in Britain, and severe competitive problems.

No country in the West has attempted to emulate the Japanese system of enterprise unionism, and none is likely to. On the other hand, in response to the economic pressures of the 1970s there was a remarkable growth in almost all of the Auto Program countries of institutions for consultation, bargaining, and participation at the company level. In the United States there was extensive experimentation with participation programs and information sharing at both the plant level and the company level. The most visible such event was the election of the president of the UAW to Chrysler's board of directors. Significant changes were also underway in Sweden and West Germany. Developments within the United States, West Germany, and the United Kingdom are described in more detail in appendix C.

Potential Patterns in the Development of Industrial Relations in the West

The impressive success of the Japanese has led many in the West to argue that their own industrial-relations systems should be reshaped to imitate Japanese practices. The lifetime-employment system and the use of quality circles have been singled out for much praise and some emulation.

The difficulty with adopting individual Japanese practices is that the various features of an industrial-relations system interact with one another and may not be separable from other features of the total system. For instance, the method of setting pay interacts with the union representation structure (enterprise-based bonuses are supported by the system of enterprise-based unions in Japan) and also with the form of worker participation. Even if they chose to, it may not be possible for Western producers and unions to adopt Japanese industrial-relations practices in a piecemeal fashion.

It is also unclear to what extent the Japanese industrial-relations system is determined by and demands particular Japanese cultural attributes. The origins of the Japanese system are complex, involving cultural and historical factors whose relative importance is extremely difficult to weigh. Although culture undoubtedly played a role, recent research suggests that historical factors were a significant influence in the 1950s when much of the present Japanese system was put in place.[5] Pivotal events in that period included the long strike at Nissan and the restructuring of the union movement which included a replacement of radical leadership. This historical perspective suggests that the industrial-relations system in Japan's auto industry comprises a set of institutions successfully introduced in a period of crisis and not strictly determined or bound by cultural traditions. Consistent with this view is the fact that not all Japanese industry follows this labor-relations pattern. In Japan's public sector there are militant unions and an industrial-relations pattern that looks more like the unionism found in the United Kingdom and the United States than the enterprise unionism of Japan's auto industry.

Although the flexibility and efficiency of Japanese industrial relations are admirable, there are features of the system that Western countries would not wish to emulate. One is the high degree of sex segregation within the Japanese production system. Women are not found in the ranks of lifetime employees of the major companies. Also, some of the supplier or "secondary" firms within Japan's auto industry have employment conditions that fall far below the high standards of the major firms. In addition, it is not clear that workers in Japan participate in corporate decision making as fully as workers in the most "cooperative" Western labor relations systems, in Germany and Sweden.

Another problem with "learning from Japan" is that there is disagreement over what the lesson is that is to be learned. It is indicative of the unique character of the Japanese industrial-relations system and the difficulties Westerners have in understanding it that the Japanese experience is cited to support two opposing recommendations on how to make Western labor relations more competitive. To some, the Japanese example demonstrates the need for the West to restore "management's right to manage." This view traces Japanese success to what its advocates believe is almost unlimited managerial discretion and an absence of interference by trade unions in company decision making. In strategic terms, it follows that the most important task in Western systems is to reassert the traditional hegemony of management in the workplace. This strategy is facilitated and encouraged by high and persistent unemployment and government policies that no longer give full employment a high priority. Since it relies basically on market forces as a source of labor discipline and compliance, this can be characterized as a "neo-liberal" approach to restructuring Western industrial relations. Others see the essential element of Japanese industrial relations as an exceptionally high degree of cooperation and mutual trust between management and labor. They conclude that Western industrial relations should be rebuilt with institutions that facilitate organized, negotiated accommodation of interests at the level of the individual enterprise. Those who hold this "cooperative" view are critical of the "neo-liberal" approach on two grounds: that it will work only in the presence of an economic crisis that the strategy is itself designed to overcome, and that it is not likely to mobilize sufficient support for company goals and to achieve the institutional stability essential to long-term growth and innovation. This view also holds that, because successful management of an automobile company requires stability and continuity of labor relations to meet long lead times for product development and planning, managements pursuing the neo-liberal option may find that initial advantages are eroded by prolonged instability and continued low trust.

These two strategic alternatives are sometime difficult to distinguish. Neo-liberals are not opposed to labor-management cooperation as such;

however, they think this can be useful only if labor is in a clearly subordinate position. They also tend to believe that managerial unilateralism and high trust between workers and management are not mutually exclusive, although this belief may be the most important difference between the West and Japan. Advocates of a cooperative strategy argue that they are not against efficient management, but that it cannot be obtained without an accommodation of interests between management and labor.

Another confusing factor is that the two strategies share the aim of strengthening industrial relations at the company level at the expense of the sectoral level and the shop level. Nevertheless, substantial differences emerge clearly on two central dimensions: the role assigned to unions and the structure and functioning of companies' labor markets.

What conditions the strategic choice of management and unions between the two alternative paths of development? To management, five factors seem to be of importance. The first of these is the extent of the crisis the industry is suffering. The deeper the industry's difficulties in a given country or company, particularly if accompanied by sharp drops in output, the greater the temptation, and perhaps the need, for management to choose a neo-liberal solution. The erosion of union power that inevitably accompanies a severe economic crisis gives management more strength and permits restructuring without union cooperation. A second factor is the existence of institutional rigidities that affect employment changes. Where hiring and firing are easy and inexpensive, an important incentive for firms to rely on their internal labor market is absent. In a country whose legal system provides high employment security and makes dismissals costly, companies already have experience with managing stable employment and mobilizing their internal labor market to achieve flexibility in the use of human resources. Legally protected participation and co-determination rights of unions at the company level are a third conditioning factor. Where collective co-decision rights of workers are legally enshrined, they are less endangered by economic fluctuations than where they are based on voluntary agreements or on "custom and practice." The market segment in which a company's products compete constitutes a fourth factor. National auto industries and individual companies that compete at the upper end of the market or offer products in special market niches are more likely to develop in the cooperative direction. They are less sensitive to short-term demand fluctuations and have less need to compete on the basis of lowest production costs. Moreover, complex and superior products of high quality require the deeper worker commitment that is most likely to develop in a cooperative industrial relations environment. The fifth and last conditioning factor is the ownership of the firm. Everything else being equal, assemblers that are subsidiaries of a multinational company seem less dependent than others on developing a cooperative pattern of labor relations. The reason may be that their ability to shift production to sites in other countries gives them additional power in bargaining with their work force in a given country.

From the perspective of established unions, the cooperative option is at least as difficult to choose as it is for management. Participation in decision making, particularly in a period of crisis, carries with it joint responsibility for painful decisions. Pursuit of trade protection may be more attractive, at least initially, because it preserves the context for the traditional adversarial pattern of industrial relations and maintains union bargaining strength. Protectionism relieves competitive pressures, reduces the need for restructuring, and stabilizes union power, which makes it both unnecessary and impossible for management to impose unilateral control. On the other hand, protectionist trade policy is not a viable option for unions representing workers in national auto industries that are highly dependent on exports, or which have members in other export-dependent industries in addition to autos. In other countries protection, even if obtained initially, may be difficult to sustain over the long term, particularly when inflation control becomes a pressing political issue. When they do not have a protectionist option, unions are more likely to seek accommodation with management and accept joint responsibility for the industry's competitiveness.

Labor representatives are more likely to be accepted into management where there is a tradition of institutionalized cooperation, and trade unions that have long been operating under such conditions are more likely to have developed the organizational capacities needed to cooperate with management than trade unions whose role has been limited to collective bargaining.

Pressures for Change, Emerging Patterns, and the Role of Government

Heightened international competition has brought pressure for cost reduction, rapid technological change, and improvements in product quality. These pressures have in turn created the need for changes in the conduct of labor relations. At the same time, rapid prospective advances in productivity and moderate forecasts for growth in sales point to an overall employment decline for in auto industry in the Auto Program countries. How then can labor and management respond?

We conclude that piecemeal adaptation will not be possible and that the parties must eventually choose between the neo-liberal and the cooperative approaches. Changes made initially to only parts of the industrial-relations system will eventually force the parties into systemwide change. Furthermore, a series of piecemeal changes will probably not be sufficient to adequately improve a national industry's competitiveness.

Given that systemwide changes are needed in the long term, the actors must choose between the clear alternatives. While the specific steps to be taken will vary significantly among Western nations, we believe that labor and management should pursue a reform strategy that is based on enhanced cooperation and participation, because this approach offers the most joint gain with the least costly social conflict. In addition, we believe that any strategy for change that risks high degrees of conflict and denies labor's role in decision making will, in the end, fail to generate the required improvements in quality and productivity.

What would a cooperative strategy look like? Put simply, labor would accept increased work-rule flexibility and moderation in compensation, linking it closely to firm performance. In exchange, management would provide workers with greater employment security and more information on production and technological changes, and would help to sustain institutions giving labor direct participation in decision making.

Flexibility in work rules would help in the introduction of new technologies and the new forms of work organization associated with those technologies. Moderation in compensation would help return Western producers to competitiveness and avoid the need for even more drastic employment cuts. Enhanced job security would increase workers' commitment and ease their fears of displacement by the new technology. Increased worker participation would help reduce costs and heighten attention to quality.

Governments have never been indifferent to employment trends and the evolution of industrial relations in the automobile industry. Because changes in the industry will continue and intensify in coming years, governments will need to sort through their options and develop a labor-market policy consistent with these structural changes.

Governments can encourage the pursuit of a cooperative reform strategy in response to the challenges confronting the industry by, first, resisting pressures to remove the legal employment protections, such as the lay-off notification requirements, that now exist in many European countries. Managements should be encouraged to engage in manpower planning so that long-term employment cuts and a company's long-term manpower policy can be subject to early and extensive consultation and negotiation with labor to enable the two sides to exhaust all available alternatives to dismissals. Publicly funded programs should help manage short-term cyclical changes in labor input.

The "voice" of labor at the company level can be strengthened by the promotion of greater worker participation in decision making. This is a prerequisite for the cooperative strategy. In this approach, government aid to ailing companies should be contingent upon management and labor agreeing on a scheme that provides for accountable and responsible participation of labor representatives in decision-making, this coupled with other accomodations, such as adjustments in compensation, which will make the company competitive.

Governments should also encourage share ownership by workers. In some countries, this will require changes in tax and other legislation. The considerable legal and political difficulties associated with this should be overcome by governments in order to strengthen workers' interest in their company's performance and competitiveness and, at the same time, to offer them another opportunity to participate in the making of company policy.

Finally, governments should facilitate the creation of flexible compensation systems that will be more responsive to economic conditions. Governments could encourage a shift toward the payment of employee bonuses through appropriate changes in tax and legal policies. Such policies can help improve competitiveness when they are accompanied by compromises on labor's part that make work rules more flexible and link the growth of compensation to the firm's health. Without these compromises, adoption of the other policies in the West might well add to the Western companies' competitive disadvantage with the Japanese.

Reforms along these lines may improve competitiveness and prevent dramatic shifts in employment between national auto industries while also helping avoid industrial conflict. However, these strategies cannot forestall substantial employment declines in the Auto Program countries as a group over the next 20 years. Governments need to create programs to cope with the social costs associated with these declines by encouraging retraining and relocation and by providing temporary income support for displaced workers. Sweden and West Germany have a long and successful tradition of "active labor-market policies," including relocation assistance, retraining programs, and income support. Much could be accomplished through the expansion and imitation of these programs, which would also greatly aid the political acceptability of industry restructuring and serve to reduce pressures for long-term trade protection.

Government policies such as these can make a significant contribution to a stable structure of cooperative labor relations in the auto industry that will encourage high economic efficiency and competitiveness. However, these policies do not create this structure. All they can do is provide favorable conditions under which management and labor can work together in the pursuit of common economic interests. Whether or not labor and management respond to those conditions is ultimately up to them.

10   Nations in Competition: The Trade Dilemma

Open trade has been a frequently stated ideal of Western leaders during the postwar era. Where it is achieved, they have claimed, the pressures of competition yield economic efficiency, high rates of innovation, and low consumer prices. Additionally, the interdependence among national economies that it fosters is said to be a powerful long-term force for peace.[1] Even when the practices of OECD governments conflict with the principles of open trade, they typically pay it obeisance by explaining that what they have done is temporary, a product of very special circumstances, and/or really intended to accomplish domestic social purposes (as in the case of product regulations designed to preserve public health) rather than impede competition. Thus, the rhetoric of OECD statesmen might lead one to conclude that impediments to free trade are unusual in international commerce.

In practice, however, they have been more nearly the norm, and public policies have played as great a role in the international economy as they have in the domestic economies of the OECD countries. In this discussion of trade policy we will apply the label "trade interventionist" to policies that discriminate between domestic and foreign enterprises for the purpose of shaping international trade and investment flows. Examples include direct import restrictions such as tariffs and quotas, regulatory and tax discrimination against foreign products, restraints on foreign investment, and subsidies to domestic producers of internationally tradeable items.

The Balance of Political and Market Forces: Trends and Countertrends in the Postwar Era

The Trend toward Liberalization

As was related in chapter 2, the three decades after World War II witnessed an unprecedented relaxation of traditional barriers to trade. The General Agreement on Trade and Tariffs (GATT) was adopted by 24 of the world's richest nations in 1947 (the current membership is 89), and effective tariffs on traded goods fell sharply in the decades that followed. Tariff reductions were to some degree offset by the growth of nontariff barriers (such as quotas and discriminatory regulations) and of public aid (such as direct subsidies, guaranteed loans, special tax incentives, and preferences in government procurement) to favored enterprises. Nevertheless, the overall trend was clearly toward liberalization, and global commerce expanded dramatically. From 1913 to 1948, world trade in goods and services rose only about one-fourth as rapidly as production: on an inflation-adjusted basis, about 0.5 percent annually versus 2 percent. From 1948 to 1973, on the other hand, trade expanded 1.4 times as rapidly as production: 7 percent annually versus 5 percent.[2]

In the auto sector, and among the major auto-producing nations, tariff rates of 30 percent and more were still common as of 1960. However, tariffs dropped sharply thereafter and were entirely eliminated within the European Common Market. Trade barriers were also greatly relaxed between the United States and Canada by means of individual trade-balance agreements negotiated between the major auto producers and the Canadian government under the Auto Pact of 1965. While not absolutely freeing trade, these allowed considerably more leeway in trade flows than the tariffs that preceded them. Although the pace of liberalization slowed after 1973, the pattern of declining tariffs continued with the Tokyo Round tariff negotiations of 1979, which call for progressive reductions in the already low auto tariffs of the Auto Program countries through 1987.

In retrospect it seems clear that the success of tariff reductions in auto trade since World War II was a product of five opportune factors.

First, the world auto market was growing so rapidly that very large changes in market share could occur without any national industry or its employment being thrown into absolute decline.

Second, the entire world economy was also booming, so the situation in many other industries was similar to that in the auto industry. This all tended to be reinforcing: The economic boom facilitated the lifting of trade barriers in many industries, and wide-ranging trade liberalization gave a further boost to international prosperity.

Third, World War II transformed the political and economic balances of the noncommunist world in ways that strongly favored trade liberalization for nearly 30 years. During this period the leadership of a single nation was universally acknowledged, and it was powerfully motivated to champion more open trade. The United States accounted in the late 1940s for more than half of the world's industrial production and for one-third of the world's exports even though its economy was among those least dependent on trade.[3] It enjoyed vast trade surpluses and a leading position in virtually every industrial sector. Its currency was the standard medium of world trade. Its supremacy was political and military as well as economic. At the same time, it felt significantly threatened by communism and by the specter of a return to the economic conditions of the 1930s. These fears provided the vital spur for the United States to throw off a long historic legacy of protectionism, while its great margin of economic leadership enabled it to pursue tariff reductions with a minimum of domestic turmoil. Its ability to lead was further enhanced by its willingness, through the 1960s, to accept less than full reciprocity from its trading partners as barriers were gradually negotiated down. The U.S. commitment to open trade during these years was nowhere stronger than in the auto sector. Having little to fear from imports throughout most of this period, the U.S. auto industry concentrated in the area of trade policy on securing opportunities for foreign investment.[4]

Fourth, the Bretton Woods system of fixed exchange rates prevailed through the 1960s, with the dollar becoming increasingly overvalued (in terms of prices for comparable goods) as the world's other leading economies recovered from wartime devastation. This was extremely significant, because nations tend to be far more amenable to trade liberalization when their trade balances are improving than otherwise, and to become more interventionist mainly when their trade balances are worsening. Exchange-rate stability meant that abrupt changes in international production-cost relationships (which are often devastating for the producers whose relative costs increase) were rare. The trend toward dollar overvaluation meant that most leading economies other than the United States could experience gradually improving trade balances. This pattern was necessarily impermanent, because it depended on U.S. acceptance of a continuously worsening trade balance. It was able to persist for nearly three decades, however, because the United States had entered the postwar period with a vastly favorable balance and because, even after the United States began to run visible trade deficits in the 1960s, foreign demand for dollars as a reserve and international-trading currency continued to grow.

Finally, trade liberalization was achieved within Western Europe by a group of nations with intense economic and political interdependence, similar costs of production, and relatively similar patterns of government-business-labor relations. The predominant sense in this situation was that more open trade, while spurring all companies to improve their performance and imperiling some of the least efficient, should not mean great instability for national market shares in basic industries. This confidence that competition and stability were compatible on the microscale was an essential element in the creation of the European Economic Community. The effects of this initiative reverberated widely, moreover. American and Japanese tariff reductions during the 1960s were substantially motivated by a desire to ensure that the vast European market did not retain high tariffs against outsiders as it became more open internally.

The Countertrend toward Protection

These liberalizing forces have all ceased to operate or today operate in severely weakened fashion. Steady economic expansion has been replaced since 1973 by a pattern of extreme cyclical volatility around a long-term trend of very sluggish growth. The leadership will and capacity of the United States have been severely eroded, and no other nation is in a position to assume its former role. The momentum for European integration seems exhausted. Exchange rates have become increasingly volatile since the breakdown of the Bretton Woods system in 1971, and the perception is widespread that the dollar is misaligned in terms of merchandise trade.

The dollar's valuation remains critical, not simply because it affects the ability of the United States to maintain a free trade stance but also because the dollar remains the world's primary medium of international exchange. The obstacle to achieving a dollar valuation that would keep U.S. trade in balance is that, while the dollar remains overvalued in terms of tradeable merchandise and service prices, it is apparently valued quite reasonably in the eyes of the world's financial managers. The latter, of course, are mainly in search of safety, liquidity, and competitive interest rates, all of which the dollar has consistently provided even when the United States was running large trade deficits. In consequence, though the United States has experienced high inflation and low productivity growth since 1973 in comparison with its leading industrial competitors, the exchange value of the dollar throughout 1982 and 1983 was just about as high as a decade earlier when calculated on a trade-weighted basis against the other leading currencies.

These adverse trends in the broader economic situation have had remarkably little effect on the downward trend in auto tariffs. As a result, auto trade across the Atlantic and from the West to Japan is more open then ever. At the same time, the emergence of the Japanese challenge in the midst of general economic stagnation has led since 1975 to a wide range of nontariff barriers against Japanese imports to the other Auto Program countries. These have sharply reversed the liberalizing trend in auto trade of the preceding decades.

The paradoxical emergence of country-specific nontariff barriers in the midst of generally declining tariff barriers has been a general phenomenon of recent years. It has occurred partly because the very success of multilateral tariff-cutting negotiations has channeled protectionist impulses onto other paths and partly because many trade dilemmas have involved competitive challenges from producers in a single country or region.

Tariffs, as the simplest and most obvious form of trade restraint, were historically highly suitable for application by governments that did not attempt to manage their domestic economies, and they have proved to be the simplest trade restraints to negotiate away. The newer methods of intervention—quotas, "voluntary" export restraints, veiled warnings, local content requirements, subsidies, discriminatory regulations—are far more difficult to monitor, to debate publicly, or to negotiate about internationally. Their complexity, their variety, and their frequent informality breed pessimism that these emergent forms of trade interventionism can ultimately be controlled.

Even if feasible, the banning of one or more specific instruments of nontariff intervention would probably have little impact on trade in the current environment. Other measures would always be available to take their place, and there is endless room for bickering about whether particular actions constitute formal breaches of international rules. In the auto sector specifically, the central issues are competitive imbalance, excess capacity in a framework of market stagnation, and the determination of all major producing nations to avoid employment shocks and to maintain a vigorous long-term industrial presence. In this environment, even if protection consists at a specific moment of no more than veiled warnings, the effect on trade is likely to be chilling. Given the massive investments and multiyear lead times required for capacity expansion in auto production, investors are particularly sensitive to signals that governments may not permit them to market a car after it has gone into production.

Current Auto Trade Policies of the Auto Program Countries

While varying among themselves, the Auto Program nations still, by and large, profess strong support for open trade in principle. But they are committed as well to the values of industrial stability, job security, and long-term strength in their basic industries. These latter commitments are neither new nor absolute, but they have increasingly come to the fore during the late 1970s and the early 1980s. Within this general framework, national trade-policy positions tend to vary chiefly as a function of sectoral competitive position and secondarily as a function of general trade orientation.

Sweden, the nation most committed to free trade, is a country of 8 million people that depends overwhelmingly on the prosperity of a few export industries. Its auto manufacturers export about two-thirds of their production, and Sweden's export revenues are nearly twice the magnitude of its auto import costs. Nonetheless, Sweden's Foreign Trade Minister announced early in 1983 that his government had "recently informed Japan that we shall be keeping under close scrutiny developments relative to auto imports from that country." Although Japanese producers commanded only 15 percent of the Swedish market, and competed primarily with imports from the rest of Europe rather than with the larger, more rugged vehicles that are the hallmark of Swedish manufacture, he maintained that this warning was appropriate "due to the risk that exports 'voluntarily' diverted from the U.S. and the European Community may flood our market."[5]

West Germany is another nation whose prosperity rests squarely on large industrial trade surpluses, and its auto trade position remains exceptionally strong. It exports half its vehicle production, twice as many vehicles as it imports. Moreover, Germany specializes in the export of luxury vehicles. Even excluding intra-EEC trade, its export revenues are consistently more than triple its import bill. And, as in Sweden, Japanese gains in the German market have come mainly at the expense of other imports rather than of domestic models. After the conclusion of the U.S.-Japan Voluntary Export Restraint Agreement (VER) in April 1981, however, the German Economics Minister engaged in "informal" conversations with Japanese officials. While stressing his own commitment to open trade, he apparently informed them that his government might well be compelled to take protectionist action if Japanese vehicles kept out of the United States were diverted to Germany. The Japanese, whose market share in Germany had tripled during the preceding 3 years (to 10 percent), reportedly noted that they did not expect exports by their producers to rise by more than another percentage-point share of the German market (i.e., to 11 percent) during 1981. In fact, Japanese sales remained at 10 percent during 1981 and 1982. German officials point to various commercial reasons for this stabilization, notably a sharp depreciation of the Deutschmark relative to the yen and the introduction of some attractive European models. Others speculate that an additional factor has been Japanese export moderation meant to keep Germany a strong advocate of open trade in councils of the EEC.

The United States is a nation thoroughly divided on the issue of auto trade in the 1980s. Having enjoyed trade surpluses in the auto sector for half a century until the 1960s, it currently runs the world's largest automobile trade deficit. Excluding trade with Canada (because American and Canadian production have been fully integrated since 1965), the United States in 1980 imported nearly 13 times as many vehicles as it exported (2.76 million versus 0.22 million). Between 1978 and 1981, moreover, the constant dollar value of domestic sales by the U.S. producers fell 36 percent while the value of import sales rose 24 percent.[6]

Having led the postwar trade-liberalization movement, the United States remains one of those nations most committed to open trade ideologically. Nonetheless, with automotive production at the lowest level in two decades and its auto companies reporting multi-billion-dollar losses, the U.S. government negotiated a "voluntary" export restraint (VER) agreement with Japan in 1981. The Japanese government accepted responsibility for ensuring that Japan's exports of passenger cars (including vans and station wagons) would not exceed 1.76 million in the year beginning April 1, 1981, a drop of 7.7 percent from the prior 12-month period. During the second year of the VER, Japanese exports were to be permitted an increase equal to one-sixth of any growth in the total U.S. market. A third-year target was left for future determination. At the time, U.S. passenger-car sales were expected to reach 9.8 million units in the first year (up from 8.8 million during the previous 12 months) and 11.5 million in the second year. Had these forecasts been realized, the Japanese share of the U.S. market would have slipped from 21.5 percent in the last pre-VER year to slightly below 18 percent in each year that the VER remained in effect. As it happened, though, demand fell in the first two VER years, with the result that the Japanese market share actually increased, to nearly 23 percent in the second year. The U.S. administration insisted that it remained committed to open trade, and that the VER agreement was purely for the purpose of providing "breathing space" for the American auto industry to adjust to recent shocks. On the very day that the third year of the automotive VER began, however, President Reagan imposed an elevenfold increase in the tariff on motorcycles with engines larger than 700cc, from 4.5 to 49.4 percent. Again, the impact fell almost exclusively on Japanese producers. The ostensible purpose of the action was to save the nation's sole remaining domestically owned motorcycle producer, Harley-Davidson. Whether intentionally or not, however, it also signaled that the United States would probably act decisively if the import share of its auto market again began to rise significantly. Late in 1983, although a major recovery was underway in the U.S. auto market, the American and Japanese governments agreed to extend the VER for a fourth year from April 1, 1984, with a 10 percent increase in the ceiling. Numerous observers commented that it would have been very difficult for President Reagan to terminate the VER in a presidential election year, but that a major controversy could be expected over the question of whether to extend it beyond the new scheduled termination date of March 31, 1985.

The United Kingdom's priorities have shifted dramatically toward intervention since the mid 1970s. In 1975 the British government encouraged the negotiation of an "unofficial" agreement between its auto-industry association and that of Japan that has effectively limited Japanese passenger-car imports to 11 percent of the British market. This agreement is open-ended, and there is no indication that any thought has been given to its termination. Since 1977, moreover, when it nationalized BL, the British government has provided over 3 billion dollars to finance new models and production equipment. These interventionist measures have not, however, been attempts to freeze the size and structure of the British auto industry. The BL program was designed to yield a much smaller but more competitive company rather than simply to prop up existing operations. In addition, the United Kingdom has accepted a reduction by half from 1972 to 1981 in the number of motor vehicles produced domestically, and has permitted imports to capture nearly 60 percent of its market (up from 8 percent in 1968). Britain also remains among those nations most open to foreign investment, having succeeded at the beginning of 1984 in a multiyear effort to convince Nissan to commence domestic auto manufacture.

Italy and France have both consistently been disposed toward strong trade intervention throughout the automotive era. While accepting open trade within the European Common Market since the 1960s, they have insisted on Common Market policies guaranteeing them net benefits, such as subsidies for the development of depressed regions in the case of Italy and agricultural subsidies in the case of France. Both have typically favored prompt trade intervention when imports have threatened European industries. In countering Japanese imports they have not hesitated to rely on formal quotas holding the Japanese market share to very low levels.

Italy imposed a formal ban on auto imports from Japan as the latter was negotiating for full membership in the GATT during the early 1960s. Subsequent negotiations led to a 1969 agreement whereby Italy and Japan each agreed to accept up to 1,000 of the other's cars per year beginning in 1970. The ceiling has been 2,200 since 1976. Italy has also sought unsuccessfully within the Common Market to block intra-European trade of BL's Acclaim model, which is produced in Britain by BL under license using many components supplied by Honda from Japan. Historically, the Italian government has also prohibited foreign direct investment. During the early 1980s, however, over the vociferous opposition of Fiat, it modified this position somewhat by approving a joint venture between state-owned Alfa Romeo and Nissan; this resulted in the Arna car, which entered production in late 1983. Italy's will to keep trade with Japan under tight rein is not in doubt, however. During 1980, when the Common Market as a whole ran an $11 billion deficit with Japan, Italy accounted for only $20 million of this total (about 0.02 percent). Whereas total exports by the Common Market states to Japan covered only 37 percent of their import bill, the Italian figure was 98 percent. Italy had actually run small bilateral surpluses with Japan during each of the previous years.

France imposed a 3 percent market-share limit on Japanese imports in 1977, reportedly judging that this was just below the level at which Japanese producers would find it worthwhile to develop a strong French distribution system. In 1980, concerned that this cap might be exceeded, France resorted to a drastic, openly publicized slowdown in customs clearance procedures to ensure that it held. Generally, French leaders have made clear their belief that the European market should be predominantly reserved for European industry. It is now appropriate to think in terms of Europe rather than France alone, they note, because only Europe can provide a large enough market for the nurturing of world-class enterprises in some critical sectors. But they have indicated as well that they consider open trade a tactic normally advocated by nations feeling confident about their competitive position and not as a principle for all seasons. Michel Jobert, when French Foreign Trade Minister, inquired rhetorically in his address to the opening session of the 1982 GATT Ministerial Conference: "[Is not] dogmatic liberalism finally the most disguised form of protectionism—that of the absolute power of the strong over the weak?"[7]

In February 1983 the European Economic Community as a whole for the first time reached a series of VER agreements with Japan, involving cars, motorcycles, light commercial vehicles, video cassette recorders, several categories of consumer electronics, and numerically controlled machine tools. The automobile agreement specified merely that Japanese exports would be "moderate in relation to past export and market performance and future market developments." This appeared to mean that Japanese automakers would not substantially exceed their prevailing 9 percent share of the EEC market during 1983. Nevertheless, there was every indication that this pattern of trade management between the EEC and Japan would prove long-lived.

Japan itself, prior to achieving global competitive superiority in several mass market segments, protected its domestic auto market more thoroughly than any Western nation other than Italy. It also prohibited any direct foreign investment that would entail enterprise control.[8] Since the late 1970s, however, Japan has eliminated automotive tariffs completely, dismantled many of its nontariff trade barriers, such as prohibitions on foreign ownership of auto companies, and loosened many others, such as onerous type-certification requirements for imported vehicles. The question remains of how deeply committed the Japanese are to an open domestic auto market, but their resolve will only be tested if the Japanese industry suddenly faces a serious import threat—an event highly unlikely for many years to come.

In sum, the auto trade policies of the Auto Program countries are highly correlated with the competitive positions of their domestic producers, although this tendency is moderated somewhat by the overall national orientation toward trade policy. Thus, the traditional American ideology of open trade has held protection of the industry to a lower level than the industry's weak competitive position after 1979 might otherwise have suggested. Nevertheless, the most striking feature of these trade policies is the strong determination of every Auto Program country to preserve large-scale domestic production. Even the Swedes and the Germans, who have not experienced major Japanese market penetration in their home markets at the expense of their domestic producers, have urged export moderation on the Japanese.

The Future Context of Auto Trade Policy

What does the future promise in the way of an auto trading regime? Political forecasting is even more hazardous than economic forecasting, but it is possible to suggest the boundaries of the world's economic and industrial situation in the remainder of this century and the types of trading regimes that are likely to result. Five dimensions seem particularly important: the state of the macroeconomy, the exchange-rate regime, the condition of the auto industry in the Western nations, employment patterns in the auto industry generally, and the strategies of the Japanese producers.

The most optimistic scenario combines stable prosperity with Japanese producer caution about exports:

• Economic growth in the OECD countries would be 3 percent a year, with only modest cyclical instability. In short, the economy would once more grow steadily, as it did in the 1950s and 1960s, although not so exuberantly.

• Unemployment would decline gradually from one business cycle to the next.

• The OECD countries would make significant progress toward an exchange-rate system able to maintain rough commodity-price parity among the world's major trading currencies. This would mitigate balance-of-payments pressures for trade intervention.

• Western auto producers would make rapid strides toward closing the competitive gap with Japanese producers in mass market segments. As a result, they would be sufficiently profitable that they could obtain needed investment capital without government help.

• Japanese automakers would avoid export surges of finished units and components, particularly during economic downturns.

Under this scenario, the Western political balance would gradually but inexorably shift back toward open trade. The shift would be gradual, because fears of a renewed Japanese export surge would persist. It would be most pronounced in the United States, which experienced the most severe auto-industry slump during the early 1980s and which consequently strayed the furthest from its general ideological orientation. This swing of the pendulum would be echoed in Sweden and Germany, which have never concluded formal restraint agreements with Japan in any event. There would not likely be any relaxation of French and Italian quotas, however, and any easing of British import curbs on the Japanese would occur very slowly because of the time needed to make British manufacturing systems fully competitive.

The most pessimistic scenario combines slow growth with intense Japanese competitive pressure:

• Economic growth in the OECD countries would be only 2 percent per year, with cyclical instability resembling that of the decade following 1973.

• Unemployment would rise from one business cycle to the next.

• The exchange rates would continue to exhibit their recent volatility.

• Western automakers would close the competitive gap in mass market segments only very gradually and would face crises at each economic downturn due to their position as high-cost producers.

• Employment would contract substantially across the world auto industry because of automation, competitive pressure to improve productivity, and sluggish sales growth.

• Japanese producers would make vigorous efforts to increase their exports of finished units and components.

Under these conditions, the Western political tide would flow strongly toward reinforcement of the current system of caps on finished unit imports from Japan. In addition, pressures would build for supplemental trade restrictions to stem the flow of Japanese components. These flows would otherwise surely increase, as they are the simplest way for Japanese producers to continue export growth in the presence of barriers to finished units. Supplemental restrictions might take the form of local-content requirements for vehicles sold by Japanese producers in each Western country or net trade-balance requirements imposed on Japanese producers in each country.

If some Western producers improved their competitiveness faster than others, particularly through collaboration with Japanese producers, trade barriers might be extended much further to include vehicles produced in other Western countries with substantial amounts of Japanese value added. This issue is already emerging in Europe, where the BL-Honda, Alfa Romeo–Nissan, and Nissan U.K. ventures are provoking warnings from other members of the EEC about the acceptability of growing volumes of vehicles assembled in Europe but with some Japanese components. Thus, the liberal trading regime within Europe and across the Atlantic might also be dismantled as a ripple effect of the Japanese challenge. Finally, restrictions on Japanese direct investment might be raised in order to protect the domestic market share of troubled existing producers.

Achieving a New Balance in an Era of Slow Growth and Competitive Disequilibrium: The Trade Debate

Either of the above scenarios is possible, but the trend in world affairs in recent years has convinced many of the participants in the Auto Program that economic and competitive conditions in the remainder of this century are likely to be much closer to the second scenario than to the first. Thus, it is hardly surprising that the most intensely debated issues in the Auto Program were what the trade policies of the Auto Program countries ought to be in the years to come and how the most desirable trading regime might be brought about. Two broad intellectual positions emerged during the course of the Program; we will label one "open trade" and the other "interventionist." Their main points follow.

The Open-Trade Position*

This position begins with a diagnosis of the present disequilibrium in the world auto industry, which goes as follows: The competitive dis-

---

*A more detailed formulation, prepared by Gunnar Hedlund of the Stockholm School of Economics in collaboration with a number of other Auto Program researchers, is given in appendix D.

advantage of the American and some European auto producers is a matter of high factor costs, notably for wages and capital, and of inferior production processes. The latter means simply that many American and European auto producers require more than their Japanese competitors of each factor (again primarily labor and capital) to build a comparable product. This is the result of uncompetitive systems of production organization, outmoded approaches to the design of production facilities, and so forth. The Western producers therefore have a choice. They can reduce employee compensation, find some way to reduce the amount of labor and capital needed to produce an automobile, or pursue some combination of these. But they must make some decisive move in the direction of lowering factor costs and/or improving their production processes. Otherwise they must exit the industry.

In this situation, protectionist measures can only delay the inevitable. Their strong tendency is to remove the pressure to address the fundamental problems, so the cost of protection to the national economy rises steadily. At some point the cost becomes so great that political support for protection crumbles and the industry faces new competitive pressures from an even weaker position. Meanwhile the cost to society of failing to allocate resources more efficiently is very great.

This scenario is not just hypothetical. Those Western auto industries that have had the most protection in the postwar era—notably the British, the French, the Italian, and the American (by virtue of the government's energy-price policy that made very large autombles predominant)—are today in the weakest competitive positions. Recent British experience suggests what is likely to happen in the long run: The cost of protection and the inability of protected enterprises to compete even against Western rivals leads eventually to public refusal to tolerate uncompetitive products produced at high cost. Large-scale retrenchment, such as that undertaken by BL since 1979, is then the only solution. The net effect of protection, therefore, is only to delay industrial reform at great cost.

This is the core of the open-trade position, but its proponents also sought to counter several arguments sometimes cited to justify protection of the auto industry: that the current situation warrants short-term protection because of discontinuities in world auto markets, that autos are a vital industry for national security, that autos are a key industry for any nation wishing to assure itself a strong position in long-term industrial competition, and that political realities dictate some sort of government assistance to troubled producers in periods of extreme competitive imbalance in a major industry such as autos.

With regard to market discontinuities, the open-traders argued that short-term protection might have been appropriate in 1979 to prevent an import surge while the American industry developed new models suited to the new energy order. However, the Americans now have a suitable product line, and the European mass-market producers could never claim this excuse. The continuing competitive problems in both industries must now be labeled for what they are: the consequence of uncompetitive production systems and factor costs. Thus, further protection simply delays the need to adapt.

The argument that a nation may wish to maintain its auto industry in order to convert it to defense use in wartime ignores the nature of modern weapons and warfare. The notions that auto plants could quickly be converted to build complex defense hardware (as happened in World War II) and that another protracted war between the major powers will be fought are quite out of date. The military need for heavy-duty vehicles could be met at much less cost through a combination of dedicated plants and stockpiling. For other transportation tasks during the period a modern war is likely to last, the existing fleet of civilian trucks and off-road vehicles should be adequate, and in any case it will have to suffice because of the lack of time to put the auto industry on a war footing.

Finally, the idea that a nation ought to maintain a domestic auto industry with the aid of protection because this industry will be a key market for electronic components, flexible manufacturing systems, new materials such as ceramics, and other products of potential domestic growth industries is self-defeating. A protected and inefficient auto industry will soak up resources that ought to be going to such growth sectors and will not make rigorous demands on them with regard to product quality and cost. Thus, a nation may build new industries, but they may be no more competitive on a world scale than the protected auto industry to which they are linked. The result will be a highly diversified but second-rate economy.

With regard to the large-scale disruptions that open trade in a period of severe competitive disequilibrium may produce and the political pressures these may generate for protection, the open-traders argued that direct compensation to displaced workers is a much better means of addressing the problem than protection of uncompetitive companies. The former can provide retraining and transition to new jobs in growth sectors; the latter tends only to halt adjustment in the short run while building up explosive pressures for industrial restructuring in the long term.

The open-trade position has an additional political dimension: It warns that once the idea takes hold that exceptions to free trade may be justifiable, the tendency is for actual exceptions to proliferate indiscriminately. Persons whose jobs and businesses are threatened at any moment by foreign competition are far more likely to mobilize than consumers or persons engaged in export-oriented activities. Government officials are poorly equipped to make judgments about who to protect on the basis of technical analyses of the potential for reestablishing competitiveness, and in any case they have limited maneuvering room in pursuing market-oriented adjustment policies. Consequently, the main counterweight to interventionist pressure is the widespread public conviction that free trade represents the overall national interest. The great danger is that trade intervention on behalf of troubled industries will come to seem routine and that public support for the principle of open trade will become *pro forma*. In short, the idea that a nation can protect a giant industry such as autos as an isolated case is naive.

This political argument has an international dimension as well: The system of international agreements on which open trade depends is itself quite fragile. In practice, the domestic political balance in nearly every country tends toward interventionism, and the openness of trade is prone to atrophy except when there is forward momentum. Forward momentum exists only when the governments of the advanced industrial nations are actively negotiating for the reduction of trade barriers. When such negotiations are in progress, national leaders achieve heightened sensitivity to the views of their foreign counterparts and are frequently emboldened to defend open trade at home with reference to the concessions they seek abroad. Such multilateral cooperation is extremely difficult, however, when individual governments are regularly intervening on behalf of their own producers. The emphasis is likely to shift in this context (particularly in hard economic times) toward retaliatory reciprocity, ending in trade warfare. In short, protection limited initially to autos can easily spiral out of control.

The Interventionist Position

Whereas the open-trade position was advanced in reasonably similar form by most participants in the Auto Program who labeled themselves "open-traders," the interventionist position had a number of somewhat disparate points which were held in varying combinations by proponents of intervention.

Many of the interventionists accepted the open-traders' diagnosis of the basic problems in the auto sector, along with the proposition that long-term adjustments will be necessary. However, they argued that it does not follow that intervention always retards adjustment or that the long-term cost of some types of protection is greater than the short-term dislocation costs open trade can produce. This is particularly true because the need to change production processes—agreed by many interventionists to be the key problem—is mainly a matter of widespread organizational learning. That is, the members of the vast industrial enterprise that is an auto industry must learn new ways of working together. Facilities must be rationalized and relocated to permit the use of the just-in-time method and other inventory-reducing and capital-equipment-reducing manufacturing techniques. New relationships between assemblers and suppliers and new approaches to labor-management relations will be necessary. The difficulty is that this process requires a number of years and cannot be successfully conducted in a panic atmosphere. Thus, some sort of protection over an extended period is required—particularly during economic downturns, when the higher-cost Western producers will absorb most of the sales losses, which will drive their unit cost of production even higher and can easily lead to a rout rather than to orderly restructuring.

If a rout does occur, it causes enormous dislocation costs while capital and labor are reallocated in other sectors. These sectors may suffer from the same inadequate production processes but may escape scrutiny because the products or services produced are not internationally traded. Thus, what is called adjustment is in fact permanent acceptance of approaches to production organization that are below world best practice. Any nation facing this situation is justified in taking some risks with inefficiency in the short-run in an effort to see if a viable auto sector can be rebuilt.

All of this would be beside the point if the clear evidence was that the invariable result of protection was to halt adjustment. Those defending intervention cite the rebirth of the European auto industry in the 1950s and the 1960s after many years of protection and the extraordinary export success of the Japanese industry from a completely protected domestic base as examples that protection does not inevitably lead to declining competitiveness. They maintain that those who believe this focus on factor costs as the key to competitiveness, assuming that production processes are hard or impossible to change. However, the transformations in automotive history can be traced more to innovations in production systems and products than to low wages or cheap capital, and this provides a strong argument that production processes do change.

The interventionists cite the cases of Chrysler and BL as two recent illustrations that governments can nurture firm-specific turnarounds in the context of some market protection that moves domestic producers toward rather than away from the highest standard of international competitiveness. In each of these cases, the troubled company benefited from a substantial inflow of resources that the private sector would never have provided on its own and also from restraints on Japanese imports. The government attached numerous conditions to its aid in each instance as well, striving to hold down its costs and to ensure that vigorous adaptation was occurring. In the Chrysler case this involved requirements of major concessions by private lenders, suppliers, and employees. In the case of BL, it involved nationalization and the government's insistence on the closure of numerous plants, massive layoffs, and wage moderation. There is still considerable room for controversy about the future prospects of Chrysler and BL, and in particular about whether they can overcome their remaining competitive weaknesses against the Japanese now that they are once more able to compete against their American and European rivals. Nevertheless, there is little doubt that their performance has improved vastly and that in the absence of government assistance they would have collapsed.

A second and entirely different interventionist argument was that the exchange-rate system and national tax and fiscal policies were producing distortions in the trading regime. These matters should be addressed at their source, but the OECD nations have exhibited little capacity to do this. These interventionists argued that trade policy must therefore be used as a second-best but still appropriate technique. In effect this position holds that the world's auto producers would currently be near a competitive equilibrium if macroeconomic conditions were only as they should be, so that talk of the need for massive adjustment and adaptation is vastly exaggerated.

Other interventionists, who accepted the existence of the competitive imbalance and acknowledged the cost of protection in the short term, justified their interventionism with the argument that industrial linkages are important and that the auto industry remains a key to future industrial growth in each of the Auto Program nations. Most obviously, the auto industry is a leading purchaser of computers, flexible manufacturing equipment, semiconductors, high-strength lightweight materials, and electronic control systems. Indeed, the continuing technological revolution in the auto industry may provide the single largest market opportunity over the next 10–20 years for many emerging growth industries. However, because the trend in auto manufacturing (motivated by the Japanese example) is to make as much of the car as possible at the point of final assembly, the hope that suppliers of these new technologies will find foreign markets in the absence of a strong domestic industry is naive. In addition, other more mature industries such as steel, aluminum, glass, and rubber depend critically on auto-industry sales. Although less glamorous, they account today for more employment than the "high tech" industries, and they form significant parts of each nation's industrial infrastructure. The economy cannot prosper by propping up these producers in inefficient form, but the effort to restructure auto manufacture and to geographically concentrate it around final assembly sites is an opportunity to revitalize these industries as well.

In a similar vein, some interventionists defend protection as a matter of national security. This is not because the auto industry may be directly called upon in a future war but because a diversified manufacturing base is undeniably vital to any country's defense posture in the modern world. Autos are a vital element in the industrial system, and measures that improve the efficiency of the auto sector will have a demonstration effect all across heavy industry. If the alternative in an open-trade regime is "deindustrialization" in some leading countries, which would sharply reduce their manufacturing base, then some types of protection may be justified on grounds of national defense.

With regard to the politics of protection, most interventionists acknowledged the danger of indiscriminate proliferation but accepted this as a risk worth bearing. They argued that for a nation to adopt many welfare-state measures carries the risk that the efficiency of competition in the marketplace will be sacrificed. No doubt this is true to some extent, but all modern nations have accepted the need to balance market-efficiency values against those of social justice and equity. And by building a basis of individual security into the system, governments make the social disruptions caused by marketplace competition acceptable. Similarly, in the case of key industries, governments' efforts to cushion and guide the adjustment process make marketplace competition over the long term socially and politically tolerable.

Regarding the alleged fragility of the GATT system and the likelihood that protection in the auto sector will spiral out of control, many interventionists argued that the GATT rules are incomplete precisely because the GATT member nations have never been prepared to give up all, or even most, of their freedom to intervene in trade. The result is a system of international economic relationships with a remarkable capacity for tolerating exceptions to free trade without breaking. In addition, a trade war between Japan (the object of automobile trade restraints) and the West is very unlikely. Japan runs enormous trade surpluses with the United States and the European Economic Community. There is no disposition in the West to eliminate this imbalance or even to markedly reduce it. The real question concerns future growth, and in this situation Japan has every reason to seek accommodation rather than a trade war. This is precisely what has been happening.

Styles of Intervention

The intervention case, of course, must be specified in terms of the type of intervention, a topic of further debates within the Program. Not only were open-traders paired against interventionists; there were also debates among those with differing approaches to intervention.

The open-traders noted that, although intervention *per se* is nearly always inadvisable, intervention techniques vary in the degree to which they distort markets, tend toward permanence, and undermine the overall system of international trading rules. Thus, the following rank order among methods of trade intervention should be borne in mind: Explicit subsidies to domestic producers are the "least bad". Nondiscriminatory tariffs (tariffs applying equally to all foreign sellers) rank next, then nondiscriminatory quotas. The worst methods commonly proposed or employed are discriminatory quotas and local-content rules.

The major advantage of explicit subsidies is their visibility. Appropriations for them normally have to be reviewed annually, and they are obvious targets for budget cutters. By contrast, the costs of direct trade restraints are concealed in consumer prices and generally attract little public attention. Thus, politicians have little motive to attack them, and they are likely to continue indefinitely.

Though less so than subsidies, tariffs are also fairly visible in that they represent explicit costs of bringing foreign products into the domestic market. The GATT provides an international framework, more-over, for ensuring that they are applied in nondiscriminatory fashion. And the market-distorting effects of tariffs are less pernicious than those associated with quantitative restrictions. Governments do not have to allocate market shares to specific firms. Buyers are left free to obtain whatever quantities they desire if they are willing to pay the tariff-influenced price. Finally, a domestic advantage is that tariffs raise revenue from foreign producers and typically cut into their profit margins because they still must compete on price with domestic producers.

Quantitative restrictions involve governments in allocating firm-spe-cific market shares. Their costs are difficult to estimate. They are in-flationary, and they have a strong tendency to harm those protected rather than those protected against. To the extent that they are expressed in terms of finished units, they spur foreign competitors to move into "up-market" segments, where domestic producers may previously have faced little competition. In this way importers can continue to increase their share of revenues even while selling the same number of units.

Other likely responses of foreign producers to quotas on finished units are to increase exports of components to domestic manufacturers and to establish local final-assembly operations. From the perspective of open-traders, component exports are a virtue, since they dilute the market-distorting effect of the quota. From the standpoint of some interventionists, however, this trend is unsatisfactory and may create the need for a tightening of restraints in the direction of local-content requirements.

Yet another problem with quotas is that, by neglecting to impose a windfall-profits tax on quota-imposed price increases (or by selling quota allocations, which would accomplish the same purpose), quotas also yield high unit profits for foreign producers. These profits are likely to be invested in the next generation of products and production pro-cesses. In short, finished-unit quotas combine strong tendencies toward market distortion and inflation with weak or even negative long-term effectiveness.

What is worse, the recent tendency is toward discriminatory and "informal" quotas, sometimes labeled "voluntary"and sometimes con-sisting merely of "warnings" about the unpleasant consequences that might flow from further export expansion. In restricting only a subset of foreign sellers, such restrictions violate one of the central tenets of the GATT. Designed as they are to evade the postwar system of inter-national trade agreements, they may severely discourage future export-oriented investment. They are particularly difficult to negotiate away because in many cases they are scarcely admitted to exist.

From the open-trader's perspective, local-content requirements are even worse because they restrict every company's pursuit of efficiency and because they are intrinsically designed to become permanent by attracting long-term capital investments. Indeed, foreign companies making large investments in internationally uncompetitive local manufacturing operations may themselves become vigorous supporters of permanent protection. In addition, because much of the future growth in automotive trade is likely to occur in the area of components, any system designed to inhibit this trade and to require the production of most components by every producer in every market will severely inhibit the rationalization of the industry. In many configurations, moreover, local-content rules are likely to prove counterproductive at the most obvious level. The leading proposed U.S. legislation, for example, would gear the percentage of local content to sales volume, beginning at 10 percent for automakers selling more than 100,000 vehicles annually and rising to 90 percent for those selling more than 900,000. Though designed to avoid trade friction with Europe by exempting lower-volume sellers, this legislation would prohibit many competitive responses by the U.S.-based producers while facilitating sales growth by the smaller Japanese sellers.

For the interventionists, the choice of methods was also vitally important; however, there was no general agreement on which approach was best. There was agreement that subsidies may be a useful approach, particularly when one of a nation's automakers is in a weak competitive position threatening its survival and a government is intent on maintaining competition among domestic producers. However, it was also argued that in the situation faced by some Western auto industries at present—one of severe competitive disadvantage for many firms—some forms of market protection may be necessary as well.

There was general agreement that, although tariffs may be the most economically efficient method of protection and among the methods easiest to repeal, the existence of the GATT and the strong continuing commitment to it by all the Auto Program countries make tariffs an unrealistic approach, especially in an industry such as automobiles where the competitive imbalance originates from one country. The interventionists argued that it is precisely because there is a broad consensus in favor of preserving the current multilateral trading regime that governments feeling a need to engage in trade intervention have turned increasingly to nontariff methods such as quotas imposed on a single country whose producers are displaying a marked competitive superiority. The prime advantage of this approach is precisely that it enables governments to confine their breach with open-trade principles as narrowly as possible, to limit the number of nations among whom disputes must be negotiated to the smallest possible number, and to focus trade restrictions on nations with the least incentive to retaliate. Thus, although the American quota on Japanese automobiles strains a single bilateral relationship, an across-the-board tariff large enough to produce the same level of restraint on the part of the Japanese would provoke widespread retaliation from European auto-producing nations, and this retaliation would spill over into many other sectors.

From the standpoint of many interventionists, the fact that finished-unit quotas leave restrained producers with attractive opportunities to enhance export revenue through component exports and domestic final assembly is a virtue rather than a vice. Over time, fixed quotas do lose their effectiveness as competitors find their way around them. However, they provide a breathing space for domestic industries threatened by imports, because it takes time for their foreign competitors to develop and implement new strategies. Also, many of these strategies focusing on some local manufacturing will spur the existing producers to precisely the organizational learning about new approaches to domestic production that they need.

For other interventionists who accorded overwhelming weight to the aim of job preservation, these alleged advantages of quotas were in fact their greatest fault. Local-content requirements were proffered as more effective approach. These interventionists argued that such requirements would not necessarily lead to production at inefficiently small scale in many markets (as claimed by some open traders) provided that producers were allowed to count exports from world-scale components or assembly plants located in a given market against their local content requirement for the vehicles sold in that market.

Common Long-Term Goals amid Short-Term Disagreements

The many disagreements about trade policy among those participating in and analyzing the automotive world, as reflected in the Auto Program's policy forums, should not obscure the broad underlying agreement that the appropriate long-term goal is an integrated auto market with all producers in the Auto Program countries achieving the highest level of competitiveness. No one, that is, defended protection and market isolation as a desirable end point of the auto industry's evolution or suggested that some producers should permanently be allowed to lag behind world best practice. However, it was also agreed that the current imbalance in the world auto industry, the likely future state of the world economy, and powerful political forces within each of the Auto Program countries will make the path to the goal of an integrated world auto market arduous.

11   Walking the Tightrope: Choices in an Era of Transformation

We began this inquiry by asking if automobility could endure. We found that the automobile's future as the prime means of personal transport is quite secure because of the flexibility of the basic concept and the robustness of automotive technology. Autos can be produced in more fuel-efficient, less polluting, and safer versions, as future conditions demand. In particular, a broad range of new technologies are becoming available as auto designers race to keep in front of changing consumer preferences and social requirements. Auto producers may need several years to adjust when changes occur abruptly, but there is no basis whatever for projecting that in the end auto technologists will fail to cope. Thus, the auto industry can continue to be one of the world's foremost manufacturing activities far into the future, serving the need for personal transportation in developed and developing nations.

Challenges of Adaptation

If the future of the auto industry on a world scale is ensured, the future of individual producers and national industries is far less certain. All producers and producing nations face many challenges of adaptation in the years ahead. First among these is the necessity of adapting to the competitive challenge from the Japanese producers which, we have called the third historic transformation in the world auto industry. These producers have discovered ways to reduce the amount of labor needed to design and manufacture automobiles while improving quality. This has been achieved through advances in social organization that can be employed with conventional manufacturing machinery and techniques.

The new approaches to production organization are rooted in a social system and a culture very different from those of the West. Consequently, Western producers cannot simply copy Japanese methods. The challenge they face is to become fully competitive once more, but to find their own means of doing so—drawing on Japanese experience, to be sure, but adapting it imaginatively to their own circumstances. The consequence is a far more dynamic type of competition in the world industry, and considerably more uncertainty, than would exist if the challenge were simply to bring about the diffusion of a major technical breakthrough among producers with similar organizational systems.

However, there are also dramatic technical advances in prospect, and these must be accommodated at the same time. These constitute a fourth transformation in the world auto industry, one that will fundamentally alter its structure. Flexible design and manufacturing technologies rooted in microelectronics are sharply reducing both the minimum economic scale and the manpower requirements of automobile production. The auto industry has been characterized conventionally as one with massive scale economies, a mature product, and a mature production process. Until recently most observers concluded that these factors were driving the industry inevitably toward dominance by a few giant producers carrying out an increasing share of their manufacturing activity in less-developed countries, where they could take advantage of low labor costs. Thus, it was widely predicted that by early in next century the OECD auto industry would consist of perhaps six "mega-producers" performing design, marketing, and management functions in the advanced industrial countries and much of the actual production in the less developed countries.

The new logic of industrial evolution, however, is that automobiles can be produced competitively by organizations of widely varying forms and sizes. Flexible manufacturing systems can perform multiple functions, shifting rapidly among them as demand dictates. The consequence is to reduce dramatically the volume required for many components and most car models in order to gain full scale economies. New approaches to cooperative production will facilitate the efforts of smaller producers to gain full scale economies in engines and transmissions, the two components that will still have scale economies up to very large production volumes.

As scale economies have declined and cooperative production arrangements among competitors have proliferated in recent years, it has become apparent that there is no technical reason why the number of world automakers must contract over the remaining years of the twentieth century. It is quite reasonable to expect that the number of major final assemblers (now 20 in the Auto Program countries) will remain essentially stable, and that those nations with only medium-sized independent producers, such as Sweden and the United Kingdom, can continue as participants in the world industry.

The new production technologies also mean that the shift to low-wage locations will not occur on the scale once expected. The markets of the developed countries are demanding precise, high-quality production. Flexible manufacturing, in combination with the redesign of products to gain its full benefits, can provide this while sharply increasing labor productivity. These innovations have shifted the focus of thought about the future geography of production location from the less developed countries to concentrated production of most components near the point of final assembly in the developed countries.

The combined challenges of the third and fourth transformations would be quite enough to keep participants in the world auto industry in a frenzy of adaptation for many years to come. However, in addition, these challenges must be met in economic circumstances that are likely to prove trying. The demand for new cars, which rose at a dizzying pace from the end of World War II until the oil shock of 1973, is unlikely ever to grow again so rapidly over a sustained period. This reflects both the approach of saturation in developed markets and the expectation of slow economic growth rates, in the range of 2–3 percent per year, over the remainder of the century. The demand for automobility itself typically rises, even during periods of economic stagnation. In addition, national auto fleets grow even when new-car sales are depressed—an apparent paradox explained by the great discretion consumers have in deciding when to scrap older vehicles. But the auto industry, concerned with the volume of new-vehicle demand, will face the continuing challenge of how to cope with slow growth.

In the past there was always the hope that as auto markets matured in the developed countries the industry could continue to expand by exporting to developing markets. To some extent this will be possible in the case of small growth markets, but the clear trend of the past decade is for countries with substantial growth markets to insist that high percentages of manufacturing value be added locally. In addition, the heavy international debt of many countries with growth markets makes it apparent that fundamental economic forces going beyond government trade policies will tend to limit auto exports to the less developed countries from the established production locations in the developed countries.

Finally, the markets within the three main auto-producing regions have been converging. The mix of products demanded in each major market remains distinctive, but the areas of overlap have become large. Most of the output of every substantial producer in the OECD countries could in principle be sold in all three regions if the price and quality were right and if government policies permitted. The main exception is the "very-large-car" segment of the North American market, but it has declined substantially in importance since 1973 and remains vulnerable to any future energy shocks.

To note this growing overlap in the demand mix is by no means to forecast that total convergence will occur in the decades ahead. It is to stress that in the next 20 years each producer may come to pose a threat to every other producer in every OECD market. This represents an unprecedented intensity of competition. It entails particular uncertainty for those Western producers whose product lines are most similar to those of the major Japanese automakers and who compete in markets, export or domestic, that are fully open to international competition. More generally, it is apparent that differences in competitiveness among the auto producers of Japan, Western Europe, and North America, which could once be ignored, will henceforth be continuously in the spotlight.

Paths to a New Equilibrium

There are three broad paths to a new equilibrium in the world auto industry. The most direct of these is the elimination of the least competitive producers and national industries, accompanied by the shift of a considerable share of the developed countries' auto production from the United States and parts of Europe to Japan. This could not occur overnight or even in a decade, because capacity expansion entails large investments and multiyear lead times. If Japanese automakers could be confident that open trade policies would prevail regardless of any export successes they might achieve, however, it is certainly plausible to imagine that they might invest boldly to realize this scenario.

An alternative development path is rapid learning and cost reductions by Western mass-market producers, enabling them to close the competitive gap within a few years. The result would be a new equilibrium

Rainbow Bridge National Monument, 309 feet high, is the world's largest known natural bridge. Located on 180-mile long Lake Powell, which is one of Arizona's most popular water playgrounds, Rainbow Bridge is just one of the scenic wonders in the state's northeast section that includes Monument Valley, Canyon de Chelly, the Petrified Forest, Painted Desert, Glen Canyon National Recreation Area, Meteor Crater, and more. For travel information, contact the Arizona Office of Tourism, 1100 W. Washington, Phoenix AZ 85007, (602) 542-TOUR.

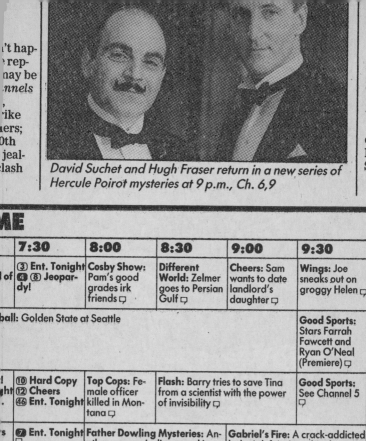

David Suchet and Hugh Fraser return in a new series of Hercule Poirot mysteries at 9 p.m., Ch. 6,9

Partial right-column fragments:

Sea
(Cl

run
see
The
p.m

cyc
PB:
Suc

ME

	7:30	8:00	8:30	9:00	9:30	10
of	**③ Ent. Tonight** **④ ⑧ Jeopardy!**	**Cosby Show:** Pam's good grades irk friends ▯	**Different World:** Zelmer goes to Persian Gulf ▯	**Cheers:** Sam wants to date landlord's daughter ▯	**Wings:** Joe sneaks out on groggy Helen ▯	L.A mu a p
ball: Golden State at Seattle					**Good Sports:** Stars Farrah Fawcett and Ryan O'Neal (Premiere) ▯	Kn sigl me
ght	**⑩ Hard Copy** **⑫ Cheers** **㊻ Ent. Tonight**	**Top Cops:** Female officer killed in Montana ▯	**Flash:** Barry tries to save Tina from a scientist with the power of invisibility ▯		**Good Sports:** See Channel 5 ▯	Kn sigl me
s	**⑦ Ent. Tonight** **⑩ ⑬ Current Affair** ▯	**Father Dowling Mysteries:** Another woman is discovered impersonating Sister Steve ▯		**Gabriel's Fire:** A crack-addicted baby is left in Josephine's restaurant ▯		Pri leg ▯

	7:30	8:00	8:30	9:00	9:30	10
er o ▯	**Family Feud**	**Simpsons:** Homer files a lawsuit ▯	**Babes:** Charlene plans a reunion ruse ▯	**Beverly Hills, 90210:** While their parents are out of town, the twins throw a party ▯		Ne
	Hometime	**This Old House**	**New Yankee Workshop** ▯	**Mystery!:** "Peril at End House" See Channel 9 ▯		Sov
	Wild, Wild World of Animals	**Aboard the QE2:** Alan Whicker explores the relationship between passengers and crew		**Mystery!:** "Peril at End House" A young woman becomes hysterical after her fiance is killed		Che Our Prir

among the world's major auto-producing regions at the level of world "best practice."

The third path is for governments to back up failing producers and national industries with subsidies or trade restraints. This would ensure that most production for each of the world's largest markets would occur domestically, but it might entail progressive widening rather than contraction of competitive imbalances.

Governments can prevent major shifts in production location over the short term. If they use their power to simply hold back the tide, however, they are likely to find the cost rising inexorably. By way of illustration: At the moment, automotive trade restraints by Western governments are directed almost exclusively at Japan. Thus, even if Japanese export growth were shut off altogether, competition in the West would be intense. Moreover, at least a few Western auto industries will make great strides toward matching Japanese practice in the years ahead through copying, collaboration with Japanese producers, or by means of direct Japanese investment. Individual producers and national industries who count on government protection for long-term security, therefore, are likely soon to need protection from Western as well as Japanese-based competition. For any nation this is a bleak prospect indeed. Its implications for the continuation of an integrated economy in the developed countries are alarming.

Thus, the only path to rebalancing the world auto industry that is both feasible and desirable is for the auto-producing nations with competitive weaknesses to catch up so that open competition may be carried on across the developed world. This competition may well lead to gradual shifts in production to one region or another but shifts that publics, governments, and work forces may find acceptable because they will not portend the imminent and total collapse of whole industrial sectors. The question is how to move rapidly to achieve a new competitive balance at the highest level of best practice while avoiding the collapse of Western auto industries over the short term.

The Central Challenge

If wise paths of adaptation are pursued by producers and labor unions as well as governments, the challenge of rebalance along with the introduction of new manufacturing technology creates extraordinary opportunities for industrial vitality. An industry once considered mature, perhaps even stagnant, has already encountered some extraordinary market and public-policy challenges and demonstrated remarkable vigor in meeting them. At present it is pioneering new manufacturing strategies—organizational and technological—that promise to boost productivity dramatically while improving product quality, and to stimulate other industries by their demonstration effects. The end result of this process may be a world system of auto production that will be highly dynamic for decades to come and will be widely distributed geographically throughout the OECD world and, increasingly, in developing countries as their demand for automobiles grows. This would entail competition among the automakers of these regions on relatively even terms in a widening international marketplace.

The obstacles to this bright future are daunting. The root problem is that the current and future transformations in the auto industry entail great insecurity for vast numbers of people. Policies adopted to mitigate this insecurity may severely retard the progress of the global auto industry and heighten tensions among the leading democratic nations.

At the macroscale, it is apparent that the best solutions are those that will optimally advance global economic progress. However, the perspectives of decision makers in firms, unions, and governments are invariably more micro. They are primarily concerned with the effects of change on their own institutions and constituencies rather than with global optimality.

The central challenge, then, is to reconcile this macroaim with the wide diversity of microperspectives. This challenge must be met in a highly decentralized fashion. There is no supreme manager. To achieve a bright future, leaders of business, labor, and government in numerous countries must understand the "logic of the future"—the powerful underlying forces of industrial transformation, which demand creative initiatives and adjustments by many parties. Understanding this logic has been a key objective of this volume and of the Auto Program.

Acting on this knowledge, however, requires unusual levels of statesmanship in balancing the parochial and short-term concerns that immediately preoccupy leaders everywhere against the broader, long-term prospect. Because the constituency pressures for parochial strategies are extraordinarily intense, the leaders who reach for such statesmanship will be walking a tightrope.

Choices for Industry Participants

Leaders of organized automotive labor in the West undoubtedly face the most difficult choices. After three decades in which they moved from one membership gain and negotiating triumph to another, they now confront the prospect of continuous membership decline along with intense competitive pressure on compensation levels and work-rule agreements. Competitive pressures, moreover, are calling upon them to lead their members toward more positive, quality-conscious shop-floor attitudes.

The inexorable tendency of the auto industry's development over the remaining years of the century will be toward labor-force contraction virtually everywhere. First, Western producers will be driven to match Japanese labor-content levels. Second, the Japanese themselves will be exploiting the labor-saving potential of flexible manufacturing technologies, and the Western producers must match these gains as well. Third, changes in materials and manufacturing techniques threaten membership losses in established unions, because the sharpest employment declines will occur in areas (such as metal fabrication) that are at the heart of current auto-related union membership. These losses will be partially offset by gains in the electronics, plastics, and other "new" supplier industries whose employees are generally unorganized or represented by other unions.

The short-term interest of the leaders of auto workers' unions is to preserve existing levels of employment and compensation by any and all means, including the erection of impermeable trade barriers. This approach meshes well with labor's view that compensation and manning levels should reflect social negotiations oriented toward conceptions of social justice rather than mere market forces. As labor is organized nationally rather than at the OECD level, it seems to face a choice between abandoning its fundamental ideology and striving to insulate the markets of the Auto Program countries from one another.

If there were no more to it than this, labor might well concentrate exclusively on restraining international trade. In practice, however, short-run success on this path may increase future vulnerability if it leads to a widening of international competitive imbalances. A union able to persuade its nation's government to impose trade restraints today may be unable to secure their renewal or reinforcement at a later time. As foreign producers develop strategies to circumvent initial restraints (such as imports of components rather than finished units, or domestic manufacturing facilities with superior production systems and lower wage rates) reinforcing measures will often be necessary to preserve union jobs and wage levels. However, political leaders may be focusing on inflation control when the renewal and reinforcement proposals come up, or overall trade deficit concerns may have abated. Even worse, critics of trade restraint may sway the public mood as they stress that restraints once justified as temporary are becoming permanent and ever more costly.

Labor is most secure, therefore, where its negotiated benefits can be sustained without government assistance. Most leaders of auto workers' unions in the West understand this and recognize that they have a stake in cooperating with management to pursue competitive balance, but at the same time they are political leaders with constituents. Their "tightrope walk," consequently, involves serving both the members who elect them and the social values closest to their own hearts by preserving employment and the terms of past negotiated agreements while cooperating with management to pursue world-scale competitiveness over the longer run. Unfortunately, the long-run aim often requires very painful measures in the here and now, including employment contraction, productivity-enhancing changes in work rules, and wage concessions (or at least relative declines in comparison with employees in other domestic industries).

The task of accommodation is least difficult for union leaders in those national auto industries such as the Japanese, the Swedish, and the German, which run large export trade surpluses. Rank-and-file union members in these countries understand that they must remain internationally competitive if their negotiated gains are to be preserved and expanded. At the other extreme, the American and the British auto industries have no substantial export markets to lose. Their employees are thus much more susceptible to arguments that government intervention in trade can effectively contain the Japanese competitive challenge (and the European challenge as well, in the case of the United Kingdom).

The critical choices for producers include the commercial, labor-relations, and political strategies that make up a corporate strategy of adaptation. These elements of the corporate strategy are directly related. For example, commercial decisions about production, marketing, and distribution must be adopted with an eye toward actual and prospective government policies (in the areas of taxation, trade, subsidies, and regulation) in all those countries where the company is active. Some key commercial options were discussed in chapter 8, and a central message of this study is that the automotive system as a whole is likely to evolve most dynamically if these decisions are left to the companies—provided that they face intense competition from one another.

Labor-relations strategies are perhaps the most critical for many Western manufacturers, because these must somehow nurture new skills and patterns of human organization in the production system while simultaneously holding down costs. One approach is to bring costs and quality into line with Japanese competitors by actively working with labor at home. This strategy acknowledges that capital facilities and human skills are at present heavily concentrated in the home country, and that producers must concentrate on getting the most from these resources even if they desire to gradually shift production and procurement abroad or to lower-cost domestic sources.

Additionally, labor's support is critical whenever government must be lobbied for regulatory relief, trade intervention, or financial assistance. For companies that are owned wholly or largely by governments (BL, Renault, Alfa Romeo, and Volkswagen) or that otherwise feel highly dependent on the good will of the home government (PSA), no other course besides the accommodation of labor may be feasible. The elements of such accommodation are likely to include guarantees of job security for employees with substantial seniority, promises to keep work in house even where significant short-term savings might be realized by contracting it out, and only modest pressure on levels of compensation.

The alternative is an aggressive strategy of "outsourcing." The advantage is that this constantly dramatizes the possibility that in-house jobs will be lost unless changes occur that are of sufficient magnitude to overcome the competitive advantages of outside vendors. The disadvantage, of course, is that this strategy is likely to embitter domestic labor relations and frustrate efforts to improve productivity and worker involvement.

No company is likely to adopt one or the other of these strategies in pure form. Illustratively, Ford is the U.S. producer that seems most committed to a strategy of accommodation. It announced in mid 1983, however, that it would close down its in-house steel plant unless employees accepted a substantial pay cut. (They did.) In short, it made clear that its commitment to accommodation could not involve the indefinite acceptance of large cost differentials.

General Motors, on the other hand, has moved vigorously toward outsourcing. It has contracted to bring in its next generation of subcompact cars primarily from Japan. Moreover, after closing down a major assembly plant at Fremont, California, GM reached an agreement with Toyota on joint production of a new model, with day-to-day management under Toyota's direction. The former employees were informed that, although they would receive consideration for re-employment, decisions on whom to hire would be discretionary, seniority would be irrelevant, and work rules would be negotiated afresh. General Motors has also increased its domestic outsourcing, turning in many cases to non-union vendors. Even so, GM continues to place great emphasis on its in-house Quality of Work Life program and to strive generally for improved relations with its employees. While recognizing that the two prongs of their strategy are partially in conflict, GM officials perceive them even more significantly as reinforcing. The pressure of outsourcing more generally serves to remind employees of the outside competition they and the company face.

The issue, again, is one of delicate balance. No company can afford to ignore the outsourcing alternative. Nor can any succeed in the long run without eliciting the commmitment of its own employees. The balancing task would be difficult in any circumstances, but it is particularly so when the prospects are for an overall decline in employment and when competitive pressures necessitate rapid adjustment. This means walking the tightrope in a hurricane.

Unfortunately, the option of waiting for milder weather is not available to many of the Western auto companies. Or is it? Some producers believe that government can and should provide an effective shield from the winds of competition until larger economic problems are solved—that is, until the economies of the West are again experiencing sustained growth and perceived problems with currency alignments and comparative taxation are solved. Companies that adopt this viewpoint are likely to be driven toward policies of accommodating their unions, because government assistance is most obtainable when management pursues it in alliance with labor. Companies doubting that this can be an effective path to long-term competitiveness, however, are likely to favor relatively open markets as a means of keeping pressure on employees to match global best practice.

Even where companies and unions cooperate initially to secure government assistance, they are likely to divide subsequently over its precise objectives and methods. The primary aim of the unions will be to save existing jobs. Corporate leaders, on the other hand, are likely to view state aid as regrettably necessary for the moment but a very weak reed on which to rely for the longer term. They will typically favor adjustment strategies under the umbrella of public assistance that entail investment in the most advanced production technologies, sharp contraction in the labor force, and cuts or freezes in wages.

In this situation, companies may well hedge their bets. The GM case is again instructive. By 1983 the company was positioned to profit either from the continuation of Japanese export restraint or from its elimination. If export-restraints continued, GM would prosper because it was well positioned in the American market in relation to its Western competitors. Additionally, it would begin marketing in 1985 the cars it planned to produce jointly with Toyota in the United States without having to face additional Japanese competition. Alternatively, if the restraints were lifted, GM had contracts in hand to import several hundred thousand Japanese small cars beginning in late 1984 for marketing under its own brand names.

The Western transnational automakers, in short, are under great pressure to prepare for a variety of governmental policy contingencies. Over the long run, however, those that remain important producers on the world scale will be those that are able to compete without significant government assistance. Thus, whether pursuing government assistance or stressing the desirability of open international competition (or both simultaneously), Western corporate leaders will have little justification for claiming success in the years ahead unless they have made progress toward closing the competitive gap.

The Japanese producers are also trying to hedge their bets in devising competitive strategies that depend crucially on predicting the future evolution of Western government policies. They are going slow on capacity expansion at home while rapidly expanding their commitment to production abroad. They are also working hard to develop collaborative agreements with a wide range of Western producers, which they believe will help them gain market access (particularly for components).

Finally, with regard to the critical choices facing governments, it is essential to distinguish among the situations facing the different Auto Program countries. For Japan the critical choice is whether to simply insist on open trade, using whatever bargaining levers are at hand, or to accept that there are broad limits on the size of its automotive trade surplus that Western governments will tolerate. The former strategy may yield modest short-term concessions if the world economy resumes moderate growth in the years just ahead, but it is primarily a path toward heightened trade tension between Japan and many of the Western auto-producing nations. The latter path, on the other hand, would urge Western acceptance of the existing vast surplus along with a modest rate of growth in times of economic expansion, coupled with encouragement from the Japanese government for direct investment by Japanese producers in Western production facilities, both alone and in collaboration with Western producers.

The governments of the Western auto-producing nations as a group face more difficult choices than the Japanese, because their aim is not simply to facilitate growth but rather to avert or mitigate declines in their industries and in employment. On the one hand, political time horizons are short, and elected leaders are sorely tempted to preserve domestic producers and employment even if they fear that the long-term effects may be counterproductive. On the other hand, most believe that competition is the long-term key to economic advance and that the OECD economies can be insulated from each other only at considerable risk to world prosperity.

During the 1950s and the 1960s, the view that trade intervention is normally counterproductive provided a critical ideological base for Western trade-liberalization initiatives. The advocates of this view pointed to the trade wars of the 1930s as an object lesson about the probable end result of protection. So long as the OECD economies were thriving, with close to full employment, the idea that more open trade was in every nation's interest had few critics. Special-interest groups might obtain protection by the sheer weight of their political influence, but they did so by claiming acute hardship rather than by successfully challenging the dominant ideology.

Of late the choices before Western governments are perceived as more complex, and new ways of thinking will be needed to preserve the momentum for economic integration over the remainder of this century. First, there is increasing recognition that trade intervention is not an all-or-nothing proposition. Competition may be intense and may move producers toward world best practice even where it is not completely open—as in Japan before import liberalization and as in several Western markets today. Moreover, large institutions such as auto production chains can only be transformed over a period of years. Consequently, governments may have legitimate choices to make about whether to mitigate some of the pressure to which threatened producers are exposed during a period of adjustment to new competitive forces, and about the rate at which assistance should be withdrawn. Second, the problems faced by Western auto manufacturers are similar to those faced by a growing number of other Western industries. In light of the

linkages of the auto industry to many of these industries and the un-
likelihood that new high-wage growth sectors can generate vast numbers
of jobs over the remaining years of the century to offset massive losses
in mature industries, there is great reluctance among the Auto Program
governments to sacrifice the auto industry on the altar of any abstract
theory of efficiency. Rather, the tendency is to view the auto industry
as one of the critical arenas in which the lessons of Japanese productivity
must be absorbed and the potential of flexible manufacturing technology
achieved, so that progress can be made toward restoring confidence in
the future of Western industrial competitiveness more generally.

The question therefore is just how to move national auto industries
toward world best practice while protecting them against short-term
collapse or massive employment shocks. For each of the Western nations
the policy path is probably different. In the case of the Germans and
the Swedes, who are now highly competitive because of their strong
market position in high-performance and luxury segments, the challenge
is to avoid falling into the American position of the 1950s and 1960s
where security in uncontested market segments diverted attention from
production costs that failed to keep pace with world best practice.
Clearly, trade restraints are not the proper way to address this issue.
Instead government, industry, and labor must form a clear vision of
future competitive needs and take steps to deal with the employment
consequences of adjustments that may be necessary as the introduction
of flexible automation continues and as Japanese producers began to
offer larger high-performance and luxury models.

The challenge for U.S. policy is how to protect the domestic auto
industry from catastrophe during economic downturns and dramatic
demand-mix shifts (which tend to occur together) while maintaining
steady pressure on management and labor to continue moving along
the still lengthy path toward world best practice. The Voluntary Restraint
Agreement has sent a powerful signal to the Japanese that the United
States intends to maintain a major domestic auto industry, and this
device may well find use again in future economic slumps. However,
it will be vitally important to remove import barriers in periods of strong
market growth and healthy industry profits lest the true competitive
situation be forgotten.

A second challenge for the United States, tied closely to the first, is
how to manage its energy policy. The present Corporate Average Fuel
Economy (CAFE) standards run directly counter to the industry's need
to maintain volume in the "large" and "very large" segments, where

American producers still face little competition from the Japanese. However, the fear in the U.S. government is that relaxation of the standards will instill another sense of false security and lead to a catastrophe if energy prices ratchet upward once more and these market segments shrink dramatically. Some type of industry-government understanding is clearly needed so that the government can be assured of the industry's intentions to continue emphasizing fuel efficiency in new products and the industry can have reasonable freedom to seize competitive advantages in the near term.

In moving its automotive sector toward full competitiveness, the United States is helped by its historic willingness to permit foreign direct investment and by recent decisions not to block the internationalization efforts of U.S. producers on structural (anti-trust) grounds. Direct investment and cross-national collaborations are key means by which new systems of production organization are diffused from one country to another. In the anti-trust area, the key challenge for the world during the next two decades is not too little competition due to mergers and short-term alliances; rather, the greater danger is so much competition that some nations will find the threat to their producers intolerable and seek to isolate their markets.

Britain, France, and Italy face situations with many similarities, notably domestic industries with many competitive weaknesses and a long tradition of market protection. Their government-policy challenge is to find ways to move their producers toward best practice so that the prospect of open competition will not appear so threatening. A key advantage of Great Britain's policy is a willingness to invite both foreign collaboration and direct investment, an approach thus far accepted only haltingly by Italy and rejected by France. The common argument against these measures is that they will exacerbate overcapacity in the European industry. However, in the current situation, where there are such broad differences in the competitiveness of different production facilities, new investments in more advanced systems of production organization and in technology will be pushing out obsolete capacity rather than adding to excess capacity. In the absence of willingness to push hard on less competitive producers and facilities, the imbalance in the world industry can only become worse. Indeed, the greatest problem in Europe is that some national industries may avail themselves of the most promising catch-up measures while others will not, which may lead to severe trade tensions within the EEC.

The Prospects

The great question, then, is whether all the competing interests and perceptions of reality, within each country and across the developed world, can be balanced. From the global standpoint, is the goal of a new competitive balance at the level of world best practice a reasonable one? From the standpoint of individual nations, companies, and labor unions, does it make sense to walk the tightrope toward this goal rather than to stake out simple positions and insist on them?

We have no final answers, but there are many positive signs. The pace of copying, collaboration, and direct investment has stepped up dramatically in the United States and Europe since the late 1970s. The major producers and component suppliers, both in Japan and the West, seem to be internationalizing rapidly. Honda and Nissan are assembling vehicles in the United States and have announced plans to gradually expand the number of models produced and to increase their local content. General Motors and Toyota have received government permission to embark on a collaborative manufacturing venture in the United States which GM managers describe as a benchmark by which other elements of GM's domestic manufacturing system will be judged in the future, and on its own GM has made impressive advances in manufacturing systems such as "Buick City" and the Pontiac Fiero production system. BL is continuing a thoroughgoing process of organizational learning through a series of collaborations with Honda (not just in manufacture but also in vehicle design), and the pace of competition in the whole British industry will be stepped up in the late 1980s when Nissan begins to assemble vehicles locally and move toward a high level of local content. In addition, a long list of cooperative ventures have been announced between other Japanese and Western producers which will diffuse innovation and aid in restoring the competitive balance.

However, there are also many question marks. The full process of rebalancing and assimilation will take many years. Individual producers inevitably will make catastrophic errors from time to time, which governments will be hard pressed to ignore or to remedy creatively. Labor leaders and company heads will face a difficult task in explaining the demands of the future to the rank and file. Finally, the trade cycle and the general sluggishness of the world economy will put periodic pressures on the weakest producers and national industries, which governments will feel compelled to alleviate. Thus, the auto industry on a world scale faces a long tightrope walk to a brighter future. If concentration on the task of creative adjustment wavers, serious problems for the developed countries lie in wait. If the players continue to increase their understanding of the underlying logic of industrial evolution and adjust their microperspectives accordingly, the whole world will benefit.

Appendix A
National Research Teams Participating in the International Automobile Program

Federal Republic of Germany—Wissenschaftszentrum (Science Center), Berlin

National Team Leader: Meinolf Dierkes, President, Science Center

Hermann Appel, Technical University of Berlin
Andrew Black, Science Center Berlin
Joachim Blödorn, Technical University of Berlin
Rob Coppock, Science Center Berlin
Manfred J. Dirrheimer, Science Center Berlin
Knuth Dohse, Science Center Berlin
Gertraud Foos, University of Karlsruhe
Rolf Funck, University of Karlsruhe
Klaus Peter Hilber, Technical University of Berlin
Andreas Hoff, Science Center Berlin
Thomas Hübner, Science Center Berlin
Ulrich Juergens, Science Center Berlin
Uwe Kunert, Technical University of Berlin
Thomas Malsch, Science Center Berlin
Wolfgang Streeck, Science Center Berlin
Harro Volkmar, Technical University of Berlin

France—Institut de Recherche des Transports, Paris

National Team Leader: Michel Frybourg, Conservatoire des Arts et Metiers

Jacques Anthonioz
Jean-Pierre Barbier, SEMA
Marie Antoinette Dekkers, Institut de Recherche des Transports
Laurent deMautort, CEPII
Armand Leinekugel-le-Cocq, SEMA
Claude Moinet, Renault
Jean Pierre Orfeuil, Institut de Recherche des Transports
Francis Pave
Rémy Prud'homme, University of Parix XII

Italy—NOMISMA, Bologna

National Team Leader: Patrizio Bianchi, NOMISMA

Nicola Bellini, NOMISMA
Ettore Santucci, NOMISMA
Maria Luigia Segnana, NOMISMA

Japan—Nihon Kotsu Seisaku Kenkyukai, Tokyo

National Team Leaders: Hideo Nakamura and Yukihide Okano, University of Tokyo

Doichi Aoki, Japan Automobile Manufacturers Association
Haruki Fujii, Toyota Motor Co., Ltd.
Takahiro Fujimoto, Mitsubishi Research Institute, Inc.
Takahiko Furuta, Institute for Social Engineering, Inc.
Kenichi Goto, Japan Automobile Research Institute, Inc.
Shigeru Handa, Japan Economic Research Institute
Reijiro Hashiyama, Japan Development Bank
Waichiro Hayashi, University of Tokyo (and MIT)
Noboru Hidano, University of Tokyo
Hitoshi Honda, University of Tokyo
Shoji Honda, Daihatsu Motor Co., Ltd.
Chisato Hoshino, Daihatsu Motor Co., Ltd.
Tadashi Ide, Fuji Heavy Industries, Ltd.
Masakazu Iguchi, University of Tokyo
Mitsumasa Inoue, Nissan Motor Co., Ltd.
Yoshio Ishii, Mitsubishi Motor Co., Ltd.
Kiichi Kageyama, Chiba University of Commerce
Ichiro Kaneshige, Isuzu Motors., Ltd.
Shigeru Kashima, Chuo University
Kozo Kitoh, Japan Automobile Research Institute, Inc.
Fumihiko Kobayashi, Toyota Motor Co., Inc.
Toshiyuki Kono, Japan Automobile Research Institute, Inc.
Masaki Koshi, University of Tokyo
Kazutoshi Koshiro, Yokohama National University
Eiichi Kumabe, Toyota Motor Co., Ltd.
Atsushi Kusano, International University of Japan
Hiromitsu Kusano, Mitsubishi Motor Co., Ltd.
Renpei Matsumoto, Fuji Heavy Industries, Ltd.
Yasunobu Mitoya, Toyo Kogyo Co., Ltd.
Masao Miyazaki, National Police Agency
Shigeru Morichi, Tokyo Institute of Technology
Yoshio Nakamura, Honda Motor Co., Ltd.
Masakatsu Ono, Toyo Kogyo Co., Ltd.

Makoto Osawa, Honda Motor Co., Ltd.
Taku Oshima, Osaka City University
Koichi Shimokawa, Hosei University
Haruo Simosaka, Meiji University
Yoshio Suzuki, Industrial Bank of Japan, Ltd.
Yoji Takahashi, Japan Regional Development Corporation
Kengo Teranishi, Daihatsu Motor Co., Ltd.
Shunichi Toshida, Nissan Motor Co., Ltd.
Hiroshi Tsuda, Suzuki Motor Co., Ltd.
Yoshio Tsukio, Nagoya University
Keiichi Tsunekawa, University of Tokyo
Atsushi Watari, University of Tokyo
Taizo Yakushiji, Saitama University
Tokuro Yamashita, Isuzu Motors, Ltd.

Sweden—Institute of Management of Innovation and Technology (IMIT), Göteborg

National Team Leader: Lars Sjöstedt, Chalmers University of Technology

Christian Berggren, Royal Institute of Technology
Åke Claesson, Royal Institute of Technology
Tomas Engström, Chalmers University of Technology
Lars-Erik Gadde, IMIT
Bruce Grant, Chalmers University of Technology
Rolf Gustafson, Linköping University of Technology
Gunnar Hedlund, Stockholm School of Economics
Jan Owen Jansson, National Road and Traffic Research Institute
Christer Karlsson, IMIT
Ulf Karlsson, Chalmers University of Technology
Stefan Liljemark, Chalmers University of Technology
Olof Lundin, University of Göteborg
Bertil Nilsson, IMIT and Lund Institute of Technology
Hans-Åke Petterson, Chalmers University of Technology
Leif Ringhagen, Royal Institute of Technology
Dag Rolander, Stockholm School of Economics
Lars-Erik Sjöberg, Swedish National Road Administration
Roland Steen, Stockholm School of Economics
Ove Svidén, Technical University of Linkoping
Henrik Swahn, Stockholm School of Economics
Örjan Sölvell, Stockholm School of Economics
Jans-Erik Vahlne, Stockholm School of Economics
Thure Valdsoo, Royal Institute of Technology
Christopher von Schirach-Szmigiel, Stockholm School of Economics

United Kingdom—Science Policy Research Unit, University of Sussex

National Team Leader: Daniel Jones, Science Policy Research Unit

Paul Gardiner, Science Policy Research Unit
Tony Manwaring, London School of Economics
David Marsden, London School of Economics
Anthony May, University of Leeds
Neville Patterson, University of Leeds
Paul Weaver, University of Leeds
Stephen Wood, London School of Economics

United States—Massachusetts Institute of Technology, Cambridge

National Team Leaders: Alan Altshuler and Daniel Roos

Martin Anderson, MIT
James Dunn, Rutgers University
Jane Fraser, Purdue University
Ann Friedlaender, MIT
Waichiro Hayashi, MIT (and University of Tokyo)
George Heaton, MIT
William Johnston (private consultant)
Harry Katz, MIT
Mary McShane, MIT
John Menge, Dartmouth College
Thomas Sparrow, Purdue University
James Utterback, MIT
William Wheaton, MIT
Robert Whitford, Purdue University
Clifford Winston, MIT
James Womack, MIT

Appendix B
Participants in the
International Automobile
Program Policy Forums

Three-day policy forums for invited participants, their designated associates, and members of the national research teams were held at Philadelphia, Pennsylvania (June 28–30, 1981), Hakone, Japan (May 16–18, 1982), and Stenungsund, Sweden (June 13–15, 1983). These sessions were followed by 2–3-day research meetings for the research teams and the Policy Forum associates. Each participant was asked to designate an associate who would be able to consult with Program researchers on an extensive basis and who would keep the participant informed about Program activities.

Those listed were asked to attend as individuals with extensive knowledge about the automobile and the auto industry rather than as representatives of their organizations. The meetings were held on an off-the-record basis in the sense that no direct attribution of observations and comments was allowed in Program research reports. This volume, as we have noted, is the work solely of its authors. Although the participants and the associates were given full opportunity to comment on draft versions at several points, their participation in the Program and their attendance at the forum sessions do not mean that they or their organizations subscribe to the findings and recommendations of this volume.

Forum Participants

France

Pierre Amouyel
Chef du service de l'énergie et des
activitiés tertiaires
Commissariat Général du Plan

Pierre Eelsen
Délégué Général
Régie Renault

M. Emmanuel Euverte
Director, Strategic and Corporate
Planning, Automobile Sector
Régie Renault

Michel Frybourg
Ingénieur Général des Ponts et
Chaussées
Professeur-associé au Conservatoire
National des Arts et Metiers

Pierre Gadonneix
Directeur
Direction des Industries métallur-
giques, mécaniques et électriques
Ministère de l'Industrie

Christian Hue de la Colombe
Directeur, Automobiles
Direction des Industries métallur-
giques, mécaniques et électriques
Ministère de l'Industrie

François Perrin-Pelletier
Conseiller en innovation auprès du
Directoire
Peugeot S.A.

Federal Republic of Germany

Achim Diekmann
Vice-President
Verband der Automobilindustrie e.V.

Meinolf Dierkes
President
Wissenschaftszentrum Berlin

Hans Joachim Förster
Director of Research
Daimler-Benz AG

Peter Frerk
Member, Board of Management
Volkswagen AG

Hans Jürgen Fröbose
Deputy Assistant Secretary
Ministry of Transport

Bernhard Molitor
Assistant Secretary
Ministry of Commerce

Lorenz Schomerus
Head, Industrial Sector
Ministry of Commerce

Albert Schunk
Head of International Department
Industriegewerkschaft Metall für die
Bundesrepublik, Deutschland

Italy

Luigi Arnaudo
Director, Strategic Planning
Fiat S.p.A.

Patrizio Bianchi
NOMISMA

Pasquale Calderale
Director
Istituto della Motorizzazione del
Politecnico di Torino

Antonio Lettieri
Member, Executive Committee
Conferazione Generale Italiana del
Lavoro

Japan

Yoshiharu Aikawa
General Manager
Europe Office
Toyota Motor Company

Naohiro Amaya
Special Advisor
MITI

Shigeru Aoki
Managing Director and General
  Manager
Tokyo Office
Toyota Motor Co., Ltd.

Nobuo Araki
Director of International Affairs
Confederation of Japan Automobile
  Workers' Unions

Mitsuya Goto
General Manager
Europe Office
Nissan Motor Company

Makoto Itabashi
Executive Vice-President
American Honda Motor Co., Ltd.

Hidenari Ito
Manager of Administration and
  Finance
U.S. Representative Office
Toyota Motor Company

Tsutomu Kagawa
General Manager
Planning & Public Relations
Japan Automobile Manufacturers
  Association

Setsuo Kashiwagi
General Manager
Planning & Public Relations
Japan Automobile Manufacturers
  Association

Yutaka Kume
Managing Director
Nissan Motor Co., Ltd.

Teruo Maeda
General Manager
Product Development Office
Nissan Motor Co., Ltd.

Yoshiharu Matsumoto
General Manager
Tokyo Research Department
Toyota Motor Company

Kiyoshi Mori
Executive Chief
Europe Head Office
Honda Motor Company

Hideo Nakamura
Department of Civil Engineering
University of Tokyo

Yukihide Okano
Faculty of Economics
University of Tokyo

Keiichi Oshima
Professor Emeritus
University of Tokyo
Co-Chairman
International Energy Forum

Hiroto Oyama
Senior Research Fellow
Institute for Social Engineering

Seizaburo Sato
Professor
College of General Education
University of Tokyo

Moriharu Shizume
Paris Office
Japan Automobile Manufacturers
  Association

Eishi Takahashi
Director
International Affairs Bureau
Confederation of Japan Automobile
  Workers' Association

Hideo Takeda
Director
Honda R&D Co., Ltd.

Toru Toyoshima
Director-General
Machinery and Information Industries Bureau
MITI

Chikao Tsukuda
Director General
Japan Trade Center
Paris

Sweden

Henrik Gustavsson
Director of Quality and Technical Public Affairs
Passenger Car Division
Saab-Scania AB

Per-Olof Holmqvist
Head of Automobile Department
Swedish Metalworkers Union

Lars Sjöstedt
Department of Transportation and Logistics
Chalmers University of Technology

Carl-Olof Ternryd
Director General
Swedish National Road Administration

Dan Werbin
Senior Vice President
Product Planning
Volvo AB

United Kingdom

Michael J. Callaghan
Treasurer, European Credit Operations
Ford Motor Credit Co. Ltd.

Alan A. Gaves
Director, Group Strategic Planning
Lucas Group Services, Ltd.

Malcolm J. Harbour
Director, Marketing
Austin Rover Group, Ltd.

Daniel T. Jones
Senior Research Fellow
Science Policy Research Unit
The University of Sussex

Karl E. Ludvigsen
Vice-President, Governmental Affairs
Ford of Europe, Inc.

J. Mark Snowdon
Commercial Director, Cars
BL Cars Ltd.

United States

Irving Bluestone
University Professor of Labor Studies
Wayne State University

Thomas J. Busch
Vice-President and Group Executive
Business Strategy and Marketing
Bendix Corporation

Michael Driggs
Deputy Assistant Secretary for Automotive Industry Affairs
U.S. Department of Commerce

Theodore Eck
Chief Economist
Standard Oil Co. (Indiana)

Donald Ephlin
Vice-President
Director, GM Department
United Automobile Workers Union

R. Eugene Goodson
Group Vice-President
Hoover Universal, Inc.

Maryann N. Keller
First Vice-President
Paine Weber Mitchell Hutchins, Inc.

Frederick T. Knickerbocker
Acting Director
Economic Policy Staff
U.S. Department of Commerce

C. Kenneth Orski
President
Corporation for Urban Mobility

Raymond A. Peck, Jr.
Administrator
National Highway Traffic Safety
  Administration
U.S. Department of Transportation

David S. Potter
Group Vice-President, Public Affairs
General Motors Corporation

Will Scott
Vice-President, Government
  Relations
Ford Motor Company

Diane K. Steed
Administrator
National Highway Traffic Safety
  Administration
U.S. Department of Transportation

Russell Train
President
World Wildlife Fund, U.S.

John S. Trees
Senior Vice-President
Allstate Insurance Group

Roger Vincent
Vice-President, Automotive Affairs
Bankers Trust Company

At Large

David Bayliss
Chief Transport Planner
Department of Transport and
  Development
Greater London Council

Paolo Cecchini
Deputy Director
Directorate General for Internal
  Market and Industrial Affairs
Commission of the European
  Communities

Collin Gonze
Director, Auto & Aerospace
  Department
International Metalworkers'
  Federation

Herman Rebhan
General Secretary
International Metalworkers'
  Federation

Ricardo Garcia Saenz
General Director
Diesel Nacional, S.A.

Dale R. Weigel
Manager, Promotion Department
International Finance Corporation
World Bank Group

Forum Associates

France

François Beaujolin
Chargé de mission
Service de l'Industrie
Commissariat Général du Plan

Gerard Gastaut
Ajoint au Directeur de Planification
Renault

Jean Houot
Direction des Plans et Produits
Peugeot S.A.

Felix Melin
U.S. Technical Research Company
P.S.A. Peugeot-Citroen

Federal Republic of Germany

Klaus-Dieter Burchard
Department Head for Auto Industry
Ministry of Commerce

Frank Neumann
Ministry of Commerce

Udo Reber
Assistant to Director of Research
Daimler-Benz AG

Hans Viggo von Hülsen
Director for Foreign Legal Matters
Volkswagen AG

Italy

Piera Balliano
Strategic Planning Division
Fiat S.p.A.

Patrizia de Battisti
Planning Division
Alfa Romeo S.p.A.

Maria Teresa Schutt
Industrial Relations Division
Fiat S.p.A.

Japan

Tooru Gejima
Manager, Marketing Department
Daihatsu Motors Co., Ltd.

Akira Hasegawa
Corporate Staff
Business Research & Administration
Nissan Motor Co., Ltd.

Toshihiro Iwatake
Assistant Director
Washington Office
Japan Automobile Manufacturers
  Association

Shin Kanada
Chief
Tokyo Research Department
Toyota Motor Company

Ryuichi Kasahara
Manager, Comptroller Section
Subaru General Administrative Div.
Fuji Heavy Industries, Ltd.

Shinichi Kashiro
Manager, Research Section
Mitsubishi Motors Corporation

Isamu Kawashima
General Manager, Automobile De-
  sign & Technical Division
Suzuki Motor Co., Ltd.

Hiroshi Kimura
Project Manager
Office of the President's Staff
Toyo Kogyo Co., Ltd.

Akio Kotani
General Manager
Corporate Planning Office
Nissan Motor Co., Ltd.

Hiroshi Mitani
Director, Section of International Af-
  fairs, Planning Department
Ministry of Construction

Hiroyuki Nishimura
Staff Engineer
Wako R&D Center
Honda R&D Co., Ltd.

Shinziro Nishinaka
Manager, Automobile Division
Machinery and Information Indus-
  tries Bureau
MITI

Yutaka Nochiide
Director, Regional Planning Division
Ministry of Transportation

Tomizo Ohnoda
Manager, Forward Planning Office
Research and Engineering Division
Isuzu Motors Ltd.

Shoichiro Sugiura
Europe Office
Toyota Motor Company

Tatsuo Suzuki
Secretary General
International Association of Traffic
& Safety Science

Katsuhisa Takiyama
Manager, Economic & Legal Re-
search Affairs Department
Toyota Motor Co., Ltd.

Isao Tanaka
Manager, Planning Section, Plan-
ning and Public Relations
Department
Japan Automobile Manaufacturers
Association, Inc.

Etienne van Buynber
Master Staff Engineer
European Office
Honda Motor Company

Yukimasa Yamada
Counsellor, Traffic Safety Counter-
measures Officer
Prime Minister's Office

Masaru Yamaki
Staff Engineer, Technical Division
American Honda Motor Co., Inc.

Sweden

Jan Helling
Organizational Consultant
Saab-Scania AB

Stieg Ingvarsson
Project Coordinator
Saab-Scania AB

Lars-Erik Sjöberg
Assistant Director
National Swedish Road
Administration

Stephen Wallman
Manager, Technological Analysis
Product Planning
AB Volvo

United Kingdom

William Horton
Manufacturing Planning Director
Austin Rover Group, Ltd.

United States

Russell D. Archibald
Director, Business Development,
Special Programs
Bendix Corporation

Robert Coleman
Automotive Industry Manager
Bureau of Industrial Economics
U.S. Department of Commerce

Michael Finkelstein
Associate Administrator
National Highway Traffic Safety
Administration

Sheldon Friedman
Research Director
United Automobile Workers Union

Edwin R. MacKethan
Director
Business Environment Evaluation
Corporate Strategy and Analysis
  Staff
Ford Motor Company

Craig Marks
Executive Director
Environmental Activities Staff
General Motors Corporation

Thomas G. Marx
Director of Economic Policy Studies
General Motors Corporation

David C. May
Staff Director
Industry Demand Analysis
Standard Oil (Indiana)

John Mowinckel
Europe Office
Bankers Trust Company

John Rindlaub
Tokyo Office
Bankers Trust Company

H. Paul Root
Associate Chief Economist
General Motors Corporation

Stephen Soderberg
Securities Analyst
Wellington Management Co.

Richard L. Strombotne
Chief, Energy and Environment
  Division
Office of the Secretary
U.S. Department of Transporation

Donald Trilling
Executive Assistant to the Deputy
  Secretary
U.S. Department of Transportation

Curtis S. Vail
Director of Research and
  Development
Hoover Universal, Inc.

At Large

Francisco de Paula Magalhães
  Gomes
Technical Director
Empresa Brasileira de Planajemento
  de Transportes, GEIPOT

Gerhard Lohan
Administrator
Directorate General for Internal
  Market and Industrial Affairs
Commission of the European
  Communities

Yusuf Ozal
Senior Economist and Investment
  Officer
International Finance Corporation

R. Des Shaw
Assistant to the Commercial
  Counselor
Delegation of the European
  Communities

Juan Wolffer
Director of Planning and
  Development
Diesel Nacional, S.A.

Appendix C
Industrial-Relations
Systems in the
United States,
the United Kingdom,
and West Germany

The following accounts of recent developments in the labor-relations systems of three Western countries provide some of the detailed background for chapter 9. West Germany is an example of a country in which labor relations are remarkably stable and tend strongly toward a cooperative path of development. In the United States and the United Kingdom, the many recent changes in the conduct of labor relations have made the long-term course of labor relations unclear.

Labor Relations in the United States

A prolonged recession and shifts in the demand for automobiles led to enormous employment declines and layoffs of both blue- and white-collar workers in the U.S. auto industry after 1979. The employment of production workers in the auto industry (SIC 371) dropped from a peak of 802,800 in December 1978 to 487,700 in January 1983. The social hardship caused by these layoffs in the United States was exacerbated by the concentration of motor-vehicle production in a few urban areas in a few north-central states. In 1980, unemployment rates in some metropolitan areas in this region exceeded 20 percent; for example, 22.2 percent in Flint, Michigan, and 20.2 percent in Anderson, Indiana.[1]

In response to these dire social and personal hardships, unions have focused their national lobbying on efforts to provide a more stimulative macroeconomic policy, to gain trade protection, and to cushion the social impacts of the employment decline. Along these lines, the United Auto Workers has campaigned for modification of the social-welfare policies of the Reagan administration, which had reduced trade-adjustment assistance and unemployment-insurance benefits to laid-off auto workers. By late 1982, some federally funded extensions of state unemployment-insurance benefits were reinstated, although the Reagan administration's sharp cuts in trade-adjustment assistance benefits were not reversed.

In the face of severe economic pressure, major modifications were made in the U.S. labor-relations system which suggest the possibility of even more significant changes in the future.[2] In particular, automotive collective bargaining agreements have been adjusted in a number of ways. For example, revisions have been made in the wage formulas (cost-of-living escalator and annual improvement factor) used to set wages in the national company agreements with the UAW over the last 30 years. These changes include pay concessions negotiated at Chrysler in 1980 and 1981 and at Ford and General Motors in 1982. At Chrysler, formula wage increases were deferred in 1980 and canceled in 1981. At General Motors and Ford, the two and one half year re-negotiated agreements signed in March of 1982 (before the scheduled expiration of the existing contracts in September) deferred some scheduled cost-of-living adjustments, did not include the traditional 3 percent annual improvement factor, and cut real pay 4 percent by removing 10 paid holidays.

Major changes in work rules, negotiated at the plant level, led to significant interplant divergence in contract terms. At many plants the work-rule changes included a broadening of job classifications and the introduction of more flexibility into human-resource allocation through modifications in job bidding, seniority, and transfer rights. Meanwhile, steps taken at the national level have produced a shift toward an employment system containing more extensive guarantees. These include company-funded retraining programs, plant closing moratoriums, and income security programs for permanently displaced workers with high seniority.

A number of other steps that have been taken involve a more cooperative relationship between labor and management. Among these are the expansion of worker participation programs at GM and Ford and more extensive information sharing between labor and management at the shop-floor and corporate levels. Information sharing has been increased by formal mechanisms such as "mutual growth forums" and "quality circles" and by the informal exchange of information between company and union officials. Through these channels workers have begun to provide input into production decisions, thereby assisting in cost-reduction efforts. In some plants workers now communicate directly with plant industrial engineering staffs and with suppliers. Workers and union officials in these locations typically now receive advance warnings of layoffs, production plans, and new technology.

The net effect of these changes has been to begin moving the labor-relations system in the U.S. auto industry away from its traditional form. The new contract terms and participation programs represent an effort to substitute communication and participation for detailed contractual regulation. They provide greater employment security for the work force through employment guarantees and greater reliance on training and internal promotions, and they bring greater worker recognition of business considerations. Changes in workers' attitudes at the shop-floor level are borne out by their willingness to amend work-rule practices to maintain competitiveness and expand employment opportunities. Change at the national level is signaled by the 1982 contract terms, which partially substitute profit sharing for the traditional pattern bargaining and formula wage increases.

Two questions about the future course of labor relations in the U.S. auto industry remain. One is whether the 1982 contract changes and the worker participation programs will be expanded and will lead to more significant alterations in labor relations. The second is whether these changes will contribute significantly to the economic recovery of the industry. It is difficult to answer either question, because the future course of labor relations is intertwined with the success of change efforts. However, some patterns can be detected.

There are recent signs that auto workers view the 1982 contract changes as temporary and are reluctant to go further in modifying compensation levels or labor-relations practices. Recent bargaining at Chrysler provides an example. In the face of threatened bankruptcy, in 1980 and 1981, compensation levels were modified significantly, $1.15 of accrued cost-of-living-adjustment payments and future cost-of-living increases were canceled, paid personal holidays were eliminated, and the traditional 3 percent "annual improvement factor" wage increase was removed.

With the success of the "K cars" and cost-cutting measures, Chrysler's financial situation had improved enough by mid 1982 that company president Lee Iacocca could boast of $1 billion in cash reserves. This evidence of recovery may have bolstered Chrysler's standing in the financial community, but it also destabilized contract negotiations. In the fall of 1982, workers resoundingly rejected a tentative agreement reached by the UAW national leadership and the Chrysler management. Prior to these negotiations, the president of the UAW, Douglas Fraser, took a temporary leave of absence from the Chrysler board of directors to "avoid any conflict of interest."

A five-week-long strike ensued among Canadian Chrysler workers. The eventual settlement reinstated cost-of-living increases, removed the newly introduced profit-sharing plan, and narrowed the roughly $2.50-per-hour wage gap that had developed between Chrysler workers and those at Ford and GM. In the fall of 1983, when the Chrysler-UAW contract was reopened and renegotiated, the settlement fully restored the traditional cost-of-living and annual-improvement-factor wage increases. This new agreement will almost completely close the wage gap with Ford and GM.

The effect of this new settlement is to reverse some of the concessions agreed to between 1979 and 1981. This episode shows that there is substantial worker loyalty to the traditional wage-setting mechanisms, such as the cost-of-living formula and pattern bargaining. These institutional procedures have a long history in the industry. Despite recent modifications, workers clearly are not prepared to abandon wage-setting procedures or the high wages they provide. More broadly, events at Chrysler suggest the difficulty of sustaining a "cooperative" labor-relations strategy.

Troubles at Ford and GM were also signaled by the slow pace of local-contract renegotiation at the plants designated as pilot employment-guarantee sites in the 1982 national contract. As part of that 1982 national settlement, four GM and three Ford plants are to negotiate new local agreements to qualify for a guarantee under which 80 percent of the existing hourly work force will not be laid off during the new national contracts ending in September 1984. The presumption was that labor and management at these plants would significantly modify their local agreements to provide increased flexibility in human-resource allocation. This would facilitate reassignments during future downturns in auto sales and also lower labor costs, to lessen the financial burden to the company of guaranteed employment. In this process, it was assumed that the personnel rules and procedures in these plants would become more like those in Japanese auto plants. However, although negotiations began during the summer of 1982, they have progressed extremely slowly. Only one plant has ratified an agreement. In another plant a tentative agreement was rejected by the plant's workers by a margin of four to one.

These examples illustrate problems that the U.S. industry has already encountered in its efforts to expand worker participation and move away from the traditional formal labor-relations system. When one speculates about the future, additional problems become apparent. For example, it may be difficult for cooperative solutions to flourish in an environment that also includes pay concessions or moderation in the growth of wages and fringe benefits. Workers may become so angered by such concessions that they block shop-floor participatory efforts. One could even project a scenario in which national pay negotiations become so heated that a difficult strike ensues which is reminiscent of the long strikes that occurred in the U.S. industry in the immediate postwar period. This strike might then block any expansion of participatory programs and could even lead to the demise of existing programs. Yet if the production-cost differentials discussed in chapter 7 persist, further compensation concessions may be required for the restoration of U.S. competitiveness.

Changes in labor relations are also being hampered by the need for systemwide rather than piecemeal change. This is because the various features of a labor-relations system interact and reinforce one another in a number of ways. For instance, the heavy use of written procedures within collective bargaining goes along with and is reinforced by the "arms-length" nature of labor-management relations, which provides limited involvement of workers in decision making. Also, the use of formula mechanisms to set wages (such as the cost-of-living escalator and pattern bargaining) are parts of the U.S. labor-relations system that fit together well with other attributes of the system.

Alternatives to these wage-setting mechanisms that tie compensation more directly to company performance might make sense in a different system where labor and management exchange information on corporate plans and workers participate in business decision making. But this is not characteristic of the U.S. system. Consequently, unless there is comprehensive change in many features of the U.S. labor-relations system, it is unreasonable to expect that marginal changes in labor relations will eventually add up to more fundamental change or contribute significantly to cost reduction. The point is not that significant change in the conduct of labor relations is impossible. Rather, it is that these interconnections present a problem that makes a major transition difficult.

As discussed earlier, the 1982 negotiations at GM and Ford represent a serious effort on the part of labor and management to redirect the course of labor relations. Other hopeful signs exist at a number of plants where even farther-reaching changes have been adopted. A handful of GM plants have gone so far as to organize all production workers (but often not craft workers) into "operating teams." Within these teams there is only one job classification and workers receive higher pay after learning a wider variety of job tasks. This "pay for knowledge" compensation system creates direct rewards for worker flexibility. In these plants, workers also receive extensive information about production plans and business decisions.

These team systems involve a major shift away from the traditional job-control focus. It remains to be seen whether these experimental programs at the local level can mesh with new efforts at the national level to produce a broad transformation of labor-management relations.

The developing labor relations at new foreign-owned plants (such as the Honda facility in Marysville, Ohio, the Nissan plant in Smyrna, Tennessee, and the proposed joint GM-Toyota plant in Fremont, California) also critically affect the evolution of the collective bargaining system. The UAW will try hard to organize these plants. In the fall of 1983 the UAW agreed to reduce the number of job classifications and make other work-rule changes in the proposed GM-Toyota joint venture. In exchange, the joint-venture agreed to recognize the union and to recruit primarily from the ranks of former workers at the GM Fremont plant. As part of its efforts to organize other foreign-owned plants, the union may reveal further willingness to modify traditional labor-relations practices. Alternatively, novel labor-relations practices that may emerge at the new foreign-owned plants may induce reactions or imitations in the GM, Ford, and Chrysler plants.

Recent research does suggest that alterations in labor relations can have a major impact on productivity and cost competitiveness.[3] This research, which analyzes plant-level data from one U.S. auto company, indicates that economic performance, measured by product quality and labor costs, varies by 40 percent among plants that make the same product and have the same technology. Furthermore, this research provides evidence of a strong association between the industrial-relations performance of a plant, measured by grievance rates, absentee rates, and other indicators, and the economic performance of the plant. The implication is that improvements in labor-management relations can con tribute significantly to improving cost competitiveness. This research also offers evidence that Quality of Working Life programs in these plants in the late 1970s led to improvements in product quality. The critical remaining question is whether programs involving operating teams as described above, or some other major transformation of labor relations, can build on these early cooperative programs and produce much greater improvements in economic performance.

Two factors will determine whether a cooperative reform strategy is aggressively pursued in the years ahead. One is the degree to which labor and management view the recent recession as just another cyclical downturn, deep but not fundamentally different from other postwar business cycles. An alternative perspective, and one consistent with the conclusions of this volume, is that structural long-term changes have occurred in the world auto industry and that these changes require structural changes in labor relations.

The other critical factor is the extent to which labor and management are able to achieve the necessary balance of cooperative and distributive modifications. If "cooperative" change is defined as givebacks from labor rather than the design of new institutions that provide the potential for joint gains, or if labor tries aggressively to exploit periodic short-run improvements in its bargaining position, a shift from traditional labor relations practices is unlikely.

Labor Relations in the United Kingdom

Industrial relations are often seen to be at the heart of the problems of the British motor industry. The importance of employee relations in overall corporate strategy has increased because the companies are aware that improved productivity and quality depend on active support from their labor forces.

The Donovan report on industrial relations in 1968, an important product of such thinking, focused largely on the engineering industry.[4] Many of the changes proposed by Donovan or subsequently were attempted within the auto industry, but not always successfully. BL, for example, tried during the 1970s to centralize bargaining, move away from payments by result toward measured day work, and rationalize its industrial-relations system. All the car firms gave increasing recognition to the shop-floor movement within the trade unions. Yet, at least until the end of the 1970s, productivity remained low, strikes continued to plague the industry, and industrial-relations reform progressed slowly.

Throughout the 1970s BL and Vauxhall faced severe profitability problems. The oil crisis, in particular, exposed certain weaknesses in the British car industry that went far beyond industrial relations. BL, for example, had failed to reinvest enough of its profits in the 1960s, to rationalize its management structure after its formation, to develop a viable product range, to modernize its plants and machinery, or to improve the quality and delivery standards of its component suppliers.

When the world crisis in the auto industry intensified in the late 1970s, the various manufacturers in Britain were in very different positions that reflected their histories and corporate identities. All were, by this stage, advancing programs to improve their position. BL underwent major internal changes, completing earlier mergers, centralizing its pay negotiations, and abandoning the old payment-by-results system for production workers. BL was also collaborating with a Japanese firm, slowly reforming its industrial relations, rationalizing its management structures, reducing its number of plants, and developing a new and viable product range. Meanwhile, Vauxhall had increasingly integrated its British base into GM's world operations, concentrating on assembly. Ford's products were already integrated into its world production system, and the firm was highly profitable in Britain.

All the firms were nevertheless faced with common problems of productivity and quality posed by the increasing competition from Japan. They had long been aware of their low productivity relative to continental plants. (Ford and Vauxhall were in a position to compare their British plants with their counterparts elsewhere in Europe.) A joint management council of BL reported in 1978 that "unless our productivity levels improve quickly and by a large amount, our ability to compete with European and other foreign manufacturers will continue to deteriorate."

Each of the companies appears to have different priorities in seeking to adjust to the change in the automobile market, despite common recognition of the problems of productivity and quality. BL has placed the greatest emphasis on new production technology and on changing demarcations among skilled maintenance workers. Vauxhall has placed greater emphasis on changes in management practices and much less on robotics. Ford has put particular emphasis on comparisons of performance and productivity with Ford plants in other countries, notably West Germany.

Thus, there are many different angles from which productivity and quality problems have been tackled. Each company has tended to choose its angle of attack according to its own external constraints and labor-force problems. Vauxhall, lacking internally generated profits or the backing of its parent company or the government, has had limited funds for new technology, so its main emphasis has been on increasing productivity and quality through improvements in management and work organization. BL, on the other hand, has been able to invest heavily in robotics on the Metro and the Maestro body and paint lines with government support, and has sought to improve its management and work practices around these new lines. Starting from a stronger position, Ford has gone less far in investment in robotics than BL, and less far in the development of multi-skilled workers. Of course these are differences of emphasis or priority in the manner in which all three companies are seeking greater efficiency in manning and in the organization of production.

Production standards, the allowance for nonproductive time, and the amount of below-standard output in British plants all exceeded the levels in most of their foreign competitors' plants in the 1960s and the 1970s, and may still. Reasons include industrial-relations problems in the narrow sense, such as the high strike record of the industry and the way in which strikes delayed new-model introduction dates. Industrial relations in a broader sense was also at least partly responsible for low productivity due to overmanning, inflexibility, high absenteeism, and "over-generous" work standards. Yet these were often difficult to distinguish from other factors that were contributing to low productivity. At BL, such factors included inadequate products, design, and planning, as well as inadequate control of the parts supply and of working methods.

Many recent changes in working practices have been aided by increasingly high levels of unemployment and by the Conservative government's attitude and policies toward trade unionism. For example, the facilities of shop stewards and their involvements in many issues have been considerably reduced. But many such changes have been brought about through negotiation with worker representatives, including full-time union officials. At Ford and Vauxhall, many of the changes did not require revisions of bargained agreements, but only firmer implementation. At BL, mandatory discussions between labor and management over any proposed changes ("mutuality") ended and a new agreement was accepted by the trade unions during their annual wage negotiations. More flexible work practices have been more readily achieved during the introduction of new technology and products. Work practices on the Metro line at Longbridge provide an example.

The British auto-industry unions have been concerned mainly with the loss of jobs and (especially at BL) with what they perceive to be a loss of their power, an autocratic management style, and higher work levels. In their 1983 dispute with Vauxhall, the trade unions were negotiating not so much to stop the S-car from being produced in Spain as to limit the number of GM cars entering the country from other parts of Europe, a demand which to some extent they achieved. The dispute in March 1983 at Cowley, a BL plant, is an example of the discontent of workers and their representatives with the tenor of labor-management relations.

Recent changes in the British auto industry intended to improve productivity and quality have been introduced in a climate of crisis, often with an implication that without their acceptance many more jobs in the industry would be lost. Success could then be greeted with a feeling of improved job security. Indeed, and at BL in particular, the feeling of management is that increased job security has been an implicit *quid pro quo* throughout the change process. However, this cannot be interpreted as a move toward lifetime employment. Firms will continue to use the external labor market when necessary, train and define jobs much as before, and hold onto labor as required.

Another aspect of adjustment has been the major manpower reductions that have occurred at BL and Vauxhall and have been announced at Ford. Both BL and Vauxhall have reduced their work force by about one third since 1979. In both cases management has stated in interviews that manpower reductions are somewhat easier to obtain in Britain than in West Germany, where redundancy laws give the works councils considerable powers. BL has made closures and reorganizations which have led to layoffs. However, many of BL's separations, like all those at Ford and Vauxhall, have been voluntary. Furthermore, there has been little or no overt struggle against these closures.

Is there a trend toward longer-term employment for individual workers in the British auto industry as in the large Japanese car companies? Several factors might cause a move in this direction. First, technical change has altered traditional job boundaries and created bundles of skills which are less easily transferred to other employers. Second, the increased emphasis on flexibility of deployment within the firm may require some commitment from the companies to offer more stable employment in return.

However, there has been no equivalent in Britain to the agreement at Ford and General Motors in the United States to experiment with lifetime employment. With the major manning reductions, the British companies have not needed to recruit from the outside in any case. Also, the companies have always had a high proportion of long-service production workers. At BL's Longbridge plant the median length of service of production workers was 10.5 years in 1982, and at Vauxhall's Luton plant it was 9.9 years. This casts doubt on the proposition the the British car industry has had a high-turnover labor force and a hire-and-fire management policy.

One major constraint on greater reliance on internal labor markets in Britain is the structure of external markets for skilled workers. These remain essentially local, because the apprenticeship system produces workers with transferable skills which can be used by a number of other employers in the engineering industry. The philosophy of the Engineering Industry Training Board is that companies should contribute to the general pool of skilled labor, on which they may draw as necessary.

Despite the extent of recent changes, it would be wrong to believe that union and shop-floor power and their associated institutions have been swept away. The radical changes in BL were introduced by collective bargaining in the 1980 agreement on pay and productivity, and the changes in the other two companies have also been brought in by agreement. These changes were accompanied by general tightening of industrial-relations procedures and a clearer specification of the channels to be used and the conditions under which certain questions about work organization and technical change can be raised.

Thus, the increases in productivity and the increased flexibility of manpower deployment have been achieved in large part within the established methods of industrial relations. For example, issues of limited self-maintenance and self-inspection by production workers, and of demarcation between maintenance skills and other skills, are all handled under established bargaining arrangements.

The size of the recent productivity gains achieved in the British car industry and the speed with which they have been obtained may appear surprising in light of the conventional adversarial view of British industrial relations, in which management is seen as fighting for even the slightest change in working practices. A number of factors have contributed to this. First, high levels of unemployment have undoubtedly produced a shift of power away from the shop floor and the unions back toward management. Second, this has been compounded by the urgency of the need for improved productivity and quality if the British car industry is to survive the challenge from the Japanese and other producers. However, these changes would not have had much effect if management had not developed new models and sought to change its own practices.

Labor Relations in West Germany

No dramatic labor-relations changes have occurred in the West German auto industry in recent years, and none are expected.[5] Both employers and trade unions are trying to cope with the intensified problems of industrial restructuring by using the existing institutional framework. In fact, there is agreement between the two sides that this framework has helped identify and resolve past adjustment problems at an early stage, and thus has contributed to keeping them within manageable limits.

There are three reasons why the German situation is characterized by institutional stability. First, at the sectoral level the auto industry in Germany does not constitute a collective bargaining unit of its own but is only a small part of the much larger bargaining unit of the metalworking industry. Thus, developments that are specific to the automobile industry are not directly reflected in sectoral collective bargaining. Second, at the plant level auto workers are represented by works councils, whose existence and operation is based on general legislation applying not just to the auto sector but to industry as a whole. While its legal basis makes the works-council system and the co-determination rights of works councils relatively immune to the effects of the business cycle, its comprehensiveness also makes it insensitive to special developments in individual sectors. Third, the crisis of the auto industry was and is less severe in West Germany than in other countries. The generally accepted scenarios of future developments are less gloomy, and the institutional system of industrial relations is seen as having a proven capacity to accommodate even fundamental industrial change.

The "political economy" of the German automobile industry is characterized by three basic conditions: relatively high compensation costs, well-entrenched trade unions and works councils, and limited prospects for a protectionist defense against foreign competition. German automakers have operated on the premise that none of these conditions can be removed in the near future, and the union, like the industry, has resisted protectionist temptations. To an important extent, this was due to the fact that the union organizes, in addition to the auto industry, a number of other industries (such as the machine-tool industry) that are even more dependent on exports. It also reflects the good performance of the German auto industry in export markets, which has outweighed the losses in the German market caused by increased imports.

Furthermore, the union has long recognized that high wages and strong co-determination rights require it to accept some responsibility for the efficiency and survival of the industry. This has been manifested in union and works-council support for management policies aimed at safeguarding the industry's competitiveness in an open world market in spite of high wages and the employment rigidities associated with co-determination.

The West German auto industry has made strong efforts to remain competitive through increased productivity. Though not so productive as the Japanese, it compares well with its Western competitors. Since the mid 1970s the industry has embarked on a large-scale program to modernize production technologies. The union and the works councils have generally not impeded the introduction of industrial robotics and flexible manufacturing. Together with the facts that stoppages are infrequent and production targets are normally met, this has resulted in production costs at least comparable with other European countries even though German wages are higher.

German competitiveness has also been enhanced by the industry's move "up-market." This has been combined with an effort to improve quality and to establish product superiority through engineering. Daimler-Benz and BMW have long operated in the upper section of the market. In recent years, Volkswagen, traditionally a producer of small cars, has been moving up-market, and the same applies with some qualifications to General Motors (Opel) and Ford.

Increasing product value may compensate for some of the negative employment effects of improving productivity in the face of stagnating demand, and is therefore welcomed by the union. High quality and product superiority help defend market shares, especially in export countries where the comparatively high German compensation costs might otherwise constitute a competitive disadvantage.

A planned medium-term manpower policy designed to facilitate efficient adaptation of labor to changing economic and technical conditions has been another means of improving German competitiveness. As developed in the second half of the 1970s, this policy represents a compromise between the employers' needs for flexibility and the demands by union and the works councils for steady and secure employment. Its central characteristic is an increasing reliance by employers on internal labor markets to secure their labor supply. Medium-term manpower policy combines cautious recruitment with reliance on overtime in periods of high demand, and on short-time work in periods of low demand. In particular, new workers are hired only if it seems certain that they will not have to be dismissed for lack of demand. This policy also emphasizes internal retraining as a substitute for hiring new skills from the outside; all new openings are first advertised internally. It implies an informal but nevertheless serious commitment by managements to take all possible steps to accomplish any necessary work force reductions only by attrition.

At Volkswagen, Audi, BMW, and Daimler-Benz, this policy amounts to unofficial "lifetime employment", which has become part of companies' "corporate image" and "corporate philosophy." To be able to plan their manpower input early enough to meet the targets of their employment policy, these companies make formal and elaborate efforts to assess the likely employment effects of new investment and to integrate investment planning with manpower planning. This seems to be less pronounced, however, in foreign-owned companies, where labor relations are somewhat more conflict-laden and where the option for management to transfer production to other countries is more present.

In return, works councils agree to higher internal mobility, provided pay is not affected, and frequently help persuade workers to accept internal transfers and retraining. Works councils also generally support new, more flexible forms of work organization, including the creation of new occupations as a result of new production technology (e.g., the incorporation of certain maintenance tasks in the job of the direct line worker).

In broad institutional terms, recent years have witnessed an increase in the importance of company-level industrial relations and a corresponding decline in the importance of negotiations at the sectoral or multisectoral level in Germany. Again, it is necessary to emphasize that this was a gradual, continuous development, without major disruptions or critical institutional breakdowns. Although sectoral negotiations continue to take place every year, the decline of the union's bargaining power at this level and the limits placed by the economic crisis on redistributive trade-union policies have made it ever more difficult for industrial unions to regulate the nonwage elements of the individual work situation.

With sectoral bargaining deadlocked and weakened by the general economic crisis, the workers began to concentrate on the protection of their employment opportunities in their individual places of work. To the extent that these depend on companies' manpower policies and on the functioning of internal labor markets, company-level bargaining conducted by works councils in the framework of co-determination is closer to the predominant interests of workers. The resulting pattern is one of strong identification of the core work force with the company's competitive needs as well as with the product and the "company image."

The shift of the center of gravity of industrial relations from the sectoral level to the individual company is facilitated by the fact that the position of works councils in individual firms is much better safeguarded legally than the position of industrial unions. The Works Constitution Act of 1972 and the Co-Determination Act of 1976 have helped build strong institutions of company-centered interest representation and interest accommodation that, even under normal circumstances, are difficult for industrial unions to control from the outside.

Although the traditional, formal institutions of industrial trade unionism in Germany certainly are not about to disappear, they are increasingly confronted with a new pattern of labor-capital cooperation at the level of individual firms ("cooperative syndicalism"). This pattern, which is sustained institutionally by co-determination, seems to be particularly strong in companies, such as the big auto manufacturers, that are exposed to world market competition. On the one hand it contributes to economic success; on the other hand it is reinforced by it. The emergence of stable company-based "productivity coalitions" in the strong parts of the German economy is likely to create difficult problems for industrial unions.

Both employers and unions regard the future of the German automobile industry in the 1980s with optimism. The general expectation is that the industry will remain internationally competitive, especially but not exclusively in terms of product quality and design, and that growing product value will close part of the employment gap between the development of demand and productivity.

Relations between capital and labor, especially at the company level, are generally expected to remain cooperative, and this will strengthen the industry's economic performance. Some employment cuts are anticipated, but they are likely to be smaller than in other auto-producing countries except Japan. In fact, within Germany the auto industry is emerging as one of the more stable sources of employment in manufacturing. Difficulties are expected to come primarily from the outside, the most threatening one being protectionist trade policies in major export-receiving countries. It is obvious that a diminution of the open world market in automobiles would undermine the very basis of the German "productivity coalition."

Acknowledgments

Stephen Wood and David Marsden of the London School of Economics prepared the draft of the United Kingdom case.

Appendix D
The Case for Free Trade*

Questions of Approach

Public policy should not be conducted in an isolated fashion toward separate industries. The need to look beyond the confines of the automobile industry becomes particularly evident when one considers the alternative use of resources made available by the reduction in automobile manufacturing in a particular country. A condition for stability and innovation in a national economy is instability at the firm level.[1] General macroeconomic policy is also of great importance. At present (1984), the national budget deficit in the United States exerts an upward pressure on interest rates and, thereby, on the exchange rate of the U.S. dollar. This considerably reduces U.S. manufacturers' ability to compete against imported automobiles.

Analyses of public policy options should not focus upon bilateral trade balances. These are irrelevant from an economic point of view. Indeed, bilateral imbalances constitute an indication of international specialization and a sign of health. One need only consider the dubious success of Eastern European countries in balancing trade with every single trading partner to see what opportunities are lost by this strategy.

Trade policies may reflect the varied and considered objectives of governments, but can also be looked upon as the outcomes of rather irrational political processes.[2] The recent wave of protectionism and selective industrial policy is as much, if not more, an effect of well-organized small interest groups with clear objectives extracting favors from governments at the expense of non-organized majorities. The job lost in Detroit is visible and there is somebody to fight for it, whereas the jobs lost by not investing the subsidy in other fields are not visible and there is nobody to fight for them.

---

*This appendix is a more detailed formulation of the case for open trade presented on pages 235–238. It represents the position of a number of participants in the Auto Program. It is not the position of the principal authors of this volume, whose views are expressed on pages 238–242 and in chapter 11.

It is necessary to consider the long-run consequences of government action. Much analysis of protectionist strategies neglects to consider the prospects and results of retaliation from trading partners.

Criteria for Assessing Public Policy toward the Auto Industry

The following are the most important and appropriate aims of governments' policies toward the automobile industry.

Efficient international allocation of resources, allowing international specialization to the benefit of all trading partners. This means low prices and a wide range of products offered to the consumer and, thus, a high standard of living.

Competition within each market, keeping prices down, rewarding the most efficient producers, and contributing to dissemination of best practices.

Fair distribution of the burdens of adjustment. Structural changes hurt some people and benefit others. Most societies would like to moderate these effects.

Level and quality of employment.

Time to adjust to new conditions. In a turbulent commercial and political environment, individual firms may be forced out of business because of temporary difficulties. The loss of one important competitor may be more serious in the long term than the temporary loss of helping it out.

Considerations of national security. Some industries have clear strategic importance. Weapons, airplanes, and advanced microelectronics are perhaps the best examples.

Stress on international relations and alliances.

Conclusions on Public Policy Options

•Free trade in automobiles and related products should be the rule. The losses to consumers, foregone opportunities of structural adjustment, inflation, general rigidification of the international automobile industry, and the possibility of spillover effects to other industries from interventionism in auto trade are probable and very costly consequences of continued escalation of trade restrictions. There is no empirical evidence that continued support of uncompetitive mature industries is economically defensible. The experience with interventionism in other industries is very negative.

Ineffective firms become chronically ineffective, and vicious circles of degradation of the quality of labor, management, and output set in.

The support for free trade is not only "theoretical." Practical experience clearly demonstrates the dangers of protectionism.

The Great Depression in the 1930s was to a large extent as severe as it was because of trade restrictions.[3]

The era after 1945 was characterized by increasing free trade and rapidly increasing economic growth and prosperity, at least in the OECD area. The experience of the EEC also shows the success brought by liberalizing trade, albeit only within Europe. Countries practicing protectionsm have fared worse than those that have not.[4]

The experience with sectoral protectionism is very negative. The costs of supporting the textile industry have been very large. The failures of agricultural protectionism are well known. Most of the EEC's budget is used to support inefficient farms and agricultural overproduction. The steel industry in Europe uses only around 50 percent of its capacity, being supported by its own governments as well as the EEC directly. In the automobile industry, calculations by Gomez-Ibanez, Leone, and O'Connell show that U.S. consumers' losses through the present restrictions on sales of Japanese cars in the United States are greater than the benefits accruing to workers and capital owners within the industry.[5] Furthermore, if one considers the longer-term consequences also, workers and owners stand to loose because of artificially induced upgrading of Japanese products and foreign direct investment in the United States by Japanese manufacturers. Still, the prospect of retaliation in other fields has not been taken into account.

A study prepared in 1982 by Harbridge House, Inc., and published through the American International Automobile Dealers Association estimates the surcharge paid by U.S. buyers of Japanese cars during the first 12 months of the restraints at approximately $1,900 per car and concludes that tighter restraints in the form of local-content requirements would produce a consumer surcharge of at least $3,200 per car.

Even in countries safely protected from competition from Japanese manufacturers, auto-related unemployment is high. Italy imports only 2,200 Japanese cars per year and still has severe problems. It could also be mentioned that the British automobile industry was one of the most heavily protected for years. The rate at which British auto tariffs were reduced after the Second World War was slower than for the EEC, the United States or Japan. This appears not to have had much of a beneficial effect on the British auto industry and related employment.

Thus, the burden of evidence is squarely upon the proponents of protectionism. Established economic science is firmly supported by practical experience in refuting protectionism as a remedy for maladjustment to economic realities.

•Exceptions to the free-trade rule do not apply in the automobile industry. The most important exception concerns industries of military or strategic importance. However, this is of little relevance for the automobile industry. Production of tanks and trucks for military use can be upheld in efficient scale without the production of automobiles. Furthermore, the lifetimes of motorized vehicles are rather long. With some stockpiling, it should be easy to ensure military capabilities in much cheaper ways than through supporting domestic production of "civilian" cars. The know-how of production, engine technology, etc. that follows from auto production can be acquired in other fields, where scale requirements are not so enormous, or by straight purchase of technology.

It is often claimed that there is an "infant-industry argument" for protectionism. The dominant view among economists today is that this argument is not tenable. Assumptions of imperfect capital markets, lack of information, etc., have to be introduced in order to save it. Even if the argument is tenable, the automobile industry is definitely not an infant one. It is one of the most mature branches of industry, and the present-day practitioners of protectionism have had plenty of time to learn their trade.

Are there special reasons for protecting the automobile industry because of linkages to other sectors of industry? This is another often-stated argument. It does not stand detailed scrutiny. First, many of the linkages would be left even if domestic producers were not. The service and repair sector, which is very important in terms of employment, is needed to serve foreign cars as well as domestic ones. Component manufacturers can serve foreign companies and are doing so to an increasing degree. In fact, it is likely that international trade in components becomes more important than trade in assembled vehicles, so component manufacturers have to become internationally competitive in any case. Second, it is clearly not a precondition for being a civilized and industrially advanced nation to have one or several domestic automobile producers. Third, the same argument could be used for almost any industry. It was and is used in the case of steel. Fourth, linkages to other industries make it all the more necessary to make sure the industry under consideration is competitive and not artificially protected.

•Governments' proper roles are to facilitate structural adjustment and, in extraordinary circumstances, to help individual firms absorb temporary shocks. However, capital owners are paid returns exactly because they stand the risk of shocks, and should pay when times are rough. It is also quite reasonable that wages and salaries adapt to the competitiveness of the firm. Particularly in Europe, wages and salaries need to become more flexible. Thus, government should come in as a shock absorber only when capital and labor have taken their share of the burdens.

•Protection should be geared toward individuals rather than firms and branches of industry. Training and retraining programs, relocation assistance, and temporary income support are consistent with this view, whereas subsidies to specific firms are not. Experiences in the shipbuilding and steel industries show that the cost of helping individuals by supporting firms is very high.

•If direct support of a firm or an industry is required, direct subsidies are less harmful than restrictions on international trade. Direct subsidies to Chrysler do not push up the domestic price level, whereas trade restrictions do. Therefore, the misallocation of resources (including unemployment through reduced domestic demand for cars) by protectionism is partially avoided by using direct subsidies instead. These also have the advantage of being very visible, and decisions on subsidies normally are not extended for long periods automatically, as tends to be the case with trade restrictions. As an example of the costs of trade restrictions, Hamilton calculated the cost per man-year of employment "saved" through direct subsidies to the Swedish textile and clothing industry during the period 1973–1977 as $8,300.[6] Quantitative restrictions would have cost five times as much, i.e. $40,000.

•Straight tariffs are preferable to nontariff barriers, quotas, or quantitative restrictions if the purpose is to protect domestic industry. Tariffs are clearly visible, they can easily be applied nondiscriminatorily, and it is easy to formulate phase-out timetables. Moreover, they do not have the distortive effects of some forms of quantitative restrictions.

•Local-content requirements are particularly harmful. The advantages of large-scale production are more important in components than in final assembly, and much of potential future productivity increase in the industry is likely to come from a rationalized and globally extended system of suppliers to the final assemblers. Local-content legislation severely hampers this process.

Free component trade is also crucial to the emergence of intra-industry trade in automobiles.[7] Increased exports from the United States to Japan and Europe and from Europe to Japan would considerably reduce frictions between the countries and open up new markets for the specialties of the Western manufacturers. The success of the EEC in building up intra-industry trade by a free-trade regime within the EEC is an important case in point.

Local-content requirements would furthermore favor very large, multinational firms at the expense of small producers. Only the large firms could afford to build up separate production facilities in several countries. In the long term, domestic-content rules entail the danger of collusion between the few producers in each national market. Domestic-content legislation therefore should be resisted also on antitrust grounds.

Finally, there are severe problems with the enforcement of local-content rules. There is a great risk of government bureaucracy as well as of companies adopting inefficient (from a national welfare point of view) strategies in response to such rules.

•Free trade in goods and services is essential, and free capital movements are desirable. Foreign direct investment (FDI) can be seen as a substitute for trade in goods. However, the welfare losses from not allowing trade cannot be fully recuperated through FDI. The likely consequences of a scenario of restricted trade and free capital movements are inefficient manufacturing scale, productivity losses, and international misallocation of resources. The present role of FDI in the world economy is artificially exaggerated by restraints on trade. Taking away some of the sources of economically unjustified FDI will give it a humbler, more appropriate role.

An indication of the potential dangers of cutting up the world into "investment zones" is provided by the experience of American direct investment in Europe. It is quite possible that the American auto manufacturers would have developed smaller cars for exports much earlier had they had access to the European market through direct exports.

Instead, they were forced to invest in Europe, primarily through acquisitions of European manufacturers.

The hope that FDI will save employment in the automobile industry is largely illusory. Employment will decrease and change character anyway in the future, because of technical changes in the production process. The effect is reinforced since new FDI would most likely entail the introduction of less labor-intensive methods of production than those used in the less efficient firms outcompeted by the investor. Obviously, considered globally and across all sectors of the economy there is even less ground for arguing anything but negative consequences for employment of artificially stimulating FDI.

Finally, the argument that FDI serves to teach domestic industry about foreign technology and practices has to confront the Japanese success of assimilating foreign technology with almost no FDI at all.

•"Informal agreements", "voluntary export restraints", and the like represent the least desirable form of protectionism. It is difficult to phase out restrictions that formally do not exist. The uncertainty as to the current state of affairs as well as the future discourages investment in the industry. Informal schemes always involve the risk of collusion between powerful interests against the consumers and taxpayers.

The ranking list of public policy measures is as follows, in descending order of desirability:

Free trade plus policies facilitating structural adjustment and support of individuals hurt by transitions.
Direct subsidies to firms to overcome temporary shocks or to provide time for adjustment.
Straight tariffs.
Quotas by license or auction, quantitative restrictions.
Local-content requirements, voluntary export restraint.

•All government intervention, whether involving trade restraints or not, should be strictly and explicitly limited in time, with a fixed timetable of withdrawal. A fixed schedule of de-escalation gives producers the certainty to undertake effective measures of adjustment and puts pressures on all parties to work hard at improving their competitive stances. One important aspect is the effect on the labor market. It can well be argued that the costs of "adjustment" are so high that employees should be given the chance of adjusting their income rather than being forced to relocate. The recent history of Toyo Kogyo (Mazda) illustrates how management and employees turned the company around and accepted lower remuneration when this was required, rather than insisting on unrealistic compensation. The Chrysler case also seems to indicate that such cooperation and temporary sacrifice may pay in the long run.

•A country's trade policies, even if protectionist, should not discriminate against some exporting nations. For example, there is no particular reason why the United States should restrict imports of small cars from Japan and not from Europe. Current restrictions leave room for European penetration of small-car markets closed for the Japanese, whereas the Japanese are forced to enter the high-end, higher-value-added market segments previously occupied primarily by the Europeans. Individual European nations' (notably France's and Italy's) restrictions on Japanese exports are flawed in the same respect.

•This means that multilateralism is preferable to bilateralism in negotiations over and analysis of trade policies. The risks of continued bilateralism escalating to general world protectionism are not negligible. Multilateral forums encourage attention to non-zero-sum aspects of international trade and make it more difficult for partisan interest groups to utilize political leverage on governments. The risks of spillover effects of auto protectionism to other fields are given appropriate weight in multilaterial forums, particularly if these have not only sectoral (automobile industry) responsibility.

Summary

No new barriers to trade in automobiles should be erected. Protectionism is like quicksand; the more you move the deeper you get into it and the more difficult it is to get out of it. Today, there still is a choice. If governments act responsibly and intelligently, they can avoid making the automobile industry the starting point of a new and sad era of global economic stagnation and decline. The policies of the United States are of particularly critical importance. If any single event could initiate the destruction of the entire framework for international trade, and thereby a downward spiral of world depression, it would be drastic protectionist measures in the United States. The partly justified accusations of Western European and Japanese hypocrisy, wanting the USA to stick to free trade while allowing them to be protectionist should lead to the reduction of trade barriers in areas and countries where they do exist rather than the raising of new ones where they do not.

Acknowledgments

The author, Gunnar Hedlund of the Institute of International Business at the Stockholm School of Economics, wishes to thank Andrew Black of the Wissenschaftszentrum in Berlin, Harry Flam of the Institute of International Economic Studies at the University of Stockholm, Yukihide Okano and Seizaburo Sato of the University of Tokyo, Orjan Solvell, Dag Rolander, and Jan-Erik Vahlne of the Stockholm School of Economics, and Bruce Kogut of the Wharton School at the University of Pennsylvania for valuable comments on the text. Andrew Black and Harry Flam contributed particularly actively to improve the text.

Acknowledgments

Notes

Chapter 1

1. *Transport in the Future—Some Possibilities and Their Implications*, Bruges: College of Europe, 1982.

2. In 1979 motor-vehicle fatalities totaled 255,212 among the 96 countries reporting such information to the International Road Federation or the United Nations Statistical Office. However, the countries not reporting include the People's Republic of China, India, and the Soviet Union. Although these countries have a relatively small proportion of the world's motor-vehicle fleet, they account for half the world's population and are known circumstantially to have large numbers of fatalities involving pedestrians and cyclists struck by motor vehicles. Thus, the annual fatality total for the entire world is doubtless much higher than a quarter million.

3. The phrase is from the title of a widely read analysis of the automotive future published at that time: Lester Brown, Christopher Flavin, and Colin Norman, *Running on Empty: The Future of the Automobile in an Oil Short World*, New York: Norton, 1979.

4. Calculated from U.S. Department of Transportation, *National Transportation Statistics*, Washington: U.S. Government Printing Office,1982.

5. Calculated from *International Trade*, Geneva: GATT, various years.

Chapter 2

1. James Flink, *America Adopts the Automobile, 1895–1910*, Cambridge: MIT Press, 1970, pp. 116–117.

2. Production share calculated from *World Motor Vehicle Data* (1983 edition), Detroit: Motor Vehicle Manufacturers Association, 1983, p. 9.

3. For a review of automotive technology up to the success of the Model T see Flink, *America Adopts the Automobile*, Chapter 8.

4. For a review of Henry Ford's technical innovations see William J. Abernathy, *The Productivity Dilemma*, Baltimore: Johns Hopkins University Press, 1978,

chapter 2; for a review of Ford's innovations in production organization see Allan Nevins, *Ford*, New York: Scribner, 1953.

5. Ford production data are from Allan Nevins and Frank Ernest Hill, *Ford: Decline and Rebirth*, New York: Scribner, 1962, appendix I; production and world market share data in this and the following paragraphs are from *World Motor Vehicle Data*, pp. 9 and 10.

6. The best description of "Sloanism," which also included the concept of continuous product upgrading, is still to be found in Sloan's autobiography: Alfred Sloan, *My Years with General Motors*, Garden City, N.Y.: Doubleday, 1964.

7. For an explanation of the reasons for final assembly near the point of sale see Mira Wilkens and Ernest Frank Hill, *American Business Abroad: Ford on Six Continents*, Detroit: Wayne State University Press, 1964, chapter 2. For a chronology of Ford's foreign assembly operations see ibid., appendix 2. The information on General Motors' foreign assembly operations is from Frederick G. Donner, *The World-Wide Industrial Enterprise: Its Challenges and Promise*, New York: McGraw-Hill, 1967, p. 15.

8. The United States, by contrast, was the great protectionist, having applied a 45 percent tariff to imported cars from the earliest days of the industry. Though this may have aided the development of the American luxury car industry, the mass market addressed by Ford had been ignored by European producers, whose products, including a small volume exported to the United States, were much more complex and expensive.

9. Wilkens and Hill, pp. 141–142.

10. Ibid., pp. 230–240.

11. Ibid., p. 240.

12. Calculated from *World Motor Vehicle Data*, p. 206.

13. Calculated from *International Trade 1982–83*, Geneva: GATT, 1982, tables A19, A20, and A21. This figure is for all motor vehicles, including trucks and buses.

14. Shotaro Kamiya, *My Life with Toyota*, Tokyo: Toyota Motor Sales Company, 1976, p. 105. This volume and particularly its appendix are the main source for much of this account of the growth of the Japanese motor industry.

15. Details of the types of support the Japanese government has provided favored industries are given in Chalmers Johnson, *MITI and the Japanese Miracle: The Growth of Industrial Policy, 1925–1975*, Stanford, Calif.: Stanford University Press, 1982, p. 236.

16. William C. Duncan, *U.S.-Japan Automobile Diplomacy*, Cambridge: Ballinger, 1973, chapter 3.

17. In 1962 Italy and Japan negotiated a unit limit on Japanese imports to Italy of 1,000 cars per year. This limit was retained when Japan joined the GATT in 1964. In 1976 the limit was adjusted upward slightly to 2,200 cars per year.

18. Population estimate for 1981 calculated from *U.N. Demographic Yearbook, 1981*, New York: United Nations, 1981; share of production for 1982 from table 2.3.

19. The product cycle as developed originally by Raymond Vernon (see "International Trade and International Investment in the Product Cycle," *Quarterly Journal of Economics* 80, May 1966, pp. 190–207; *Sovereignty at Bay*, New York: Basic Books, 1971, chapter 3) suggests that, as products become more standardized and markets approach saturation, competition will be increasingly on the basis of price. This will place a premium on low production costs, pushing manufacturers to relocate production from highly developed economies to countries with low wages but enough industrial infrastructure to support heavy manufacturing.

20. Such a volume will be published shortly by Rémy Prud'homme of the University of Paris, a member of the French research team. The Brazilian and Korean cases cited here are based on papers prepared by Prud'homme as part of his research for that volume: "Motor Vehicle Production and Use in Developing Countries: A Case Study of Brazil" and "Motor Vehicle Use and Production in Less Developed Countries: A Case Study of Korea," both prepared for International Automobile Program International Policy Forum, Stenungsund, Sweden, June 1983.

21. Recently the Ford Motor Company has announced plans to export Escort models from Brazil to Scandinavia to compete with Japanese products in those markets, and Fiat plans to ship some Uno models back to Europe as well. These will be interesting tests of the ability of production in a developing country to compete, particularly on quality, with the world's high quality/low cost producer. However, it should be remembered that the Brazilian government's export incentives and the excess capacity in the depressed Brazilian domestic market make assumptions about long-term Brazilian cost competitiveness in export markets premature.

Chapter 3

1. Lester Brown, Christopher Flavin, and Colin Norman, *Running on Empty: The Future of the Automobile in an Oil Short World*, New York: Norton, 1979, p. 87.

2. Calculated from *Survey of World Energy Resources, 1980*, London: World Energy Conference, 1981.

3. Calculated from *Monthly Energy Review*, Washington, D.C.: U.S. Department of Energy, Energy Information Administration, October 1982.

4. Calculated from *BP Statistical Review of the World Energy Industry*, London: British Petroleum, 1982.

5. The most efficient refineries in the United States now produce about 50 percent gasoline, 20 percent diesel fuel, 10 percent kerosene, and 20 percent "low ends" (residual fuel oil, paraffins, asphalt, coke, etc). New refinery tech-

niques now being installed in prototype plants should make it possible to reduce production of these low ends by 75 percent. (See *Synfuel*, March 1, 1983, p. 7, for a description of these new techniques.) This in turn would permit gasoline yields of up to 65 percent of each barrel of crude oil. Diesel oil also fuels cars and trucks, so eventually up to 85 percent of crude oil may be available for motor-vehicle use.

6. Calculated from *Petroleum Supply Monthly*, Washington, D.C.: U.S. Department of Energy, Energy Information Administration, 1983.

7. The fuel-economy estimate for 1973 is from D. Murrell, J. Cheng, E. LeBaron, S. L. Loos, and R. Heavenrich, "Light Duty Automotive Fuel Economy: Trends Through 1983," Society of Automotive Engineers paper 830544, March 1983. The 1983 estimate is from the U.S. Department of Transportation, National Highway Traffic Safety Administration, Office of Enforcement. Both are for the EPA "composite" driving cycle; the 1983 figure is still preliminary.

8. *The U.S. Automobile Industry, 1980*, Washington, D.C.: U.S. Department of Transportation, 1981, p. 4.

9. Joel Horowitz, *Air Quality Analysis for Urban Transportation Planning*, Cambridge: MIT Press, 1982, p. 148.

10. National Research Council, *Diesel Cars: Benefits, Risks and Public Policy* (Final Report of the Diesel Impacts Study Committee), Washington, D.C.: National Academy Press, 1982.

11. National Research Council, *Health Effects of Exposure to Diesel Exhaust* (Report of the Health Effects Panel of the Diesel Impacts Study Committee), Washington, D.C.: National Academy Press, 1981. In the report's precise words (from the council's transmittal letter to the Environmental Protection Agency):

The report provides a careful analysis summarizing and critically reviewing the less than satisfactory state of information concerning the effects of diesel engine emissions on humans. Materials moderately active as mutagens in various assays and as carcinogens when painted on the skins of susceptible animals have indeed been partially purified from diesel exhausts. However, no evidence of carcinogenesis has been noted in animals breathing diesel exhaust fumes or in epidemiological studies of relatively heavily exposed human populations. Unfortunately, almost all of the studies are reported to have been defective in some manner and, hence, do not permit definitive conclusions at this time. Nor do the limited observations concerning the effects of diesel exhaust emissions on pulmonary physiology, susceptibility to infection, etc., permit definitive conclusions.

12. The U.S. standard allows passenger-car diesels to emit 0.6 grams of particulates per mile as of model year 1982; the permitted amount declines to 0.2 grams per mile in model year 1987. The state of California will require an interim standard of 0.4 grams per mile for model year 1986. Uncontrolled engines have emitted as much as 0.8 grams per mile in the past, but all current production designs emit well under the 0.6-gram-per-mile limit. The U.S. NO_x standard for passenger-car diesels falls from 1.5 to 1.0 grams per mile for model

year 1985. No other country has yet adopted an upper limit on passenger-car diesel emissions per unit of travel.

13. This discussion on advances in particulate cleanup technology is based largely on Christopher Weaver, "Trap-Oxidizer Technology for Light-Duty Diesel Vehicles: Status, Prospects, and Current Issues", Society of Automotive Engineers paper 831713, November 1983.

14. This estimate has been calculated from data on aggregate emissions by source in *National Air Pollution Emission Estimates, 1970–81*, Washington, D.C.: U.S. Environmental Protection Agency, 1983, tables 3, 4, and 5. The calculation assumes that all NO_x emissions contribute to acid rain regardless of where emitted, that NO_x emissions have half the acid potential for SO_2 emissions, and that NO_x emitted at ground level by motor vehicles is as much responsible for acid rain as NO_x emitted from tall stacks. Light trucks account for another 1.6 percent of the acid in rain, heavy trucks account for an additional 4.7 percent. Thus, the total motor-vehicle contribution is about 11.5 percent.

15. Typical catalyst systems in automobiles today use a combination of noble metals, rhodium, platinum, and palladium, to convert HC and CO to H_2O and CO_2. They also reduce NO_2 and other nitrogen oxides to O_2 and N_2 and are therefore called "three-way" catalysts. To accomplish NO_2 reduction the amount of oxygen in the exhaust must be carefully controlled through use of an oxygen sensor. Because this sensor controls the amount of air and fuel going into the cylinders before combustion, the total system is said to be in a "closed loop".

16. "Federal Certification Test Results for Model Year 1983", Washington, D.C.: U.S. Environmental Protection Agency, 1983. Certifications of engine families at NO_x emission levels so far below the U.S. standard are not indicative simply of engineering caution to ensure compliance with a safety margin. Rather, they reflect advances in engine techology that yield maximum fuel efficiency at NO_x levels far below those which many engineers in the mid 1970s believed would ever be possible in production engines even with a considerable fuel-economy penalty.

17. NO_x control in diesels seems today to be about where NO_x control in gasoline engines was a decade ago. In addition, the problem is considerably more challenging technically because the oxygen richness of diesel exhaust makes the use of a reduction catalyst impossible. Therefore, NO_x formation in the engine must be prevented by a variety of techniques. Many of these increase particulate emissions—thus the importance of perfecting trap-oxidyzer technology if particulates and NO_x must in the future be reduced simultaneously.

18. "Lean burn" is the term applied to increasing the air-to-fuel ratio in the cylinder to a point far beyond the "stoichiometric" point where the exact proportions of fuel and air needed for complete combustion are present. "Leaning" an engine offers many fuel-economy advantages but requires careful mixing of the fuel and air and very precise electronic monitoring of fuel flow and spark timing to prevent premature or uneven burning. "Adiabatic diesels" will have ceramic cylinder crowns, cylinder sleeves, and other components designed

to raise the combustion-chamber walls to higher temperatures than metals can tolerate. The effect of the very hot chamber walls is to reduce the amount of work wasted by the fuel in heating the combustion chamber. Early prototype engines with ceramic parts and without either cooling or lubrication systems show the promise of producing low particulate emissions and roughly the same NO_x emissions. Gas engines are not candidates for adiabatic treatment, because the high temperatures of the combustion-chamber walls would prematurely ignite the fuel.

19. Compare the relatively sanguine view expressed in National Research Council, Board on Atmospheric Sciences and Climate, *Changing Climate* (Report of the Carbon Dioxide Assessment Committee), Washington, D.C.: National Academy Press, 1983, with the more alarmist conclusions announced at the same time by scientists at the U.S. Environmental Protection Agency (*Can We Delay a Greenhouse Warming?*, Washington, D.C.: U.S. Government Printing Office, 1983). The figures cited in the following paragraphs are from these two sources, which agree closely on the trend in carbon dioxide levels and the range of possible environmental effects. Their disagreement lies in their assessment of the most probable environmental efffects.

20. The fossil-fuel contribution to carbon emissions and the oil share of fossil-fuel combustion are from *Changing Climate*, p. 116. The automobile share of petroleum consumption is estimated from the *BP Statistical Review* (note 4 above). The contribution of deforestation to atmospheric carbon dioxide is from George Woodwell et al., "Global Deforestation: Contribution to Atmospheric Carbon Dioxide," *Science*, December 9, 1983, p. 1081.

21. See Ithiel de Sola Pool, "The Communication/Transportation Tradeoff," in Alan Altshuler, ed., *Current Issues in Transportation Research Policy*, Lexington, Mass.: Heath, 1979, pp. 181–192, for a review of this issue.

22. Calculated from *World Road Statistics*, Geneva: International Road Federation, 1968 and 1972 editions, table VII.

23. U.S. fatality rates for 1923–1927 are from *Safety Facts*, Chicago: National Safety Council, 1975 edition, p. 59. The 1968 rate is from *Highway Safety 1978*, Washington, D.C.: National Highway Traffic Safety Administration, 1979, table A-1. The Japanese estimate is from *World Road Statistics*, various years, table VII.

24. The estimate of vehicles in use is from "Statistical Report on Road Accident Trends", Paris: European Conference of Ministers of Transport, 1983, table 1B.

25. The information on countries with seat-belt-use laws is from *Motor Vehicle Facts and Figures*, Detroit: Motor Vehicle Manufacturers Association, 1983, p. 92. Only Italy, Portugal, and the United States lack any type of seat-belt-use requirement. In some other countries, such as Japan, use is required only on motorways; in others, such as Canada, use is required only in some provinces.

26. See, for example, B. J. Campbell, "A Comparison of NHTSA Car Safety Ratings with Injuries in Highway Crashes," in *Highway Safety Highlights*, Highway Safety Research Center, University of North Carolina, fall 1982.

27. The estimate of households without motor vehicles available is from *Nationwide Personal Transportation Study, Report Number 2: Household Vehicle Ownership*, Washington, D.C.: Federal Highway Administration, 1980, table 2.

Chapter 4

1. For an assessment of the proper role of government in the development of new automotive technology and a review of past experience see James P. Womack and Daniel T. Jones, "The Competitive Significance of Government Technology Policy in the Auto Sector," prepared for International Automobile Program International Policy Forum, Hakone, Japan, May 1982.

2. This approach to innovation and the example of the Model T are described in detail in William Abernathy, *The Productivity Dilemma*, Baltimore: Johns Hopkins University Press, 1978, pp. 12–13.

3. Three separate analyses of the future of automotive technology have been prepared: Herman Appel and Klaus-Peter Hilber, "Auto Technology Toward 2000"; Masakazu Iguchi, Hideo Nakamura, and Koichi Shimokawa, "Technological Development and Its Implication for the Automotive Industry"; and Ulf Karlsson and Lars Sjostedt, "Robots and Men." Each of these summaries draws on papers prepared by a number of auto technologists participating in the International Automobile Program. This section draws heavily on these analyses but does not attempt to summarize them or cover all the topics and technologies they examine. The authors of these analyses anticipate that the work of the technologists participating in the Program will be collected and published in the near future as an in-depth study of the future of automotive technology.

4. For a more detailed assessment of the value and limitations of R&D and patent statistics in the auto industry see Daniel T. Jones, "Technology and Competition in the Automobile Industry," prepared for International Automobile Program International Policy Forum, Hakone, Japan, May 1982.

Chapter 5

1. J. C. Tanner, "International Comparisons of Cars and Car Usage," Crowthorne, U.K.: Transport and Road Research Laboratory, 1983 (report 1070), pp. 8–9 and figure 1.5. William Wheaton carried out a similar though more limited study of 42 countries for the Auto Program, and his findings were essentially identical to Tanner's. See William Wheaton, "The Long Run Structure of Transportation and Gasoline Demand," working paper, International Automobile Program, May 1982.

2. Tanner, pp. 9–11.

3. OECD, "Long Term Perspectives of the World Automobile Industry" (note by the secretariat), November 1982, annex I, pp. 5–7.

4. Ibid., pp. 10–12.

5. *World Motor Vehicle Data Book, 1982*, Detroit: Motor Vehicle Manufacturers Association, 1982, p. 33. British automobile registrations are unavailable for 1977 due to a change in the Department of Transport's census procedure.

6. OECD, "Long Term Perspectives," annex I, table 2.

7. The assumptions about automobile scrappage rates employed in our demand forecast are as follow (by country categories):

	1979	1990	2000
Seven Auto Program Nations	7.0%	7.5%	7.5%
Other OECD Countries	7.0%	7.5%	7.5%
Centrally Planned Economies	3.0%	4.0%	5.0%
Developing Countries	3.0%	4.0%	5.0%

8. Our assumptions about future population by country categories are as follows (expressed in millions):

	1980	1990	2000
Seven Auto Program Nations	581	605	644
Other OECD Countries	181	209	252
Centrally Planned Economies	1392	1485	1652
Developing Countries	2219	2726	3550
Total	4373	5025	6098

Source:
United Nations, *World Population Prospects as Assessed in 1982*.

9. Our assumptions about economic growth by country categories are as follows:

	Annual Growth in GNP/capita	
	1980–1990	1990–2000
Seven Auto Program Nations	2.6%	2.5%
Other OECD Countries	2.6%	2.5%
Centrally Planned Economies	3.0%	3.0%
Developing Countries	1.7%	1.6%

Source:
Based on World Bank forecasts.

10. Tanner, "International Comparisons," pp. 10, 14.

Chapter 6

1. It is important not to exaggerate this trend. The American product mix remains far larger on average than that in the other OECD markets, and the "very large" car still accounts for 30 percent of total volume.

2. As this is being written the world is into another trough in real energy prices, but no survivor of the 1970s wishes to be caught short if another ratchet in energy prices occurs.

3. The exception was Toyota, which produced vehicles of its own design from the beginning of postwar reconstruction, although they were imitative of prewar Western designs.

4. See Shotaro Kamiya, *My Life with Toyota*, Tokyo: Toyota Motor Company, 1976, pp. 77–81, and John B. Rae, *Nissan/Datsun*, New York: McGraw-Hill, 1982, pp. 13–21, for detailed accounts of the early problems of Japanese producers in the American market.

5. A Ford Motor Company estimate is that a typical American car contains some 15,000 individual parts.

6. William Abernathy, *The Productivity Dilemma*, Baltimore, Johns Hopkins University Press, 1978.

7. Two of the best sources on Japanese manufacturing practice available in English are Richard Schonberger, *Japanese Manufacturing Techniques*, New York: Free Press, 1982, and, specifically for the auto industry, James Harbour, "Comparison and Analysis of Automotive Manufacturing Technology in the Japanese and North American Automotive Industry for the Manufacture of Subcompact and Compact Cars," mimeo, Harbour and Associates, 1981.

8. Note also that the inclusion of other revenues can greatly alter the size ordering of the final assemblers. Daimler-Benz, for example, while a specialist auto producer, is the same size as Nissan (which produces four times as many cars) on the basis of overall revenues. This is due to its very large revenues from truck and bus manufacturing, which slightly exceed its revenues from autos.

Chapter 7

1. For a thorough treatment of these points, of which this discussion is a summary, see Martin L. Anderson, "Japan's Strategic Umbrella," International Automobile Program working paper, 1982, pp. 44–75, and "Structural Changes in the World Auto Companies: The Emerging Japanese Role," Society of Automotive Engineers paper 820444, 1982.

2. For a thorough treatment of these points of which this is a summary, see James P. Womack, "Public Policy for a Mature Industrial Sector: The Auto Case," PhD dissertation, Department of Political Science, MIT, 1982, Chapter 7.

3. The following material is adapted from James P. Womack, "The Competitive Significance of National Financial Systems in the Auto Sector," paper prepared for International Automobile Program Interna tional Policy Forum, Hakone, Japan, May 1982.

4. See, for example, the statement of Ford Motor Company vice-president David McCammon to the U.S.-Japan Advisory Commission, July 14, 1983, in

which he argued that an appropriate value for the yen on a trade basis would be around 185 to the dollar.

5. This assessment is based on Martin L. Anderson, "Structure of the Western European and Japanese Automotive Industry," draft final report prepared for the U.S. Department of Transportation, December 1983.

6. This section is based on a special analysis prepared for the International Automobile Program by William Johnston: "Issues in Multinational Sourcing of Production," May 1982.

Chapter 9

1. Production figure calculated from *The Motor Industry of Great Britain*, London: Society of Motor Manufacturers and Traders, 1983, pp. 40, 43.

2. K. Koshiro, "Personnel Planning, Technological Changes, and Outsourcing in the Japanese Automobile Industry," in "Workforce Restructuring, Manpower Management and Industrial Relations in the World Automobile Industry" (volume II of a report to the European Economic Commission, ed. Wolfgang Streeck and Andreas Hoff, August 1983).

3. These figures include a standardized assessment of fringe-benefit costs as well as the costs of wage payments. The figures are expressed in U.S. dollar equivalents and thus are affected by exchange rates. In addition, it should be recognized that it is extremely difficult to derive a full comparative assessment of fringe-benefit costs, and also that these figures measure hourly compensation costs but take no account of productivity differentials. Nonetheless, table 9.6 provides a good approximate comparison of total hourly compensation costs for production workers. These figures are generally consistent with those derived by the International Metalworkers Federation, "International Comparison of Wages and Working Conditions," report prepared for International Metalworkers Federation World Auto Conference, Detroit, Michigan, May 1978.

4. David Marsden, "Collective Bargaining and Industrial Adjustment in Britain, France, Italy and West Germany," manuscript, London School of Economics, 1982.

5. H. Shimada, "Japan's Postwar Industrial Growth and Labor-Management Relations," in *Papers and Proceedings of the Thirty-fifth Annual Meeting of the International Industrial Relations Association*, Madison, Wisconsin: International Industrial Relations Association, 1982, pp. 241–248.

Chapter 10

1. See the joint statement by former U.S. presidents Ford and Carter on the eve of a GATT ministerial meeting (*New York Times*, November 21, 1982, p. E19) and the speech by President Reagan reported *ibid.*, p. A1.

2. *The Economist*, December 25, 1982, p. 75.

3. See *The Annals of the American Academy of Political and Social Science*, March 1982, pp. 9, 12.

4. See Raymond Bauer et al., *American Business and Public Policy*, 1963, chapter 15 (entitled "Detroit: Hotbed of Free Trade").

5. See *Wall Street Journal*, March 17, 1983.

6. The 1982 edition of *Motor Vehicle Facts and Figures* (Detroit: MVMA) provides data on unit sales and average prices. The inflation adjustment is from *OECD Economic Outlook* 32, December 1982, table 22.

7. *New York Times*, November 25, 1982, p. D1.

8. Chalmers Johnson, *MITI and the Japanese Miracle: The Growth of Industrial Policy 1925–1975*, Stanford, Calif.: Stanford University Press, 1982, pp. 17, 26, 31, 204, 217, 235–237, 243–247, 265, 276–288, 302–303; I. M. Destler and Hideo Sato, eds., *Coping with U.S.-Japanese Economic Conflicts*, Lexington, Mass.: Heath, 1982, chapter 5; Andrea Boltho, *Japan: An Economic Survey 1953–1973*, London: Oxford University Press, 1975, pp. 188–189; Wolfgang Hager et al., *EEC Protectionism*, Brussels: European Research Associates, 1981 and 1982, volume I, pp. 27–29, and volume II, pp. 59, 60, 73. These are reviews of Japanese trade intervention in the auto sector since World War II.

Appendix C

1. U.S. Department of Transportation, *The U.S. Automobile Industry, 1980* (report to the president from the Secretary of Transportation)(1981).

2. For more detail see Harry C. Katz, "The U.S. Automobile Collective Bargaining System in Transition," *British Journal of Industrial Relations* (forthcoming); Katz, *Shifting Gears: Changing Labor Relations in the U.S. Automobile Industry*, Cambridge: MIT Press, 1985.

3. H. C. Katz, T. A. Kochan, and K. R. Gobeille, "Industrial Relations Performance, Economic Performance and Quality of Working Life Efforts: An Inter-Plant Analysis," *Industrial and Labor Relations Review*, October 1983, 37, number 1, pp. 3–17.

4. The Donovan Report is the popular name given to the "Report of the Royal Commission on Trade Unions and Employers' Associations." The report is summarized and analyzed in a symposium in the *British Journal of Industrial Relations*, vol. 6, no. 3, November 1968, pp. 275–359.

5. For more details on the operation of the German system generally, see Wolfgang Streeck, "Qualitative Demands and the Neo-Corporatist Manageability of Industrial Relations," *British Journal of Industrial Relations*, (1981), pp. 149–169. For additional detail on labor relations in the German automobile industry see Wolfgang Streeck, *Industrial Relations in West Germany: A Case Study of the Car Industry*, New York: St. Martin's Press, 1984.

Appendix D

1. B. H. Klein, *Dynamic Economics*, Cambridge: Harvard University Press, 1977.

2. G. T. Allison, *Essence of Decision*, Boston: Little, Brown, 1971.

3. J. Waelbroeck, "Utsikter for varldshandeln" ("Prospects for World Trade"), *Ekonomisk Debatt*, 6 (1982), pp. 383–390.

4. P. B. Dixon, "Alternativa ansatser i makroekonomiks politik: fallet Australien" ("Alternative Approaches to Macroeconomic Policy: The Case of Australia"), *Ekonomisk Debatt*, 6 (1982), pp. 397–401.

5. J. A. Gomez-Ibanez, R. A. Leone and S. A. O'Connell, "Restraining Auto Imports: Does Anyone Win?" *Journal of Policy Analysis and Management*, 2, no. 2 (1983), pp. 196–218.

6. C. Hamilton, "A New Approach to the Estimation of the Effects of Non-Tariff Barriers to Trade: An Application to the Swedish Textile and Clothing Industry," *Weltwirtschaftliches Archiv*, 2, 1981.

7. A. P. Black, "International Trade Trends and Policy in the Automobile Industry," paper prepared for International Automobile Program International Policy Forum, Stenungsund, Sweden, June 12–18, 1983).

Index